The Best of SQLServerCe... ...om - Vol.7

Aaron Akin
Adam Aspin
Adam Haines
Alceu Rodrigues de Freitas Junior
Bennie Haelen
Bill Richards
Boyan Penev
Brian Kelley
Chad Miller
Chris Kinley
David Dye
David McKinney
David Poole
Deepa Gheewala
Divya Agrawal
Drew Salem
Francis Rodrigues
Gail Shaw
Glen Cooper
Glen Schwickerath
Gregor Borosa
Gus "GSquared" Gwynne
Ian Stirk
Jack Corbett
Jacob Sebastian
Jagan Kumar
Jason Shadonix
Joe Celko
Johan Bijnens
Jonathan Kehayias

Ken Simmons
Ladislau Molnar
Lanre Famuyide
Louis Roy
Marios Philippopoulos
Martin Cremer
Michael Cape
Michelle Ufford
Mike Walsh
Nicholas Cain
Oleg Netchaev
Phil Factor
Ranga Narasimhan
R. Barry Young
Renato Buda
Robert Cary
Roy Ernest
Rudy Panigas
Soloman Rutzky
Sylvia Moestl Vasilik
Thom Bolin
Tim Mitchell
Thomas LaRock
Timothy A Wiseman
TJay Belt
Vincent Rainardi
Wagner Crivelini
Wayne Sheffield
Zach Mattson

The Best of SQLServerCentral.com – Vol. 7

Red Gate Books
Newnham House
Cambridge Business Park
Cambridge
CB2 0WZ
United Kingdom

ISBN 978-1-906434-36-6

Disclaimer

The Simple-Talk Publishing, SQLServerCentral.com, and the authors of the articles contained in this book are not liable for any problems resulting from the use of techniques, source code, or compiled executables referenced in this book. Users should review all procedures carefully, test first on a non-production server, and always have good backup before using on a production server.

Trademarks

Microsoft, SQL Server, Windows, and Visual Basic are registered trademarks of Microsoft Corporation, Inc. Oracle is a trademark of Oracle Corporation.

Editor

Steve Jones

Cover Art

Matthew Tye

Typeset

Alice Smith

Table of Contents

Introduction

Welcome to The Best of SQLServerCentral.com – Vol. 7

SQLServerCentral crossed a million members this year and once again we are reprinting some of the best articles, the most popular, and the most read in dead tree format. We wanted to give our authors a chance to see their names in print as well as give you an off-line resource that you can take with you wherever you may need it-most likely at your bedside to help you drop off at night :), for commutes, holding your coffee cup, whatever. This is our seventh volume and it's become an annual tradition.

We would also like to thank everyone for their support both on the website as well as by purchasing this book. Your visits to the site, clicking through to advertisers, purchasing products, registering for PASS, all help us continue this community and provide you with a valuable resource that hopefully helps you learn, perform better at your job, and grow your career. We'd like to encourage all of you to submit an article in 2010!

This is a community that includes all of you and we aren't looking for only the gurus to contribute. We love hearing about the real world you all live in and deal with on a daily basis. We try to get at least one article from each author and send you a couple copies of the book. That wasn't possible this year with the economy down and a record number of authors writing content this year. However that should encourage all of you to work a little harder next year and write something great. A couple hints: real world situations and basic content on one focused area go over the best.

These are great for your bookshelf and they make a great Mother's Day present. Think about sending something in next year.

Once again, thanks so much for your support and we look forward to another volume next year.

Steve Jones

SQL Server Preproduction Tasks

By Ken Simmons

Introduction

Okay. You have a new server and a fresh install of SQL Server. What are some of the things that you need to do before you sign off and hand it over to production? What do you need to do to keep the server running smoothly? Here is a list of things I keep in mind before handing a server over to production.

Preproduction Checklist

1. **Make sure SQL Server has the latest patches.**
   This is pretty self explanatory, but before a server gets turned over to production make sure it has the latest patches. There is no need in causing downtime later because you forgot to patch the box.

2. **Enable full auditing on both Successful and Failed Logins.**
   Under the Security Tab in the Server Properties, there is an option to audit both failed and successful logins. By default, this is set to failed logins only, but I like to be able to correlate events on the server with who may have logged in around that time.

3. **Increase SQL Server log history threshold in order to maintain logs for a longer amount of time.**
   Under the Management folder, right-click on SQL Server Logs and select Configure. By default SQL Server will keep 6 error logs before they are recycled. I increase this to 99, which is the maximum value.

4. **Set a default path for data and log files.**
   Under the Database Settings Tab in the Server Properties, there is a place to set the database default locations. I like to change this in case a database gets created without specifying a location, it will not go in the install directory.

5. **Set up Database Mail.**
   Instead of reinventing the wheel here, I will just point you to a couple of articles that I used to setup Database Mail. The following articles are

script based, so they can be modified and included in your post install scripts.

http://articles.techrepublic.com.com/5100-10878_11-6161839.html
http://articles.techrepublic.com.com/5100-10878_11-6164310.html?tag=rbxccnbtr1

6. Determine Drive Structure and move system databases if necessary. Specifically, move the tempdb to its own drive if it is possible. The system database that is most likely to cause disk contention and grow the largest is the tempdb. I typically try to put the database and log file on its own drive. Here is the MSDN link for moving system databases.

   http://msdn.microsoft.com/en-us/library/ms345408(SQL.90).aspx

7. **Create a maintenance database.**
   A maintenance database is a good place to store objects that are required to perform maintenance on the system. This may also be where you store things such as the nums or tally (*http://www.sqlservercentral.com/articles/TSQL/62867/*) table that are required for certain queries.

8. **Create a job to update statistics.**
   I have heard a little on both sides of this. If you are using auto update statistics and also have a job to update statistics, you are overworking your server. But on the other hand only certain events trigger SQL Server to Auto Update. I fall on the side of forcing the update. Here is a good script that will force the update for all databases. Keep in mind all of these stored procedures unless stated otherwise, I put in the maintenance database.

   http://www.sqlservercentral.com/scripts/Maintenance+and+Management/31472/

9. **Create a job to cycle the error log.**
   Whenever SQL Server is restarted, it creates a new error log. If the server stays up for a while, this can make for a very large error log. I create a job that runs on a daily or weekly basis that executes the sp_cycle_errorlog stored procedure in the master database. This will create a new error log without having to restart SQL Server.

10. Create a job to cleanup the Backup History from the msdb.

As backups are performed the information is logged to tables in the msdb. Over time this can cause the msdb to become very large. There is a stored procedure in the msdb that can be executed to remove this history called sp_delete_backuphistory. This accepts a date parameter and will remove any history prior to the given date. I create a job that runs the following command on a weekly basis.

```
DECLARE @DeleteBeforeDate DATETIME
SELECT @DeleteBeforeDate = DATEADD(month,-
1,GETDATE())
EXEC msdb..sp_delete_backuphistory @DeleteBeforeDate
```

11. Create a job to maintenance indexes.

I don't like jobs that just go reindex everything in the database. I like to selectively reindex; only rebuild the indexes if they are beyond a certain fragmentation level. Here is a link to script I am currently using. *http://blogs.digineer.com/blogs/larar/archive/2007/07/30/smart-index-defragmentation-for-an-online-world.aspx*

12. Create a job to run a DBCC CHECKDB to run against all databases.

A lot of times this is thrown in with the backup jobs, but I like to create a separate job that may be able to run at a different time.

13. Create a job to check for long running jobs.

One of the issues I have faced in the past is not being notified that a job is having issues because instead of failing it is just hung. I create a job that runs once an hour or so to look for jobs that have been running over x amount of time. If a job is found, then the long running job fails or sends an error notification. The following article can be referenced for details. *http://code.msdn.microsoft.com/SQLExamples/Wiki/View.aspx?title= AgentLongRunning&referringTitle=Home*

14. Determine a backup and retention strategy.

There are several different strategies here. They differ by organization and even by server. The main point here is to come up with a solution and test it thoroughly.

15. **Make sure each maintenance job has an output file in a standard directory.**
    In the advanced tab under the job steps create an output file. This will allow you to see the full description of the job execution. There is nothing more annoying than not being able to see why a job failed.

16. **Determine the optimal memory settings for the server.**
    A number of factors affect the way the settings should be configured, but here are a couple of articles that may help.
    http://msdn.microsoft.com/en-us/library/ms175581(SQL.90).aspx
    http://msdn.microsoft.com/en-us/library/ms190673(SQL.90).aspx

17. **Run the SQL Best Practice Analyzer to determine if there are potential issues in the database environment.**
    http://www.microsoft.com/downloads/details.aspx?FamilyId=DA0531 E4-E94C-4991-82FA-F0E3FBD05E63&displaylang=en

18. **You may also be interested in testing your disk drives using SQLIOSim.**
    http://support.microsoft.com/kb/231619

Conclusion

Most of the items above can be scripted and applied to the servers before moving to production. Come up with the script that best suits your organization and servers and moving a server into production should be a fairly simple process.

Scope: The drastic caveat with Logon Triggers

By Johan Bijnens

The Story

Logon triggers were implemented in SQLServer 2005 with **SP2**. Now we - the instance administrators - are able to perform some stuff at the actual logon time of a user. This way, we could, for example, restrict users access during a certain part of the day, only allow connections from certain addresses. To check on my licenses, I believed I could use logon triggers to track how many users connected from how many client machines.

I developed a little logon trigger, *which executed using the 'sa' context*, so I didn't have to grant insert to my logging database and table. I didn't mind that I would have to use "*original_login_name*" to get the actual connecting user id. This all looked pretty straight forward, not much rocket science at all.

I first tested it at my dba-dev instance. It worked just fine, not much overhead to be noticed…cool. Since the test succeeded, it was time to roll out on the developers' instances (8 instances).

Once again, everything went just fine. We managed to get a good overview of the number of clients hitting our instances and were able to store all connection related data. One week after the implementation in DEV, it was rolled out to QA. Even there, no problems at all.

In noticed a number of connections being registrated, so I got at ease and planned implementation in our production environments. All needed paperwork was done and the "request for change" was submitted and approved. The rollout was prepared (including fall back scenarios, mind you) for our 15 instances of sql2005 and got launched at the approved time. (Day x at noon).

The Production Rollout

Within seconds after the launch, the first production instance dumped and crashed!

However, I didn't notice the instance being failed over to the other node of the cluster. But that wasn't the hottest issue at that time.

Alerts were coming in from our monitoring system and hell opened some doors.

Messages pointed to:

```
------

Process ID 59 attempted to unlock a resource it does not own:
DATABASE: 9 Retry the transaction, because this error may be
caused by a timing condition. If the problem persists, contact
the database administrator.

------

Process ID 108 attempted to unlock a resource it does not own:
DATABASE: 9 Retry the transaction, because this error may be
caused by a timing condition. If the problem persists, contact
the database administrator.

------

[sqsrvres] ODBC sqldriverconnect failed

------

[sqsrvres] checkODBCConnectError: sqlstate = 08001; native
error = 102; message = [Microsoft][SQL Native Client]TCP
Provider: Timeout error [258].

------

[sqsrvres] checkODBCConnectError: sqlstate = HYT00; native
error = 0; message = [Microsoft][SQL Native Client]Login
timeout expired

------

[sqsrvres] checkODBCConnectError: sqlstate = 08001; native
error = 102; message = [Microsoft][SQL Native Client]Unable to
complete login process due to delay in login response

------

[sqsrvres] printODBCError: sqlstate = 08S01; native error = 0;
message = [Microsoft][SQL Native Client]Communication link
failure

------

Logon failed for login 'thelogin' due to trigger execution.
[CLIENT:10.16.108.226]
```

It was quite obvious: my rollout might trigger this kind of errors.

The Fallback Scenario

Time to roll out the fallback scenario for the cumbersome instance. The fallback scenario was just a SQLCMD query which would disable the logon trigger. **This scenario was also tested at Dev and QA, so I was pretty at ease with it.**

I ran the SQLCMD and **it failed**!!

It failed, because it was exactly the implemented logon trigger that caused the issues. It was at that time I really appreciated the Microsoft Dev team's efforts to implement the Dedicated Administrator Connection (DAC)! That was the way to go to turn off this trigger.

```
/*
if due to a logon trigger you can nolonger connect to a
sql2005 instance you need the local DAC (dedicated
administrator connection) using the -A parameter to be
able to connect to the instance !
*/
/* There can only be ONE active DAC !! */
[DOSBOX]
sqlcmd -A -d master -S TheInstance
Or start SSMS not connecting to an instance
   (Object browser not supported with DAC !! )
then click "New Query" and connect using "admin:TheInstance"

SQLCMD will give you a commandline like this
1>
You will need to enter your statement and the command
will only be
executed after you enter 'GO' at the next line.
1> DISABLE TRIGGER S_tr_DBA_ConnectionTracker ON ALL
SERVER;
2> go
1> exit
```

After executing this at the cumbersome instance, things turned back to normal. However, because of the dumps sqlserver generated, I asked for an emergency intervention to restart the instance so it would no longer suffer any leftovers of the dumps.

It was an instance hosting *biztalk* databases, so you can imagine the scope of the impact. Off course I also immediately disabled all these logon triggers at the other production instances that were involved in this rollout operation.

The Cause

Now I started digging into the system, trying to figure out what caused all these dumps. I started a **SQLtrace** at the instance that had dumped. At first sight, nothing abnormal going on, until I noticed some of the connections were using the serializable transaction isolation level.

I double checked with my biztalk dev team....*Isolation level ??? What the* ***...** Like many developers, they were unaware of what kind of isolation level their applications are using.

Why didn't this occur in DEV or QA?

"We weren't using DEV nor QA for the last month or so"... developers on vacation, others only used their local virtual pc with their full dev environment.

No wonder I missed this kind of errors in the whole process of DEV and QA.

Back to the drawing board for the logon tracker, because its scope was actually not restricted to the little registration at the beginning of a connection, as I supposed it would be.

The Solution

Would it be worth the effort of converting it to a service broker application, by just forwarding the connection info into a *service broker (SSB)* queue, and processing that asynchronously?

As a matter of fact, that concept already exists in SQLServer 2005. **It's called "Event Notifications"**. In this case using the login events. **Asynchrone** by design and the upmost valid alternative for my quest.

Why didn't I think of that in an earlier stage?

It provided me about all the data I had available with the logon trigger, except for the ip address of the connecting device.

I started off reading this nice article and elaborated on it:

- SQL Server 2005 Logon Triggers by Frederik Vandeputte as SSC[1]
- Logon triggers by Cristian Lefter as Simple-talk[2]

My solution is very similar to the solution Frederik Vandeputte posted as SSC. So, in my stored procedure that handles the queue, I just added an extra join to see if that user was still connected via that SPID and pull out the ip address.

I didn't want to get caught twice by the same pitfall, so I made sure my *biztalk* devs tested their stuff whilst the new implementation was active.

Lessons learned

Never assume a server has a typical usage. Double check with all dev teams to test.

Always prepare fallback scenarios and make sure you know about the *Dedicated Administrator Connection* (DAC).

Just like with any trigger, be sure its scope is very small.

And last but not least: First consider if things actually need to be performed in realtime mode.

P.S. Notice to myself: Check all servers for the isolation levels that are being used.

---

[1]
http://www.sqlservercentral.com/articles/SQLServerCentral.com/sqlserver2005logontriggers/2366/
[2] http://www.simple-talk.com/sql/sql-server-2005/logon-triggers/

The Date Dimension in Analysis Services

By Vincent Rainardi

In data warehousing, date dimension is the most frequently used dimension. Consequently, when building a cube for a data warehouse in Analysis Services, we almost always have to create a date dimension. In this article I'd like to discuss things that we are likely to come across when creating a date dimension in Analysis Services, such as having several date dimensions and handling unknown rows. I'm going to refer to Analysis Services as SSAS, which stands for SQL Server Analysis Services. In this article I'm referring to SSAS 2005 and SSAS 2008, not SSAS 2000.

Role Play Dimension

In SSAS, we can have the same dimension added into the cube several times as different names. This is known as a 'role play' dimension. A dimension that has been attached to a cube is called a 'cube dimension'.

The purpose of having a role play dimension is to have identical dimensions in the cube. These cube dimensions have the same attributes, the same members, the same hierarchies, the same sorting order, the same properties, the same default member, and the same display folders. Everything is the same, except the name and the relationship to the measure groups in the cube, i.e. referenced or direct, materialized or not.

For example, in retail banking, for checking account cube we could have transaction date dimension and effective date dimension. Both dimensions have date, month, quarter and year attributes. The formats of attributes are the same on both dimensions, for example the date attribute is in 'dd-mm-yyyy' format. Both dimensions have members from 1993 to 2010. Both dimensions have Year-Month-Date hierarchy.

When we change something, for example adding 2011 dates, both transaction date dimension and effective date dimension will be affected. This way we can be sure that they will always be identical. On the other hand, if we create the transaction date dimension and effective date dimension from 2 separate date dimensions (say transaction date is from date1 and effective date is from date2) then when we change the date1 dimension (say adding a new level), only transaction date will be affected.

Multiple Named Queries

Data Source View (DSV) is a layer on an Analysis Services project where we can specify the tables and views that we use to build a cube, and the relationship between the tables/views. Instead of specifying a table or a view, we can also specify a SQL select statement that queries a table or a view, or several tables/views. This select statement is called a Named Query.

On the DSV, we can create several named queries from the same date dimension table on the relational database. The reason for doing this is to enable us select a different range of data, i.e. different sets of rows. For example, in a credit card cube, for the start date dimension we may want to select different date range compared to the expiry date dimension. Perhaps the start date starts from 1996 but the end date starts from 1998. For insurance industry, for each policy or risk we have written date, accounted date, inception date, effective date and expiry date. These dates may have different ranges.

The second reason for having separate named queries on the DSV for date dimensions is to enable us to have different sets of columns. For example, for written date, transaction date and effective date the business may need year, quarter, month and date attributes. Whereas for snapshot month, they only need month and year.

The third reason for having separate named queries in the DSV for date dimensions is to enable us to set different formats for each attribute, as well as different hierarchy structures. Some date dimension may require '2008 July' and '2008-Q1' without any hierarchy but another date dimension may require just the month name and quarter name (e.g. 'July' and 'Q1') and a hierarchy to connect the two.

Normally for each named query on the DSV we create one dimension. But in some cases we may need to create 2 or more date dimensions from a single named query on the DSV. The reason for this is to enable us to configure the dimension properties differently, such as unknown member, default member, error configuration and display folder. And also, we can specify dimensional security differently.

Before we continue, let's recap:

From one date dimension table we can create several named queries.

From one named query we can create several dimensions.

From one dimension we can create several cube dimensions.

Unknown member

An 'unknown row' is a row on the dimension table to which the orphaned fact rows are assigned. The unknown row usually has a surrogate key value of 0 or -1. For example, the date dimension table contains dates from 1/1/1980 to 12/31/2020. If on the source of the fact table we have a date of 1/1/1970, which is not on the dimension table, the date surrogate key on the fact table is set to 0 (or -1). This way that fact table row is assigned to the unknown row.

In some data warehouses, the unknown row for the date dimension is 1/1/1900. Consequently, the year column of this unknown row is set to '1900'. Some users don't like to see '1900' when browsing the cube. They prefer to see 'unknown' instead of '1900'. But year is a numeric column and we can't store the word 'unknown' in the year column. In this case we may choose not to use the unknown row but to map it to the dimension unknown member. To do this, we make the unknown member of the date dimension 'visible'. On the DSV, we explicitly exclude the unknown row like this: select & from dim_date where date_key <> 0 . On the error configuration of the cube, we set the KeyErrorAction to 'ConvertToUnknown', the KeyErrorLimitAction to StopLogging and the KeyNotFound to IgnoreError. This way, when SSAS processes the cube and found a date on the fact table that does not exist in the date dimension table, that fact row will be assigned to the unknown member and SSAS will continue processing the cube. We need to be careful when doing this because it will affect all other dimensions, not just the date dimension.

There are 3 places where error configuration for the orphaned fact row can be set: cube, measure group and partition. The error configuration on the dimension itself doesn't affect the orphaned fact row; it is for orphaned dimension rows in a snow flake schema situation.

Another benefit of using the unknown member rather than the unknown row is to capture 'orphaned rows'. An orphaned row is a row on the fact table with a dimension key that does not exist on the dimension table. In best practice this should not happen. The ETL is supposed to prevent this situation. The ETL should allocate key 0 (or whatever the surrogate key of the unknown row is) to those fact table rows, so that they are mapped to the dimension unknown row. But in reality this does happen in practice. Not intentionally of course but it does happen. A typical situation is where the dimensional key column on the fact table contains NULL rather than 0 because that key column is not applicable for that fact row.

We suppose to have a foreign key on the fact table to prevent orphaned rows, but in many data warehouse implementation I found that this is not the case. Some people argued that it is not possible to have orphaned rows on the fact tables, because all data flowing into the warehouse is controlled by the ETL and the ETL always mapped unknown fact rows to the unknown row in the dimensions so we don't need to put foreign keys. But I found in a few occasions that data warehouses without foreign keys on the fact tables do have orphaned fact rows. In chapter 6 of my book 'Building a Data Warehouse with Examples on SQL Server'[3], I explained the benefits of putting foreign keys on the fact tables and how to deal with the assumed disadvantages (such as slowing ETL load process).

In data warehousing and business intelligence, mapping orphaned fact rows to the unknown member is important because if not we will miss those fact rows, causing the total of measures to be incorrect. In SSAS, if we don't change the UnknownMember and ErrorConfiguration properties, by default orphaned rows on the fact table will be mapped to the dimension unknown member. This way we will always get the correct totals of the measures. Some people set the UnknownMember property of the dimension to 'Hidden', relying completely to the ETL to guarantee that there are no orphaned rows in the fact table. If you decide to do this, it is wise to put foreign keys on the fact tables to guarantee referential integrity.

Another benefit of using unknown member rather than unknown row is that we can specify the name of the unknown member. It doesn't have to be 'Unknown'. We can set it to 'Not Applicable', for example, to suit the users' needs.

Despite all the advantages I mentioned above, personally I would prefer not to fiddle around with the unknown member in SSAS. Rather, I prefer to set the data in the fact and dimension tables correctly and leave the SSAS UnknownMember as per their defaults. For example, I've come across a situation where the value of an attribute on the unknown row is = 'unk'. But there is another row in the dimension table with the attribute value = 'unknown'. When browsing the cube the users will find that the attribute has both 'unk' and

---

[3] http://www.amazon.com/dp/1590599314?tag=intemarkworl-20&camp=14573&creative=327641&linkCode=as1&creativeASIN=1590599314&adid=0MXTG5HDAA3C6W0T2Z5J&

'unknown' members. We could tackle this on the DSV by adding a 'CASE WHEN' clause on the named query SQL, or we could exclude the unknown row and use the unknown member instead. But I prefer to fix the data, setting the physical values of that attribute correctly in the dimension table. The physical dimension table may not only be used by SSAS; it may also be used for reporting by SSRS or other reporting/BI tools such as Business Objects or Cognos.

Another disadvantage of using unknown member rather than unknown row is that when we make the unknown member visible, when there is no unmatched record, we will still see that member (unless we suppress it on the OLAP client).

Date Hierarchies

It is a best practice to build a hierarchy and hide the composing attributes. This is more so in 2008 where AS checks if we have hidden the members used in the hierarchy and give us a warning if we haven't done so, e.g. Avoid visible attribute hierarchies for attributes used as levels in user-defined hierarchies.

For example, say we have these attributes: date, quarter, month and year.

1. Year: yyyy, e.g. 2008

2. Quarter: yyyy Qn, e.g. 2008 Q4

3. Month: yyyy-mm, e.g. 2008-10

4. Date: yyyy-mm-dd, e.g. 2008-11-15

We then create a Year-Quarter-Month-Date hierarchy and we hide the Date, Month and Year attributes. When we browse the hierarchy using ProClarity it looks like the following.

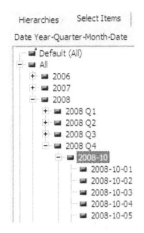

Figure 1. Browsing a date hierarchy in ProClarity

And in Excel 2007 it looks like this:

4	Year		Quarter	Month	Date
5	⊞ 2006				
6	⊞ 2007				
7	⊟ 2008		⊞ 2008 Q1		
8			⊞ 2008 Q2		
9			⊞ 2008 Q3		
10			⊟ 2008 Q4	⊟ 2008-10	2008-10-01
11					2008-10-02
12					2008-10-03
13					2008-10-04
14					2008-10-05

Figure 2. Browsing a date hierarchy using Excel 2007

My colleague John Tunnicliffe[4] advised me about ISO 8601 date format (yyyy-mm-dd), which I think is a good idea because of its clarity. It takes away the confusion caused by country-by-country custom such as dd/mm or mm/dd. He also mentioned about dd-mmm-yyyy format, e.g. 06 May 2008, which is useful to remove the confusion about month, such as 05/06/08: is it 5th June or 6th May? One caution about using mmm (short form of month) is the language, i.e. is it Mei, Mai or Mayo?

---

[4] http://sqlblogcasts.com/blogs/drjohn/

On the OLAP client, users can select members from different levels. And those members are not necessarily ascendant to each other. For example, users can still select non-ascendant months together, user can still choose 'all dates in July 2008'. This depends on the OLAP client, i.e. some OLAP clients provide facility to select all descendants of a member, but some with OLAP clients we have to select the descendants manually.

Although BIDS 2008 advised to hide the attributes used in the hierarchy, in my experience some users would still prefer to see those attributes. This enables them to use (for example) the month attribute directly either as a slicer or filter, without navigating through the Year-Month-Date hierarchy.

We should name our hierarchies properly. The name needs to reflect the levels, i.e. 'Year-Month-Date', not just 'Date Hierarchy'. Also it is better to avoid abbreviation. Calling it YMD might cause confusion among some users, wondering what YMD stands for.

It must have been quite a long read so far, so I'll end it here.

In part two, available on SQLServerCentral.com, I will discuss:

1. Date dimension that is used as a referenced dimension

2. Date dimension that is generated and stored on the SSAS server (no physical table)

3. Advantages and disadvantages of using smart date key e.g. YYYYMMDD with int data type

4. Enabling users to select a date (or month) to be used in calculated measure using 'from date' and 'to date'

5. and other things

Vincent Rainardi
Author of: Building a Data Warehouse with Examples on SQL Server.
November 2008

SCOME - Centralize Monitoring with ASP.NET - Part 1

By Drew Salem

What to do when your hands are tied?

When they discovered VMware, my employers became overly excited. For every new application, they created a new Windows Server environment with (despite my recommendations) it's own SQL Server. And so SQL Servers were popping up like wild mushrooms in a field of cows with the runs (cows have 4 stomachs). Every couple of weeks, another 2 or 3 SQL Servers would appear in the network list, and I would have no idea where they came from. Additionally, SQL Servers are a free for all where I currently work, with network administrators and 2nd line support going on and fiddling with the Servers as and when they please. There is no change control. Passwords can change  without me knowing, Servers are shut down at times during the night, out of hours, without a thought as to what it might affect. SQL Servers are installed by non-DBAs and no consideration is taken towards parameters outside the wizards default setup.

This is not a made up scenario, this is where I work. Now, I ask you from DBA to DBA, how do you manage 47 business critical servers in an environment like this? Forty seven SQL logs are 37 too many to check on a daily basis. As well as 47 x ? jobs (439 currently). Not only do failed jobs need to be checked, but their run times too. If a network fairy shut down a server during the night, SQL Server will not flag the job up as having failed. And then how do you manage disk space for this many servers when space is added and removed without any notice (due to another new toy, the SAN). And there are your test restores and log space and index rebuilds.... It's a lot to do in an uncontrolled environment for this many critical servers for one DBA. I can honestly say that during my first few months, I was losing sleep. I don't mean to go on about my own work experiences, but I'm going somewhere with this.

Despite the severity of the situation and even though little has changed, things are now very different, as through centralizing, I am one step ahead of everyone else in the department. With these scripts I am on top of every aspect

23

of monitoring and regularly find myself informing colleagues in the department of errors and warnings in their areas well before they are even aware of them.

What are these articles about?

These articles are about centralizing the monitoring of all your SQL Servers (and Oracle ones too, if you have them) and packaging the results in an ASP.Net web application. I had read many good articles on the topic of centralizing and used some of the methods, but the majority of these returned results in the query window or used SQL Mail to deliver the results to your inbox. With a heap of different areas to check daily, this felt a little fiddley and messy. I wanted a cleaner way of monitoring all the servers. I wanted reports. Daily reports in a slick page, accessible from anywhere. And so I fired up Visual Studio, and over many months developed a suite of web applications that gave me a bird's eye view of all the SQL Servers in the organization.

Through a series of articles, I'll demonstrate how I did this and will cover everything from the SQL Server side to the writing of the web application itself in ASP.Net/VB.Net. You don't need to know anything about .Net, as the format provided will be a step-by-step guide describing how to setup the Visual Studio environment, how to write the server side .Net code to display the results and to how to deliver the web pages across the network so that they are accessible from anywhere. To make this suitable for as many people as possible, I will assume you know nothing, so forgive me if I iterate over something that may seem obvious or something you already know. As there is so much to cover, I'll actually do very little explaining on how some things are the way they are in .Net, or the technology behind them, but feel free to Google these as, needless to say, there are very good web sites that do this. The aim here however is to get you up and running, so that you can systematically build your own .Net solutions in your own time, that will in-turn aid your day to day DBA duties. Whilst there are various ways of actually extracting data from databases in .Net, we will mostly use T-SQL to do this, purely so that you can combine your existing DBA SQL skills with web design abd development. If there is an ounce of creativity in you, you'll find yourself reveling in doing so. It's great when it finally all comes together.

So enough faffing[5].

---

[5] http://www.wordwebonline.com/en/FAFF

How does it work?

Here's a run down on how the system works (I'll provide scripts and step-by-step instructions in articles to come). Let's say that we want to monitor for failed jobs on two SQL Servers called Payroll_Server and CRM_Server.

1. First thing's first, you ask the boss for your own SQL Server "SQL_Admin" to run all your monitoring and auditing scripts from. You want your own server because later you'll be performing test restores on to it.

2. You chase the request for your server.

3. Six months later you've got your server. You now create your own database "DBA_Admin" that will hold all tables that will store the data regarding the SQL Servers that are being monitored.

4. You create two linked server connections from SQL_Admin to Payroll_Server and CRM_Server.

5. You create a table in DBA_Admin called "Linked_Server_Details" that holds details about all servers to be monitored (i.e. all linked servers), in this instance Payroll_Server and CRM_Server.

6. You create a table in DBA_Admin called "Failed_Job". This table will hold data regarding all failed jobs on all linked servers being monitored.

7. Now we setup the mechanism that will collect the data from all the linked servers. It's what I call the SCOME technique (Servers Coming Outa My Ears). We create a stored procedure called usp_GetFailedJob. This stored procedure accepts an input parameter; the name of any linked server i.e. usp_GetFailedJob 'Payroll_Server'. The stored procedure then fetches data from Payroll_Server's Dynamic Management Views and/or system tables and puts it into the Failed_Job.

8. But we want SQL_Admin to run this procedure on all our linked servers so that the table Failed_Job holds data about failed jobs on all servers being monitored. We have data about Payroll_Server's failed jobs but not CRM_Server's failed jobs. So we create another stored

procedure call usp_iterate_thru_servers. This proc goes through all servers in the Linked_Server_Details table one row at a time, collects the name of the server being monitored and sticks it in front of usp_GetFailedJob. Usp_GetFailedJob then does it's bit. We end up with a table of data of all failed jobs for all linked servers.

9. We create a job on SQL_Admin called Failed_Jobs and schedule this to run however often we want it to. We give this job a new category called "Monitoring_Jobs" (this is because we'll later write a web report that will tell us if any of our monitoring jobs themselves have failed!).

10. Now the fun part, we fire up Visual Studio and create a colorful web application that collects data from the table and displays it for us. Additionally, from this one page we can provide links to other pages that display the errors logs to see why it failed (saves us firing up SSMS), have a graphical representation of the number of failed jobs in the last month, the date the data was last collected etc.

11. We setup Internet Information Services to display the application as a web site so that we can access it from anywhere and then we publish the site.

12. We can now check anytime during the day if any of the hundreds of jobs across all our servers have failed.

That's it. The job is not resource heavy and completes within seconds. Now the beauty of the SCOME technique, is that this system can be applied to any type of DBA monitoring i.e. Disk Space, Unrun backups, Log size etc. Just replace the job's specific DMVs with those that hold data on backups or disk space or Log space. And replace the Failed_Job table with a table such as Disk_Space. You can have a whole suite of reports. In fact, if you can think of any that could be added to the suite, please share your idea with us in the article forum. I am genuinely open to suggestions on this and will be happy to write new articles based on these suggestions (as well as use them at work!).

Here's a figure representing the SCOME technique.

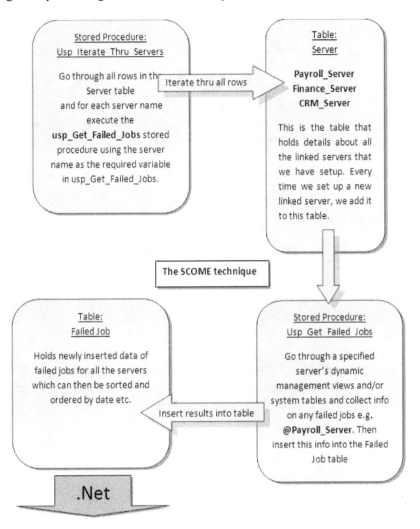

We use ASP.Net to read the results from the table and display them in a web page...

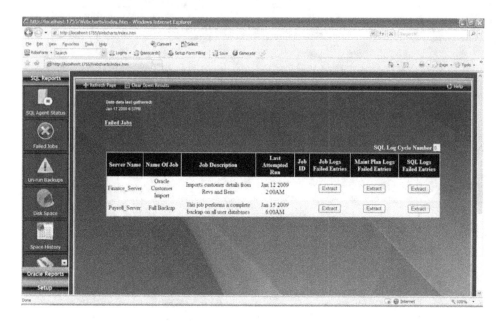

Now substitute the failed jobs system tables and dynamic management views for any other, and you can collect info about anything SQL Server, on all your linked servers.

In the next article we'll setup the SQL Server side of things; the tables, linked servers, security settings and any necessary MSDTC settings that need changing.

Monitoring Changes in Your Database Using DDL Triggers

By David Dye

Introduction

Additions, deletions, or changes to objects in a database can cause a great deal of hardship and require a dba or developer to rewrite existing code that may reference affected entities. To make matters worse tracking down the problematic alteration(s) may be synonymous to locating the needle in the haystack. Utilizing a DDL trigger in conjunction with a single user created table, used to document such changes, can considerably minimize the headaches involved in tracking and locating schema changes.

Creating the Table and DDL TRIGGER

The first step in implementing such a tracking strategy is to create a table that will be used to record all DDL actions fired from within a database. The below code creates a table in the AdventureWorks sample database that will be used to hold all such DDL actions:

```
USE AdventureWorks
GO
CREATE TABLE AuditLog
( ID          INT PRIMARY KEY IDENTITY(1,1),
  Command     NVARCHAR(1000),
  PostTime    NVARCHAR(24),
  HostName    NVARCHAR(100),
  LoginName   NVARCHAR(100)   )
GO
```

After creating the table to hold our DDL events it is now time to create a DDL trigger that will be specific to the AdventureWorks database and will fire on all DDL_DATABASE_LEVEL_EVENTS:

```
CREATE TRIGGER Audit ON DATABASE
FOR DDL_DATABASE_LEVEL_EVENTS
AS
DECLARE @data XML
DECLARE @cmd NVARCHAR(1000)
```

```
DECLARE @posttime NVARCHAR(24)
DECLARE @spid NVARCHAR(6)
DECLARE @loginname NVARCHAR(100)
DECLARE @hostname NVARCHAR(100)
SET @data = EVENTDATA()
SET @cmd =
@data.value('(/EVENT_INSTANCE/TSQLCommand/CommandText)[1]',
'NVARCHAR(1000)')
SET @cmd = LTRIM(RTRIM(REPLACE(@cmd,'','')))
SET @posttime = @data.value('(/EVENT_INSTANCE/PostTime)[1]',
'NVARCHAR(24)')
SET @spid = @data.value('(/EVENT_INSTANCE/SPID)[1]',
'nvarchar(6)')
SET @loginname = @data.value('(/EVENT_INSTANCE/LoginName)[1]',
      'NVARCHAR(100)')
SET @hostname = HOST_NAME()
INSERT INTO dbo.AuditLog(Command, PostTime,HostName,LoginName)
    VALUES(@cmd, @posttime, @hostname, @loginname)
GO
```

The purpose of the trigger is to capture the EVENTDATA() that is created once the trigger fires and parse the data from the xml variable inserting it into the appropriate columns of our AuditLog table. The parsing of the EVENTDATA() is rather straight forward, except for when extracting the command text. The parsing of the command text includes the following code:

```
SET@cmd = LTRIM(RTRIM(REPLACE(@cmd,'','')))
```

The need for the LTRIM and RTRIM is to strip all leading and trailing white space while the REPLACE is used to remove the carriage return that is added when if using the scripting wizard from SSMS. This will provide the future ability to use SSRS string functions to further parse the command text to offer greater detail.

Once the table and trigger have been created you can test to assure that it is working properly:

```
UPDATE STATISTICS Production.Product
GO
CREATE TABLE dbo.Test(col INT)
GO
DROP TABLE dbo.Test
GO
-- View log table
SELECT *
FROM dbo.AuditLog
GO
```

The results of the above query should are shown below:

	ID	Command	PostTime	HostName	LoginName
1	1	UPDATE STATISTICS Production.Product	2008-08-24T16:45:31.030	PD24546	PS\ddye
2	2	CREATE TABLE dbo.Test(col INT)	2008-08-24T16:45:31.060	PD24546	PS\ddye
3	3	DROP TABLE dbo.Test	2008-08-24T16:45:31.060	PD24546	PS\ddye

Query executed successfully.

Conclusions

By creating a table to hold all DDL actions and a database level DDL trigger we can successfully capture all DDL level changes to our database and provide greater ability to track and monitor any such change.

As performance of any such action(s) is most often the deciding factor as to whether implement such change control, I have limited excessive parsing or formatting in the above trigger. Consider this the first step, documenting. Later I will post how to utilize reporting services to provide reports showing:

1. DDL action, CREATE, ALTER, DELETE, etc

2. The schema and object affected

3. Workstation executing DDL statements

4. Drill down report to show object dependencies

That will use the *documenting objects* created above to provide greater insight and detail external of your production environment.

Imaginative Auditing with Rollback (Undo) and RollForward (Redo) Part I

By David McKinney

Imagine an audit table that allows you to rollback the changes you just made to the data. Or imagine that you ve had to restore a database from last nights backup, and you want to roll forward this morning s transactions for all tables except one. Imagine an audit table that will give you the sql insert script for the file you ve just loaded using SSIS. Imagine all this without using a 3rd party tool, and without going near the transaction log.

The code in this article is going to give you all of this, and more sort of.

Enough imagining - now for the reality. The basic idea is an audit trigger that, instead of just recording old and new values, will actually generate the sql for you to enable you to reproduce the exact same insert, update or delete. In addition, it will also generate the sql to rollback the statement.

Note: The code below was written for SQL 2005.

Auditing the Items table

ItemId	ItemName	Price
1	Chocolate bar	1.15
2	Soda	1.00
3	Chocolate milkshake	2.00
4	Mineral Water	1.30

Let's say we want to double the price of items containing chocolate. You might use an update statement like the following

```
UPDATE tblItems
  SET Price=Price*2
  WHERE lower(Item) like '%chocolate%'
```

The audit table should record the following

RollforwardSQL	RollbackSQL

| UPDATE tblItem SET Price=3.30 WHERE ItemId=1 | UPDATE tblItem SET Price=1.15 WHERE ItemId=1 |
| UPDATE tblItem SET Price=4.00 WHERE ItemId=3 | UPDATE tblItem SET Price=2.00 WHERE ItemId=3 |

An INSERT or a DELETE works in a similar way.

DELETE FROM tblItems WHERE ItemName= Soda

Should give the following in the audit table:

| RollforwardSQL | RollbackSQL |
| DELETE FROM tblItems WHERE ItemId=2 | INSERT INTO tblItems (ItemId, Item, Price) VALUES (2, Soda , 1.00) |

(Also if ItemId is an identity column, the INSERT statement must be surrounded by SET IDENTITY_INSERT ON / OFF.)

Creating the Audit database

I'm creating a specific database to store the audit table. (There is only one audit table.) If you d rather not create a new database, then you can create the audit table in an existing database but you ll have to make a couple of simple modifications to the code.

Note: This code is at www.sqlservercentral.com

Creating the Items Table

For the purposes of this example, let s create the items table in the Audit database (something that wouldn t normally happen and it ll work fine if you create it somewhere else.) The script below will create the table and populate it with 4 rows as above.

Note: This code is at www.sqlservercentral.com

Creating the Audit Trigger

Auditing is done by a regular trigger, which first examines the **inserted** and **deleted** tables to establish whether we re dealing with an insert, delete or update. In then tackles each case differently constructing the sql by selecting from the inserted and deleted tables.

The script below will create the trigger on the Items table. Once this is created, you can start playing about, by inserting updating and deleting rows from the Items table. The changes and the sql to undo the changes will be scripted for you in the table BigAudit.

Note: This code is at www.sqlservercentral.com

Now try executing the update and delete statements we saw earlier against the item table. Then take a look at the BigAudit table in the fields RollBackSQL and RollForwardSQL.

Try with your own SQL statements - an insert for example. If you want to rollback the changes just select the script from the BigAudit table

```
SELECT RollBackSQL FROM dbo.BigAudit ORDER BY Autonumber DESC
```

Copy the results into a query window and execute to rollback the changes. (By the way, this will also get recorded to the audit table.) Note the descending sort so that the changes get undone in the right order. This means, for example, that you won't get problems with foreign key constraints.

At this stage you may well be thinking, well that s quite cool, but I ve got lots of tables, with lots of fields, and it s going to take me forever to write such triggers for them. The good news is that you don t have to.

In Part II, I ll be showing you how you can generate these triggers for all tables in your database, in a matter of minutes.

There are a couple of conditions it won t generate triggers for tables that don t have primary keys, and it won t correctly audit changes when changes are made to primary key fields. Hopefully, this won t be an issue for most of us. I m a firm believer that every table without exception should have a primary key, and it s generally considered bad practice to change the value of a primary key field.

A little clue about how it's done - XML is heavily involved!

9 Things to Do When You Inherit a Database

By Sylvia Moestl Vasilik

So ... Bob's left the company to move back east, and you're the new lead database developer on the database. Or, the third-party company to which the maintenance has been outsourced is no longer working on it, so it's yours now. One way or another, you need to take over a database system that you had no part in developing. It's not in good shape, and there's not many resources for you to tap.

What do you do?

I've been faced with this situation a few times now, and have developed a list of some of the things that have helped me the most, both in getting productive, and in bringing the database system up to par.

Backups

Make sure that backups are happening. I'm assuming here that you're the database developer, and not the database administrator. However, just as minimum check, make sure that backups are occurring regularly. Ideally you should successfully restore the backup somewhere else.

Research

Look at the database. Go through and get an idea of the table structure, what the largest tables are by size, what the most commonly used stored procedures are, if there are jobs, and what documentation there is. Read through some the stored procedures. You may find it useful to create a quick and dirty database diagram if there isn't one, using the built in diagramming tool in SQL Server. This can also be a good visual aid when you talk to other people.

Talk to the former developers

This may not be an option, but try hard to have a least a few friendly interviews with the former developers. This is not the time to make comments like, "I can't believe you guys did [insert bad development practice here]". You don't know the history- maybe it was that way when they got the system. You'll want to get as much information as they can give you on current issues, items on this list, etc. Keep things friendly - and maybe try to get their cell number in case of questions. A good relationship with former developers can go a long way.

A bug database

Is there a bug database - somewhere that bugs (and sometimes enhancement ideas) are tracked for this system? This is certainly one of the things that you want to set up, if it's not there currently. I've always been lucky enough to work at companies where bug tracking was taken seriously, and there were systems already in place that I could just plug into. If there's no bug database, time to do some research. I wouldn't suggest reinventing the wheel here, since there's a lot of good systems out there -- just use what's available.

Source code control

Is the code in some kind of source code control system, such as VSS or Perforce? If it is -- is everything up to date? I'm going to hazard a guess that it's either not in source code control, or it hasn't been kept up to date. That's been a big task for me when starting work on inherited systems. There's a number of tools with which to tackle this. In the past I've used a custom written Perl tool that used SQL DMO, but I won't go into detail -- that's the topic of another article. If nothing else, you could use the built in tools that SQL Server provides to script out your database objects, and check them in. Once you have everything checked in, try running a database build from the checked in code, and compare it to production. Also -- make sure you have a good system to keep all the code updated!

Talk to the users and/or business owners

Sit down and have some conversations with the users. This is a good opportunity to get to know their problems and concerns, the improvements they would most like to see, and where things are heading in the future. You want to make sure that this database is sticking around, that it's not going to be replaced with a third party product or anything like that. If you're going to put a lot of work into improving the system, you need to know that your efforts are going to pay off for the business. Also-you'll probably be spending lots of time on issues that are important to a well-run database system (a bug database, source code control, etc), but that won't give them any new features. Make sure they understand this.

Establish credibility with the users by fixing a few things or making some enhancements

Even though you'll probably be needing to spend a lot of time on tasks like setting up source code control, bug tracking, etc, you don't want to do this exclusively. From talks with users, hopefully you've identified enhancements or bug fixes that you could get out quickly. Do what you can here. This is a great way to establish credibility with them. Let them know, too, that once you have the systems in place, bug fixes and enhancements will be much easier to roll out.

Create a development environment

If you don't have a development environment, but code still needs to be written, where are the developers going to write and test their code? I hate to tell you, but if they have access, they'll write and test in the production environment. So you may have stored procedures called CampaignEmailExport_TEST hanging around (and never getting deleted). Or -- oops -- you may accidentally overwrite the production version with your new version, and then it runs and causes hundreds of thousands of emails to be sent where they weren't supposed to. Not that I've ever heard of this happening. This kind of problem can go a long way towards convincing users that time and money needs to be spent on working on setting up a good foundation.

For the development environment-you may be able to just get a backup from production, and set it up on another server. If it's too large, you might need to be creative. Whatever you do, don't develop or test in the production environment.

Drop obsolete objects

In a system that hasn't been maintained very well, it's likely that there are a lot of database objects out there that aren't being used. They may have suffixes like 'temp' or 'bak' on them. It can be hard to identify all of these, and you may be tempted to just leave them. However, they can cause a number of problems:

- They make it difficult to figure out what the actual working code base is. If you have a lot of duplicate, backup, "working" or "temp" objects, you don't know what your code base is like, and how complex it is.

- Supposed you'd like to drop a tables because it's huge, and looks like it hasn't been updated in a long time, but it turns out that they're being used by stored procedure X. If it turns out that stored procedure X is never used, but you're keeping it around in the database anyway, then you've just lost this opportunity to enhance your code because of an obsolete stored procedure. This kind of issue, multiplied by all the obsolete objects that are in the database, can cause development to be very slow, or even grind to a halt.

Finally...

There's potentially months and months of work if you start from scratch on all of the above. It'll require good judgment on what to prioritize, where to start, and how much time to spend on all the tasks that need doing. And perhaps you're not in a position to set all the priorities. But it can be worthwhile and fun to streamline and tune-up a database that just needs a little work to become a well-oiled machine, requiring much less development time.

Thanks for reading!

Cursors for T-SQL Beginners

By Wagner Crivelini

For those who are familiar with other RDBMS's, it may sound weird to hear from T-SQL developers that cursors should be avoided. Other languages even encourage their use.

Cursors treat data in a one-record-at-a-time fashion. Data will be kept in memory, so if you are careful enough when defining the cursor, data retrieval could be faster. But in case you are not, it might be disastrous to your server.

Personally I see cursors as a useful resource, but we do need to watch them closely. Let's take a look into two situations where cursors are used. And let's discuss if they could be replaced using other T-SQL features.

CASE 1 - When concatenating a string

It may sound funny, but I bump into this kind of request (concatenating a string) over and over again. Consider when your application needs to show a person's phone numbers in one single field, as home phone number, business, mobile, fax, etc. To illustrate, let's consider the following table "dbo.tblPhone"

```
CREATE TABLE dbo.tblPhone (
 codUser INT,
 codPhoneType TINYINT,
 PhoneNumber VARCHAR(20),
 ListThisNumber TINYINT ,
PRIMARY KEY (codUser, codPhoneType)
)
GO  INSERT INTO dbo.tblPhone VALUES ( 1, 1, '1 281 444 5555' ,
1 )
GO
INSERT INTO dbo.tblPhone VALUES ( 1, 2, '55 11 4582 2752', 1)
GO
INSERT INTO dbo.tblPhone VALUES ( 1, 3, '1 471 333 1234', 0)
GO
INSERT INTO dbo.tblPhone VALUES ( 2, 1, '1 XXX XXX XXXXX', 1)
GO  CREATE TABLE dbo.tblPhoneType (
 codPhoneType TINYINT,
 PhoneType VARCHAR(50),
PRIMARY KEY (codPhoneType)
)
GO  INSERT INTO dbo.tblPhoneType VALUES ( 1, 'Residential')
```

```
GO
INSERT INTO dbo.tblPhoneType VALUES ( 2, 'Business')
GO
INSERT INTO dbo.tblPhoneType VALUES ( 3, 'Mobile')
GO
INSERT INTO dbo.tblPhoneType VALUES ( 4, 'Fax')
GO
```

To make things a bit more interesting, let's also consider our string has to deal with some business logic that demands conditional testing. In our example, let's say some users may not want to show their numbers in directory listings. The field that informs this preference is "dbo.tblPhone.ListThisNumber": when its value is 1, it means TRUE, list the number. In case it is 0, it means the number should not be listed.

For our purposes here, in the case where the number should not be listed, we would show "***********" instead of the actual number. To improve cursor performance, we will declare the cursor using the "FAST_FORWARD" option. Putting this all together, the cursor we are talking about would look like this when created using T-SQL:

```
DECLARE @AllPhones VARCHAR(1000)
DECLARE @PhoneNumber VARCHAR(20)
DECLARE @ListThisNumber TINYINT

DECLARE curPersonalPhones CURSOR FAST_FORWARD FOR
SELECT PhoneNumber , ListThisNumber
FROM dbo.tblPhone
WHERE codUser = 1

OPEN curPersonalPhones
FETCH NEXT FROM curPersonalPhones
INTO @PhoneNumber, @ListThisNumber

SET @AllPhones = ''
WHILE @@FETCH_STATUS = 0
 BEGIN
 IF @ListThisNumber = 0
 SET @PhoneNumber = '***********'
SET @AllPhones = @AllPhones + @PhoneNumber + ' & '

 FETCH NEXT FROM curPersonalPhones
 INTO @PhoneNumber, @ListThisNumber
 END

CLOSE curPersonalPhones
DEALLOCATE curPersonalPhones   SELECT @AllPhones
GO
```

To make the code simpler, I defined the cursor for one fixed User (codUser = 1) and also disregarded the fact the string will always end with an ampersand ("&").

But now we will see an easier way to do it in T-SQL. When concatenating variables, instead of using cursors, you could use a SELECT statement over the same table, storing the content of field (PhoneNumber) into a variable and concatenating this with the same variable.

This example is well described in many, many articles throughout the web. But how can this deal with the business logic? As the logic in this code is pretty simple, we can use a CASE function within the SELECT statement to have the same result. So, the new code will look like this:

```
DECLARE @AllPhones VARCHAR(1000)

SET @AllPhones = ''
SELECT @AllPhones = @AllPhones +
CASE WHEN P.ListThisNumber = 1
THEN P.PhoneNumber
ELSE '***********'
END
+ ' & '
FROM dbo.tblPhone P
WHERE codUser = 1   SELECT @AllPhones
GO
```

In this particular case, not only is the second code is simpler, but it is also much faster than the cod using a cursor. If you are curious enough, check the execution plan for each set of code. There you should look first for the Estimated Subtree Cost. (If you are not familiar to execution plans, keep in mind Estimated Subtree Cost represents the total cost for the query optimizer to execute the current "batch", combining CPU cost and also I/O cost).

You will see that, although we declare the cursor to be as fast as possible, that code has an Estimated Subtree Cost of 0.0032853 for each iteration, or in other words, each record in the cursor. In this example, we have 4 records, so we have to sum the cost of each iteration to know the cost of the whole loop.

In the other hand, for the second code, which does the exactly same output, the Estimated Subtree Cost is 0.0032859 , or roughly the same number we saw before. But notice this number represents the overall cost, as there is no loop! So, the second approach performed a lot better then the one using cursors. And it will be even better as the table we are querying grows bigger.

One important remark here: depending on the complexity of the business logic, it might turn out to be not possible to put it all together within a single SELECT statement. In those situations, we might have to keep the cursors in our code. This should not sound as a complaint. That's what cursors are for. We should be glad T-SQL has this feature so we can use it wisely.

CASE 2 - When using DML statements within Cursors.

DML (or Data Modification Language) statements include INSERT, UPDATE and DELETE statements. Some RDBMS vendors recommend using cursors together with DML statements to make sure they will run one record at a time. You can easily find examples of this when browsing the online documentation of many RDBMS's. As safe as it might sound, this can be tremendously slow. There are many situations where you can change those statements to handle several records at a time with no effort.

Let's see another example. We will use cursor to handle the data insertion into table "dbo.tblPhone". Consider the table "SouthHemisphere.tblPhone" has exactly the same structure as "dbo.tblPhone", although it collects data from customers who live in the South Hemisphere. We need to move this data to "dbo.tblPhone", which stores information for all customers through out the world. In this example, I tested the code moving 8 new records from "SouthHemisphere.tblPhone" to "dbo.tblPhone". Below you see the code:

```
DECLARE @codUser INT
DECLARE @codPhoneType TINYINT
DECLARE @PhoneNumber VARCHAR(20)
DECLARE @ListThisNumber TINYINT

DECLARE curInsertion CURSOR FAST_FORWARD FOR
SELECT codUser, codPhoneType, PhoneNumber, ListThisNumber
FROM SouthHemisphere.tblPhone

OPEN curInsertion
FETCH NEXT FROM curInsertion
INTO @codUser, @codPhoneType, @PhoneNumber, @ListThisNumber

WHILE @@FETCH_STATUS = 0
 BEGIN
INSERT INTO dbo.tblPhone
 SELECT @codUser, @codPhoneType, @PhoneNumber, @ListThisNumber
 WHERE @PhoneNumber NOT IN (SELECT PhoneNumber FROM
dbo.tblPhone)
FETCH NEXT FROM curInsertion
 INTO @codUser, @codPhoneType, @PhoneNumber, @ListThisNumber
 END
```

```
CLOSE curInsertion
DEALLOCATE curInsertion
GO
```

I did not include a transaction in this piece of code to keep it as simple as possible. But, of course, inserting one record at a time will give you more control over the process, as you can commit or rollback each individual row. But analyzing its execution plan, you see there will be a cost for each fetch (Estimated Subtree Cost = 0.0032908) plus the cost for each insert (0.0132976). This cost will exist either we insert the new record or not. Finally, we will have a final fetch, which will define the end of the loop. This also has a cost.

Doing the math, we will have the estimated cost of for each record times the number of 8 records plus the cost of the final fetch. The overall estimate cost is 0.1460048. The other approach is to insert all records at once. So, if you have transaction in the code, either you commit all records or you rollback them all. The INSERT statement will look like this:

```
INSERT INTO dbo.tblPhone
SELECT S.codUser, S.codPhoneType, S.PhoneNumber,
S.ListThisNumber
FROM SouthHemisphere.tblPhone S
WHERE S.PhoneNumber NOT IN (SELECT PhoneNumber FROM
dbo.tblPhone)
```

Besides being a lot simpler, the cost for this statement to insert the same 8 records will be 0.0298601, much faster than the previous one. As pointed out, the cons in this approach is that we do not have any control in the record level. It works as a batch: either all records are successfully inserted or they all fail.

Putting it all together.

Well, I showed a lot of numbers and I do agree this get a bit confusing. Those are real numbers (in the mathematical sense also) and it is hard to believe we humans should be able to handle such a thing.

On the next page I show a table with the Estimated Subtree Cost for all 4 scripts. Numbers represent the total cost for the whole script, as I added the cost of each statement within the script.

Estimated Cost for Each Script

c1	c2	c3	c4	c5
Script	# of Affected Rows	Total Estimated Cost with Cursor	Total Estimated Cost without Cursor	Difference $(c3-c4)/c4$ %
CASE 1: Concatenate string	4	0.0131412	0.0032859	300%
CASE 2: DML statements	8	0.1460048	0.0298601	389%

Please, remember you should not take those numbers for granted. They are valid solely for the scripts shown in this article. You should do the same kind of assessment for your own scripts and analyze the performance of those scripts.

Every Rule has an Exception

OK, from the syntax standpoint, replacing cursors looks nice and neat. From the performance standpoint, replacing cursors may boost your performance. But when replacing cursors, we are letting go some important features that only cursors can provide to your code.

Besides, remember every rule has an exception. You should not take the avoid-cursors advice as rule, but as a hint. Each situation deserves attention, as you can have a fast and well-designed code using cursors. And, in the other hand, you can also find poor-performance codes specially created to avoid cursors.

Whenever you suspect your code is not running as expected, no matter it uses cursors or not, you should check your code's execution plan. This is the ultimate information you have to assess your code's performance.

DAC - What to Execute when Connected?

By Rudy Panigas

If your SQL server is in trouble and you cannot connect then the next option is to connect with the Dedicated Administators Connection (DAC). Once connected, you can collect some information on what is happening. Since you are under pressure, it would be nice to have a stored procedure to execute that displays information? Below is my script that does just that.

You want to execute the code below in the MASTER database to create the sp_dba_DAC stored procedure. We do this in MASTER because you generally have access to this database when the server is extremely busy. Now open a CMD/DOS window and execute the following.

```
sqlcmd -A -S<server/instance name> -dmaster -E -Q"sp_dba_DAC" -
oc:\dac-results.txt
```

Replace the *<server/instance name>* with your server or instance name.

Once you execute this command, a connection is made to the server/instance and the stored procedure "sp_dba_DAC" located in the MASTER database is executed. A file called "dac-results.txt" is created in the root of C: and the connection is terminated.

Open the "dac-results.txt" file with notepad (or any other editor) and you can quickly see the information.

Below is what is collected

- Shows SQL Servers information
- Shows top 5 high cpu used statemants
- Shows who so logged in
- Shows long running cursors
- Shows idle sessions that have open transactions
- Shows free space in tempdb database

- Shows total disk allocated to tempdb database
- Show active jobs
- Shows clients connected
- Shows running batch
- Shows currently blocked requests
- Shows last backup dates
- Shows jobs that are still executing
- Shows failed MS SQL jobs report
- Shows disabled jobs
- Shows avail free DB space
- Shows total DB size (.MDF+.LDF)
- Show hard drive space available

Remember to create this stored procedure on your servers before you need to connect with DAC. Add additional stored procedure(s) or T-SQL code to provide even more information.

Note: This code is at www.sqlservercentral.com

Getting a Clue about Your Databases

By Gregor Borosa

Introduction

Once in a while most of us get a task to "get some data out of some database". I don't know if it's just me, but I keep asked to work with databases I know nothing about. I usually have no documentation and no knowledge about the data model, naming conventions, nothing much at all. Usually I only have some vague information about the things I am looking for, e.g. "all customer's data from our legacy web shop database" in which case I already expect to find some usual customers and orders related tables, like Customers, Companies, Countries, Orders, etc. However one can easily be lost among all the tables and columns.

So in order to make some starting point from which I could learn more about these databases, I've made three little stored procedures, each getting me more detailed information about the objects I'm exploring. I imagine these things might be more elegant to do in other tools, but I only have SQL Server 2000 at my disposal.

The idea is this: you have a database, but don't know which tables to look at, so first try to find the interesting ones (or at least narrow your candidate list). When you know which tables to analyze, then you need to know if these tables are somehow linked to others, so you check dependencies on them - as much as you need to (which might not always be very straightforward or easy using queries). Then you would like to get a feeling about which columns are most likely be worth checking out, so you try your luck finding similarly named columns.

The results will of course very much depend on each situation, but since the Items table usually has some columns named like %item%, then it might be worth checking the tables with similar names. During the process, a list of candidate tables is to be analyzed: how big, what columns, how many distinct values etc. While not always 100% accurate, the figures given are enough for the purpose - which is what matters anyhow. At the end, there will be some manual work with scrolling through the results, but nothing of overkill.

Since we are looking for tables which are somewhat central to the database, where all the"good data" lies, have lots of rows and lots of dependencies, we can guess that such tables will have at least a few similarly named columns. They are good candidates to review. If I'm looking at a standard Orders table, there will most likely be a column named something very close to [Customer No.]. Exactly the same column name will then probably be used elsewhere in the database, everywhere a customer is important. And that is what we're looking for in the first place.

Big tables and dependencies

The first procedure is an already known BigTables procedure, based on the system procedure sp_spaceused. I've modified and slightly expanded Bill Graziano's code[6]. This procedure lists top tables by their size (row count, space reserved/used and index size), while also displaying the number of dependant objects of each table. This is providing an important hint about the table, because "big tables" might only be some kind of dumps of data, let's say images (lots of disk space), or some tally tables (lots of rows) etc. But if I know that one particular table is used in some views or stored procedures, I can more accurately narrow my focus.

Note: This code is at www.sqlservercentral.com

Sample results are on the picture below:

	TABLE_Name	rows	reservedKB	dataPrcnt	indexPrcnt	unusedPrcnt	dependants
1	Order Details	2155	328 KB	22 %	63 %	15 %	7
2	Orders	830	496 KB	32 %	63 %	5 %	14
3	Customers	91	104 KB	23 %	77 %	0 %	8
4	Products	77	104 KB	8 %	92 %	0 %	13
5	Territories	53	32 KB	25 %	75 %	0 %	1

Note: while right-clicking on a table in Enterprise Manager or Management Studio and displaying dependencies is the most straightforward thing to do to check dependant objects, doing so with a query in SQL 2000 is not so elegant. There's a system stored procedure sp_depends which uses sysdepends table and a much more revealing, but undocumented procedure sp_msdependencies, which consists of a pile of code I'm not even trying to grasp, so I'm just using sp_msdependencies to fill a temporary table. Unfortunately, this might trigger some not really harmful errors, so I also included a snippet for using sp_depends, just in case you don't like to see any errors whatsoever). I hate to say it, but: ignore the errors and review query results.

---

[6] http://www.sqlteam.com/article/finding-the-biggest-tables-in-a-database

Searching for similarly named columns

The purpose of the second procedure is finding tables with similar column names. It lists all columns of a given table, avoiding some data types (images, timestamps etc.), and not minding the columns not used in indexes in linked tables. That is for narrowing our results. If you don't get enough rows with potentially linked tables, you can try commenting out the line with the join on sysindexes table and/or trying partial matches to column names with %s.

Note: This code is at www.sqlservercentral.com

Sample results are on the picture below:

	Column_name	Column_type	Table_name	RowsCount
1	CustomerID	nchar	CustomerCustomerDemo	0
2	CustomerID	nchar	Customers	91
3	CustomerID	nchar	Orders	830
4	EmployeeID	int	Employees	9
5	EmployeeID	int	EmployeeTerritories	49

Note: also check foreign keys, of course.

Narrowing on a table level

The third procedure returns some handy data about one chosen table, which might be of value especially if you would like to cancel out empty or almost empty columns (you've seen your tables with few hundred columns, most of those not really used). It provides data about the number of indexes, dependencies (again, review query results, ignore possible errors from sp_msdependencies), rows, columns and distinct entries in a column.

Note: This code is at www.sqlservercentral.com

Sample results are on the picture below:

	TableName	ColumnsCount	IndexesCount	DependenciesCount	RowsCount
1	KommTran	11	4	0	565621

	Column_Name	Column_Type	Count_Distincts
1	CLOSED	smallint	1
2	ERROR_CODE	int	1
3	REC_STAT	smallint	1
4	STATUS	int	2
5	T_DATE	datetime	565637

Note: with the results here one can easily get a sense of what's the deal with the table "KommTrans". Everything's stored in T_DATE field. Other columns are most likely of little use (regarding the content-oriented user).

Conclusion

It might take few seconds for all this to finish on let's say hundreds of tables, but be aware when dealing with larger numbers, as it might be a good idea to fine tune the queries to your situation (I've run it on 200 GB database with 30,000 tables: it took 5 hours to check dependencies!) - more precisely: re-think how you want to check object dependencies. **These procedures can be something to start from, but they were valuable for me a couple of times so far.** I've done this in SQL 2000 - it works on 2005 also, but there might be easier ways to do this in SQL 2005. One funny note: sp_msdependencies is behaving quite well in SQL 2005, at least in my experiments I got no errors.

Ordering Tables to Preserve Referential Integrity

By Glen Cooper

When merging two databases with the same schema, primary keys may have the same values in both databases, yet represent unrelated records. Typically you would carry over such keys as legacy values, re-create new ones in the target database, and then re-calculate all foreign keys that reference them in related tables. But in what order should these tables be ported to avoid violating referential integrity in the target database? Consider the following schema for a customer database (Fig. 1):

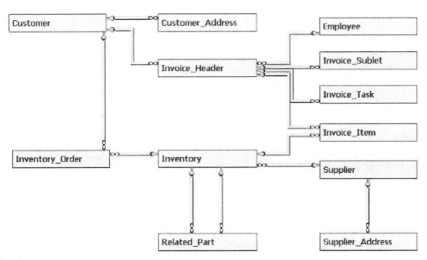

Fig. 1

If this database is appended to another database having the same schema, all primary keys in the source database must be re-calculated to new values in the target database to avoid clashing with existing values. Furthermore, all foreign keys pointing to them from other tables must also be re-calculated so they continue referencing the same records as before. That's the easy part.

The hard part is figuring out the order these tables should be ported.

In the example above, the **Customer** table must be ported before the **Customer_Address** table so that referential integrity won't be violated in the target database. In other words, when porting the latter table, all records from the former table must already be present so that the foreign key in the latter table can be re-calculated using the legacy values from the original table. Otherwise the insertions will fail.

We want to assign a "level" to each table, so that if they're ported by ascending level then no violations of referential integrity will occur. In the above example, it's easy to see that the following assignment of levels will do that:

Level	Table	Abbreviation
0	Customer	C
0	Employee	E
0	Supplier	S
1	Customer_Address	CA
1	Invoice_Header	IH
1	Inventory	I
1	Supplier_Address	SA
2	Inventory_Order	IO
2	Invoice_Sublet	IS
2	Invoice_Task	IT
2	Invoice_Item	II
2	Related_Part	RP

Here the **Customer, Employee** and **Supplier** tables may be ported in any order (so long as they're ported first). Ditto for **Customer_Address, Invoice_Header, Inventory**, and **Supplier_Address** (so long as they're ported next). But **Invoice_Item** must be ported later since it has a foreign key pointing to **Invoice_Header**.

Furthermore, it's easy to see that this assignment of levels is "optimal" in the sense that each table receives the lowest possible assignment.

The following script computes an optimal assignment of levels that preserves referential integrity. To explain how it works, it's helpful to use the language of partially-ordered sets (see ***http://en.wikipedia.org/wiki/Partially_ordered_set*** for an overview of posets).

Suppose that **Invoice_Header** has a foreign key pointing to **Customer**. We can represent this dependency as:

Customer < Invoice_Header

where the "smaller" table **Customer** must be ported before **Invoice_Header**.

Suppose also that **Invoice_Item** has a pointer to **Invoice_Header**.

Then Invoice_Header < Invoice_Item.

Of course, this now implies that **Customer** must always be ported before **Invoice_Item** even though there's no direct link between them.

To formally describe this "transitivity of dependency", recursively define the relationship << as:

```
A << B if A < B
A << B if A < C and C << B for some C
```

Prolog programmers will recognize these "axioms" as the classical ancestor relationship. In particular, **Customer** << **Invoice_Item**. More generally, << is a partial order expressing what tables must be ported before others, even if there's no pointer between two tables satisfying this relationship.

It's easy to demonstrate that << defines a partial order since closed loops in < (called a preorder) aren't possible for tables with data in them. Note that two tables violating referential integrity can still co-exist providing that no records have been inserted into either of them (and of course, it will always remain that way). This remote possibility is addressed by the script because otherwise they'll cause infinite loops.

To port these tables while respecting their dependencies, it's sufficient to list them in such a way that each table appears "before" those that are "larger" in the partial ordering <<. That's what the script does. The so-called Hasse diagram in Fig. 2 displays the above preorder (with arrows representing <). It will show us how to assign the table levels.

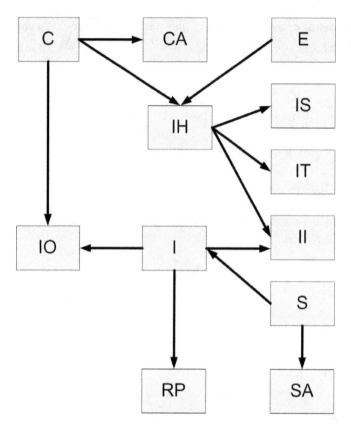

Fig. 2

What we first do is add a fictional table **F** (see Fig. 3) and enough virtual arrows so that every non-fictional table points to at least one other table (possibly fictional). By using this trick we'll avoid special cases. This virtual object is reminiscent of the well-known "point of infinity" in non-Euclidean geometry since its purpose is to simply appear "bigger" than anything else in the database for the purposes of the script.

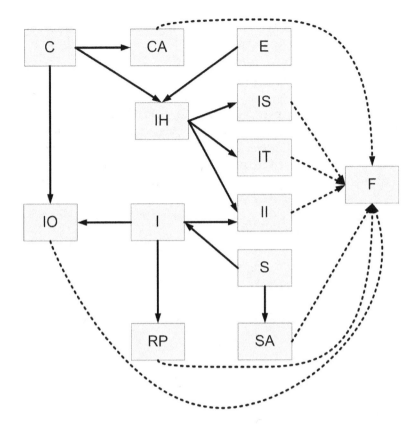

Fig. 3

Then we select those tables to which no arrow points, assign a level of 0 to them, and remove them from the diagram (along with all arrows connected to or from them). These are the tables that can be ported first, since no other tables depend on them.

For example, we would remove **S** and its two arrows. But since arrows are represented in the script by rows of an SQL Server table whose columns define the "to" and "from" tables, **SA** would suddenly disappear if the fictional table weren't present (so **SA** would never be part of the final answer). That's why we have **F**.

After this we start all over with whatever remains, but assign a level of 1. Note that **SA** has been assigned a level of 1 at this point, but it could never be assigned anything lower because an incoming arrow was originally present (from **S**). In particular, each table will be assigned its own level "just in time". In fact, levels are just the longest path lengths of any table to one of level 0, if you follow the arrows backwards. We continue this way until no more elements remain. Then we remove **F** from the answer.

Note: The script is available from www.sqlservercentral.com

I've used permanent tables to compute the answer (instead of table variables) so readers can verify the computations as the script proceeds (the last two lines will need to be deleted for this). Furthermore, since preorders appear naturally in computing, the script can be used for other purposes where you want to know the level of each object in such relationships (simply replace the snippet that uses SQL Server's sys.foreign_key_columns with one of your own). For the mathematically inclined, this exercise determines the maximum cardinality of ancestor chains for every point in a preorder.

This technique was used to join 17 faculty departments in a major university, where special processing was required on each lookup table (e.g. academic titles) since incompatible values were used before they were merged.

Creating a recycle bin for SQL Server 2005\2008

By Chris Kinley

Introduction

Recently while being shown around Oracle 10G (yes I said the 'O' word) I noticed that this product has a recycle bin. This recycle bin which stores only dropped tables falls under the Oracle flashback technology umbrella.

I was pretty sure I could do the same in SQL server using DDL triggers and schemas and prevent accidental drops of other objects as well. This article is the result of that challenge.

In a nutshell the SQL Server recycle bin is a combination of two schemas which act as bins (recycle bin and trash can) and a DDL trigger which determines which bin to place the dropped object (which is not dropped but renamed). A stored procedure (sp_undrop) is used to revert the object to its original name and schema.

Functional overview

The recycle bin holds one only copy of the most recent version of a dropped object (table, view, stored procedure or function). The trash can holds older versions of the object if the object has been dropped more than once. The trash can be purged regularly with a scheduled task consisting of a simple script.

- The UNDROP command will revert the most recent dropped copy of an object to its original location.
- If a DROP is performed on an object already in the recycle bin the object is moved to the trash can.
- If a DROP is performed on an object already in the trash can the DROP is ignored.

Figure 1 shows the Sales.vIndividualDemographics view with the most recent drop in the recycle bin and older versions in the trash can.

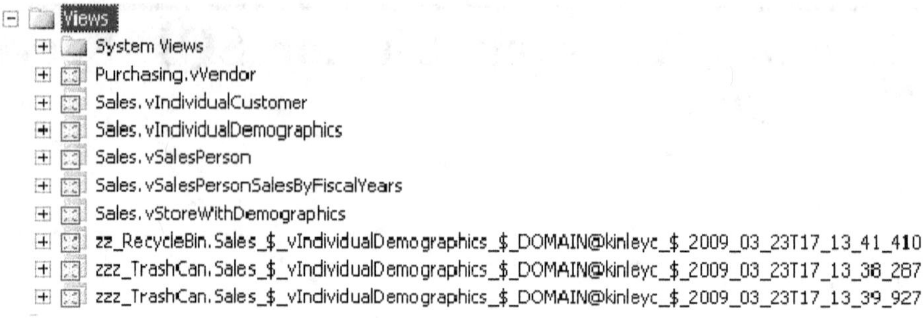

Views
- System Views
- Purchasing.vVendor
- Sales.vIndividualCustomer
- Sales.vIndividualDemographics
- Sales.vSalesPerson
- Sales.vSalesPersonSalesByFiscalYears
- Sales.vStoreWithDemographics
- zz_RecycleBin.Sales_$_vIndividualDemographics_$_DOMAIN@kinleyc_$_2009_03_23T17_13_41_410
- zzz_TrashCan.Sales_$_vIndividualDemographics_$_DOMAIN@kinleyc_$_2009_03_23T17_13_38_287
- zzz_TrashCan.Sales_$_vIndividualDemographics_$_DOMAIN@kinleyc_$_2009_03_23T17_13_39_927

Figure 1 A view of recycle bin and trash can objects

Technology overview

The SQL Server recycle bin protects spurious drops of tables, views, stored procedures and user defined functions. To enable the recycle bin the following is needed:

- Two schemas. One for the recycle bin and one for the trash can.

- One DDL trigger. This database level trigger manages objects into the recycle bin and trash can.

- One stored procedure. This is the undrop functionality and is best mounted in the master database.

Via the DDL trigger the dropped object is renamed and then moved to the recycle bin schema and the original transaction rolled back. All the information needed to undrop the object is stored in the new name so no additional metadata tables are needed.

Schemas for recycle bin and trash can

The recycle bin and trash can are simply schemas (created by the DBA as a prerequisite). The main DDL trigger will check for the existence of these schemas and abort the DROP if they don't exist. For this article I have used schema names starting with 'z' which keeps them at the bottom of the explorer view (see Figure 2 below).

Tip: The schema names for the recycle bin and trash can are declared as constants in the trigger and stored procedure. Feel free to choose your own but check they match up across all code.

```
USE [AdventureWorks]
GO
CREATE SCHEMA [zz_RecycleBin] AUTHORIZATION [dbo]
GO
CREATE SCHEMA [zzz_TrashCan] AUTHORIZATION [dbo]
GO
```

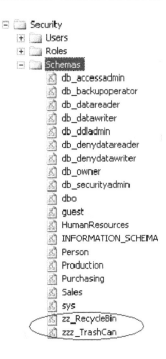

Figure 2 Recycle bin and trash can schemas

Creating the main DDL trigger

This article assumes a working knowledge of DDL triggers. For a refresher on this feature see ***http://www.sqlservercentral.com/articles/SQL+Server+2005+-+Security/2927/*** . A full code listing (commented) of this trigger is provided as a resource with this article. We will now walk through the main sections. Only one DDL trigger with database scope is required.

The trigger does the following:

- Checks for the existence of the recycle bin and trash can schemas.
- Captures the data about the dropped object.

- Builds a new object name which is the name it will have while in the recycle bin.

- If needed changes the schema of an old version of the object in the recycle bin to the trash can.

- Renames the dropped object.

- Changes the schema of the dropped object to that of the recycle bin.

First create the trigger. The trigger is at the database scope level.

Note: This code is at www.sqlservercentral.com

Then check to see if the recycle bin and trash can schemas exist. No point continuing if they don't.

Note: This code is at www.sqlservercentral.com

The next step is to extract the information need from EVENTDATA(). We're interested in:

- What was dropped (both schema and object name)?

- Who dropped?

- When dropped?

Then build up the object name as it would exist in the recycle bin. The format using the delimiter _$_ is:originalschema_$_originalname_$_domain@login _$_yyyy_mm_ddThh_mm_ss_sss

So the Sales.vIndividualDemographics view dropped by kinleyc on March 23 at 10:20:41 would be renamed to:
Sales_$_vIndividualDemographics_$_DOMAIN@kinleyc_$_2009_03_23T10 _20_41_997

Note: This code is at www.sqlservercentral.com

There is another check to see if the object being dropped is already in the trash can. If so the drop is aborted by issuing a ROLLBACK followed by a RETURN thus ending the trigger. I've chosen to engineer this way for the following reasons. Firstly it prevents objects from ever being dropped unless the DBA explicitly disables the trigger. Secondly forcing a drop would again fire the same trigger recursively and the code would have to be made more complex to allow for this.

```
IF @schema_name = @CONST_TRASHCAN_SCHEMA_NAME
BEGIN
PRINT 'This object is already in the trash can '
PRINT 'The trigger recyclebin_drop_object must be disabled for
this DROP to work'
ROLLBACK
RETURN
END
```

Now we come to the core part of the trigger where the main rename and transfer takes place. There are checks here to determine if the object being dropped is a recycle bin object or the object is in a non-recycle bin schema and an older version exists in the recycle bin. If it is an explicit drop of an object already in the recycle bin then no rename takes place and only a schema transfer to the trash can is invoked. If there is an older version of the object in the recycle bin then this is moved to the trash can to make 'space' for the new object coming in. All renames and transfer commands are prepared before initiating a transaction.

Note: This code is at www.sqlservercentral.com

It's time now to rollback the original transaction. Remember that all triggers have a transaction in progress when they are invoked. Usually it's autocommited when the trigger completes but in our case we want to stop the original drop and do our own thing.

```
ROLLBACK
```

For the final rename\transfer I've elected to use a nested transaction within the trigger the reason being I want the rename and transfer to be an all or nothing event. I've kept the transaction very short, within a try block and am not doing validation within the transaction except for variables.

See books online: *ms-help://MS.SQLCC.v10/MS.SQLSVR.v10.en/s10de_1devconc/html/650105c1-32fd-4f16-8082-f391c42c3fb0.htm* for information on transactions in triggers.

Note: This code is at www.sqlservercentral.com

The catch block is taken directly from books online to allow for uncommittable transactions. See books online:

ms-help://MS.SQLCC.v10/MS.SQLSVR.v10.en/s10de_6tsql/html/e9300827-e793-4eb6-9042-ffa0204aeb50.htm

Following the catch there are some PRINT statements back to the DBA to see the new object name.

Note: This code is at www.sqlservercentral.com

I've chosen to start a new transaction at the end of the trigger. This is solely to prevent to 3609 error when the trigger detects *@@trancount = 0*. The trigger is in autocommit mode so this dummy transaction is committed when the trigger ends. If you don't want to have it there and are OK seeing the 3609 error then remove this line. The result is the same the recycle bin will still work. The books online article for triggers mentioned above discusses this error.

```
BEGIN TRANSACTION
END
```

Figure 3 on the next page shows different objects being dropped and the results in the query results window.

```
DROP TABLE HumanResources.Manager
DROP VIEW Sales.vIndividualCustomer
DROP PROCEDURE dbo.uspGetManagerEmployees
DROP FUNCTION dbo.ufnGetContactInformation
DROP FUNCTION dbo.ufnGetAccountingEndDate
```

```
Results

Caution: Changing any part of an object name could break scripts and stored procedures.
The object HumanResources.Manager has been moved to the recycle bin
as object zz_RecycleBin.HumanResources_$_Manager_$_HAYSHPS@kinleyc_$_2009_03_30T18_42_37_243

Caution: Changing any part of an object name could break scripts and stored procedures.
The object Sales.vIndividualCustomer has been moved to the recycle bin
as object zz_RecycleBin.Sales_$_vIndividualCustomer_$_HAYSHPS@kinleyc_$_2009_03_30T18_42_37_417

Caution: Changing any part of an object name could break scripts and stored procedures.
The object dbo.uspGetManagerEmployees has been moved to the recycle bin
as object zz_RecycleBin.dbo_$_uspGetManagerEmployees_$_HAYSHPS@kinleyc_$_2009_03_30T18_42_37_430

Caution: Changing any part of an object name could break scripts and stored procedures.
The object dbo.ufnGetContactInformation has been moved to the recycle bin
as object zz_RecycleBin.dbo_$_ufnGetContactInformation_$_HAYSHPS@kinleyc_$_2009_03_30T18_42_37_463

Caution: Changing any part of an object name could break scripts and stored procedures.
The object dbo.ufnGetAccountingEndDate has been moved to the recycle bin
as object zz_RecycleBin.dbo_$_ufnGetAccountingEndDate_$_HAYSHPS@kinleyc_$_2009_03_30T18_42_37_463
```

Figure 3.

The UNDROP

It's no surprise that the undrop functionality is basically a reverse of the process from the recycle bin trigger. The undrop does not involve the trash can.

I chose to name the stored procedure *sp_undrop* and mount it in the master database so it can be called from any user database. Books online recommends not naming stored procedures with the sp_ prefix as they may clash with future system stored procedures. I figure if Microsoft introduces similar functionality they will use UNDROP as the command - that's my excuse anyway.

The full code listing (commented) of this stored procedure is provided as a resource with this article.

There are two input parameters, the combination of which makes the object unique in the database. Note that the *@undropname* parameter includes both the schema and name. An example of the stored procedure invocation.

```
EXEC SP_UNDROP @undroptype = 'PROCEDURE' , @undropname =
N'HumanResources.uspUpdateEmployeeHireInfo'
```

```
USE MASTER
GO
CREATE PROC [dbo].[SP_UNDROP]
@undroptype varchar(10) =NULL
, @undropname nvarchar(200)=NULL
AS
```

Two tables are used two store initial objects kept in the recycle bin. The first table *#sysobjects* is a temporary table so that it can be called with sp_executesql. The second table *@object_list* is the main storage table for the procedure. It stores the recycled name and various components of the original name. As this procedure is essentially about parsing there are also columns to store delimiter positions. After the initialisation of variables and constants an initial check is made to guard against execution in system databases.

Note: This code is at www.sqlservercentral.com

Now the two work tables are populated. The table *#sysobjects* table is loaded with recycle bin objects using *sys.objects* and *sys.schemas*. The table variable *@object_list* is populated with the same data plus additional information about the location of objects in the long recycle bin object name. An object count is determined and then the *#sysobjects* is then dropped. A further update of the work table is done to parse out the original object and schema names as well as deriving a full object type name.

Note: This code is at www.sqlservercentral.com

All the preparation is now done. The main conditional statement now starts and determines one of three paths:

1. At least one parameter is missing and at least one object in recycle bin.

2. Both parameters supplied and at least one object in recycle bin.

3. No objects in recycle bin.

If the first condition is met the procedure lists out all objects in the recycle bin with ready-to-go undrop syntax.

Note: This code is at www.sqlservercentral.com

EXEC SP_UNDROP results in:

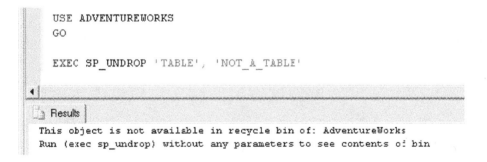

Figure 4 using sp_undrop without parameters

If the second condition is satisfied a further check is done to make sure the object exists.

```
ELSE IF (@object_list_count = 0 OR @object_list_count IS NULL)
BEGIN
PRINT 'There are no objects in the recycle bin'
END
```

EXEC SP_UNDROP 'TABLE' , 'NOT_A_TABLE' results in:

```
USE ADVENTUREWORKS
GO

EXEC SP_UNDROP 'TABLE', 'NOT_A_TABLE'
```

```
Results
This object is not available in recycle bin of: AdventureWorks
Run (exec sp_undrop) without any parameters to see contents of bin
```

Figure 5 using sp_undrop when the object does not exist

If the objects exists then the undrop is attempted within in a transaction.

Note: This code is at www.sqlservercentral.com

Taking out the trash

At the DBA's discretion the trash can be purged with a basic loop-the-loop script inside a scheduled job. There are two items of note in this script. One is the disabling and enabling of the DDL trigger to avoid any recursive trigger complications. The other is setting the trash can schema name of the *@TRASHCAN_SCHEMA_NAME* which must match the one used in the DDL trigger.

Note: This code is at www.sqlservercentral.com

Conclusion

Whether protecting your production databases from unexpected object drops or implementing a simple method of storing historical versions of objects this combination of schemas and a DDL trigger will do both

Using SQL Profiler to Resolve Deadlocks in SQL Server

By Jonathan Kehayias

It's fairly common knowledge that deadlocks in SQL Server are caused by a cyclic dependency between multiple processes, threads or sessions, for a set of resources in SQL Server. What most people don't realize is that while there are many different types of deadlocks, the methods used to resolve them all is fundamentally the same. When the deadlock monitor in SQL Server encounters a deadlock, it immediately analyzes the processes contributing to the deadlock and determines which will be the least expensive to rollback. Once this has been determined, that process is killed and a 1205 error is returned to the client.

The first thing to consider when troubleshooting deadlocks is that a deadlock in and of itself is not necessarily a problem. A properly designed and coded application will have exception handling built around all connections to SQL Server that can intercept the 1205 error and resubmit the deadlock victim request back to SQL Server. Generally speaking, the locking scenario that existed to cause the deadlock will not exist during the resubmission and the transaction will complete successfully the second time around. This however, is not actually solving the deadlock, it is just preventing the deadlock from being problematic and causing data/productivity losses to occur.

To properly resolve deadlocks in SQL Server the first that you will need is the deadlock graph. In SQL Server 2005, there are two different ways to get the deadlock graph. The first way to get a deadlock graph is to enable trace flag 1222 which is a newer version of trace flag 1204 which existed in SQL Server 2000 to output deadlock graph information. The output from this trace flag can be a bit complex to follow at first if you are not used to reading the information contained within it. The second way to get the deadlock graph is to use SQL Trace and capture the Deadlock Graph event and save the Deadlock XML Events separately from the trace file. This can be done with SQL Profiler in real time, or with a scripted server side trace which can be turned on and off as needed for deadlock analysis.

If the deadlocks are fairly frequent and you believe that you can time their occurrence, then using SQL Profiler is really fast and simple. First start up the application and connect to the SQL Instance in question. Then on the Events

Selection Tab, add the Locks: Deadlock Graph Event and then remove all of the other events from the trace definition.

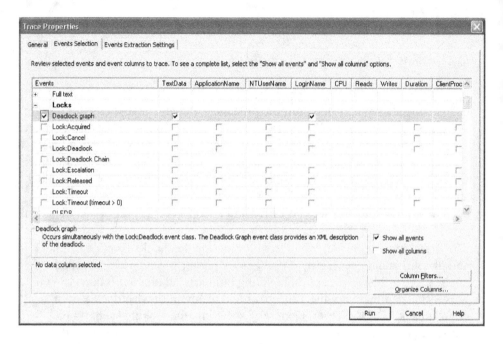

Then click on the Events Extraction Settings Tab, and check the Save Deadlock XML events separately box and specify a path and filename for saving the events to. Then select whether you want to save the events all to one file or to a separate file for each deadlocking batch.

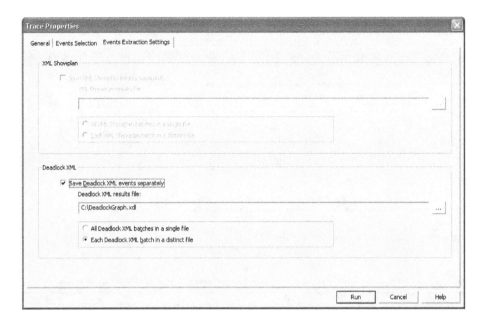

Then start the trace and wait for Deadlocks to occur and be captured by the trace. To simulate one of the more common deadlocking scenarios that I find occurring on the forums, attached to this article is a set of scripts to create a UPDATE/SELECT deadlock against a single table.

To simulate the deadlock first run the setup script. Then open the Selecter script in one window, and the Updater script in a second window. Then run both the Selecter and the Updater scripts. A deadlock will immediately be produced and captured by the Profiler Trace as follows:

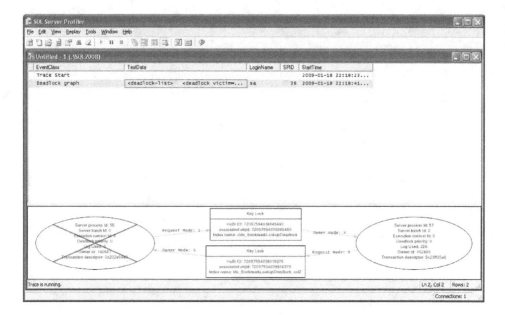

As you can see, we get a nice graphical display of what occurred during the deadlock. In the center are the lock resources involved in the cyclic locking that resulted in the deadlocks. The arrows show the lock owners and requestors and the ovals show the session_id's or SPIDs participating the deadlock. In the case of the above image, SPID 55 which selected as the deadlock victim and was killed. This is shown by the big X over the SPID information. If you hover the mouse over the SPID you can see the statement that was being executed. What this doesn't allow you to do easily is copy the information for further analysis. This is where having the extracted event information in XDL format becomes very helpful.

The XDL files output by SQL Trace/ SQL Profiler are just XML documents that are the same format as the information returned by trace flag 1222. The first place to start troubleshooting deadlocks similar to the one above is to look at the execution plans for both of the contributing processes. In this case, the plan of interest is for the Selecter process as shown below:

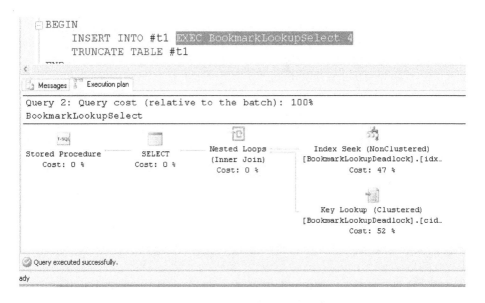

The key point of interest in this Execution Plan is the Key Lookup. When the Selecter process runs, it takes a shared lock on the non-clustered index [idx_BookmarkLookupDeadlock_col2] to maintain concurrency while it reads the data. The problem is that the index is only on one column [col2] and therefore does not contain the necessary columns to completely satisfy the select statement. Since non-clustered indexes also include the clustered index key, they can be used to lookup the missing columns from the clustered index using a Key Lookup operation. This will require a shared lock on the non-clustered index as well as a shared lock on the needed rows in the clustered index.

The deadlock in this type of scenario is completely timing based, and it can be difficult to reproduce without a looping execution as used in the attached demo. The select process gets the Shared Lock on the non-clustered index, and at the same time, the update process gets an Exclusive Lock on the Clustered Index. In order to complete, the select will need a shared lock on the Clustered Index, which is incompatible with the existing exclusive lock so it is blocked until the update completes. However, the update will also require an Exclusive Lock on each of the non-clustered indexes that contain the columns being updated, which is incompatible with the existing Shared Lock held by the select process, so it is blocked. This blocked/blocked situation is the cyclic dependency that will never resolve itself, so the deadlock monitor selects the SPID with the least cost to rollback, in this case the select and kills the session. This frees the non-clustered index for the update to complete.

To resolve this type of deadlock two things can be done. First you can remove the non-clustered index which will result in a clustered index scan to satisfy the select process, which is not ideal, and bad for performance. The other thing you can do is to create a covering index for the select query that contains all of the columns needed to satisfy the query. In SQL Server 2005, this can be accomplished by using the INCLUDED column list in the index definition. For the attached demo, the index definition would be:

```
CREATE INDEX idx_BookmarkLookupDeadlock_col2_icol3
ON dbo.BookmarkLookupDeadlock (col2)
INCLUDE (col3)
```

This allows a single index see to occur to solve the select and prevents the cross index lookup from occurring thus preventing the deadlock.

This is but one of many different ways that deadlocks can occur. Usually, deadlocks are caused by a problem in the underlying tables or index structures, by accessing tables in reverse order in code, different isolation levels between the conflicting SPIDs or a combination of all of the above. Even heap allocations with no indexes can be deadlocked against, so the solution isn't to just not use indexing. Even with "proper design" it is still possible to have deadlocking occur which is why it is crucial for applications to properly handle 1205 errors generated by the database engine. If a deadlock occurs, a properly built application should log the occurrence, but also resubmit the deadlocked transaction as a part of handling the error

What SQL Statements Are Currently Executing?

By Ian Stirk

Introduction

sp_who2 is a well known utility that shows what spids are currently executing. However the information it shows is relatively limited. For example, it only shows the type of command executing as SELECT, DELETE etc, with no reference to the actual underlying SQL executing.

Knowing what SQL is executing can be vital in debugging why a query is taking a long time, or determining if it is being blocked. It can also be useful in showing the progress of a stored procedure i.e. what statement within the stored procedure is currently executing.

The utility described in this article will obviate these limitations of sp_who2.

The utility makes use of Dynamic Management Views (DMVs), so can be used by SQL Server 2005 or greater.

What SQL Statements Are Currently Executing Utility

The SQL used in this utility dba_WhatSQLIsExecuting is given in Listing 1.

The Dynamic Management View (DMV) sys.db_exec_requests shows which requests are currently executing, the information shown includes the handle to the whole SQL text of the batch or stored procedure (sql_handle), together with offsets relating to the section of SQL within the batch that is currently executing (statement_start_offset and statement_end_offset).

To determine the current section of SQL currently executing, we need to call the Dynamic Management Function (DMF) sys.dm_exec_sql_text, passing in the handle of the SQL batch that is currently executing, and then apply the relevant offsets.

We can get more information about the query by combining the sys.db_exec_requests DMV with the sys.processes system view (joined on spid/session_id). This information includes who is executing the query, the machine they are running from, and the name of the database.

The utility selects relevant fields from the sys.db_exec_requests and sys.sysprocesses views. The selected fields are described in figure 1 (largely taken from SQL Server 2005 Books online).

Column name	Data type	Description
spid	smallint	SQL Server process ID.
ecid	smallint	Execution context ID used to uniquely identify the subthreads operating on behalf of a single process.
dbid	smallint	ID of the database currently being used by the process.
nt_username	nchar(128)	Windows user name for the process, if using Windows Authentication, or a trusted connection.
status	nchar(30)	Process ID status. For example, running and sleeping.
wait_type	bigint	Current wait time in milliseconds.
Individual Query	varchar	SQL Statement currently running.
Parent Query	varchar	Routine that contains the Individual Query.
program_name	nchar(128)	Name of the application program.
Hostname	nchar(128)	Name of the workstation.
nt_domain	nchar(128)	Microsoft Windows domain for the client, if using Windows Authentication, or a trusted connection.
Start_time	datetime	Time when the request is scheduled to run.

Figure 1 Columns in the What SQL Statements Are Executing utility.

Running the utility on my SQL Server gives the results given in Figure 2.

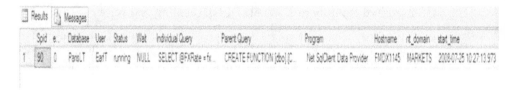

Figure 2 Output from the What SQL Statements Are Executing utility.

The results show the Parent Query that is running (typically a stored procedure), together with the Individual Query within the Parent Query that is currently executing. Additional useful information (e.g. database name, user name etc) is also shown.

Discussion

This utility allows you to observe the progress of a stored procedure or SQL batch, additionally it can be used to identify the cause of a long running query or blocking query.

Since the utility uses existing data held in DMVs it is relatively non-intrusive and should have little effect on performance.

If the identified queries are long running or causing blocking, it might be worthwhile running them inside the Database Tuning Advisor (DTA), this might identify the cause of the slow running (e.g. a missing index).

Further work

It is possible to extend this utility to report only on the database you are interested in, by providing a filter based on database name or database id.

It might be interesting to use the output to drive a trace and/or process-flow engine. This will report on process flow through a stored procedure, and could be useful in determining how much code has been hit/missed during testing, as well as getting a view on what code is executed for a given run/set of parameters.

Conclusion

The utility described in this article will allow you to identify what SQL statements are currently executing. This information can be useful in debugging the cause of both long running queries and blocking, and should prove valuable in the everyday work of the SQL Server DBA/developer

Credits

Ian Stirk has been working in IT as a developer, designer, and architect since 1987. He holds the following qualifications: M.Sc., MCSD.NET, MCDBA, and SCJP. He is a freelance consultant working with Microsoft technologies in London England. He can be contacted at Ian_Stirk@yahoo.com.

Note: This code is at www.sqlservercentral.com

Duplicate Records using SQLCMD

By Renato Buda

Overview

This article presents an approach to showing and deleting duplicate records that is concise, generic and efficient. It uses some features that were introduced in SQL Server 2005.

History and Background

Dealing with duplicate records in a table is a subject that has been covered many times in SQLServerCentral and elsewhere. Four good articles are listed below.

- 'Removing Duplicate Rows' By Neil Boyle[7], 2001/05/14. This covers a number of different methods for removing duplicates with an examples of each method.

- 'Finding and Deleting Duplicate Data' By Chris Cubley[8], 2003/07/25. This is a great article that covers identifying and efficiently removing duplicate data using an example from a Payments table.

- 'Remove Duplicate Records' By Syed Iqbal[9], 2008/05/26. This article presents a novel method for removing duplicates that involves a WHILE loop that deletes one record at a time.

- 'Handle Duplicate Records' By Erik Andersen[10], 2009/01/07 presents a nested cursor based solution that gives the DBA a chance to insert logic to combine records or audit deletions.

Why did I want to re-visit this subject again when it has been covered so many times?

---

[7] http://www.sqlservercentral.com/articles/Advanced+Querying/removeduplicate/207/
[8] http://www.sqlservercentral.com/articles/Miscellaneous/findinganddeletingduplicatedata/1075/
[9] http://www.sqlservercentral.com/scripts/TSQL/62866/
[10] http://www.sqlservercentral.com/scripts/duplicate+records/65381/

There are two features that were introduced with SQL Server 2005 that can be applied to the duplicates problem and allows an efficient piece of code that does not need much modification to deal with each different real table.

The **row_number()** function can allow a flexible identification of different records within a group.

SQLCMD mode with **SETVAR** allows table names and column lists to be replaced in scripts without the use of dynamic SQL

The row_number() function allows records in a duplicate group to be distinguished in a generic fashion that does not rely on cursors or any particular distinguishing column. This is illustrated in the examples below.

The use of SETVAR in SQLCMD mode allows SQL statements to be written generically, with variable table and column names but without using dynamic SQL. This means the script can be used without needing to re-write parts to handle different situations. Using the script is just a matter of changing the SETVAR statements. The script is easier to read than dynamic SQL, especially in Management Studio because the query editor still color-codes the keywords.

Note that SETVAR cannot replace dynamic SQL in all situations because SETVAR can only accept a constant value, not a variable or expression on the right hand side,

Let's get to the script without more ado.

The Script Sections

The following script does four things:

1. Set the SQLCMD variables using SETVAR.

2. Counts the duplicates in $(TableName) based on $(UniqueColumnList)

3. Displays a sample of the duplicates.
   The sampling is controlled by $(SampleSize) and $(MaxRowsPerGroup).

4. Deletes the duplicates. Generally I leave this commented out until I'm sure that I want to delete.

Section 1: The SETVARs

```
:SETVAR TableName Person.Contact -- Name of table to de-
duplicate
:SETVAR UniqueColumnList "FirstName, Phone" -- Comma separated
list of columns
:SETVAR JoinCondition "T1.FirstName=T2.FirstName AND
T1.Phone=T2.Phone" -- Use in WHERE clause to show sample
:SETVAR SampleSize 20
:SETVAR MaxRowsPerGroup 2
```

The SETVAR parameters above are designed to be used in the AdventureWorks database to find cases where the Person.Contact table has records with duplicate combinations of the FirstName and Phone columns. When displaying duplicates a sample of 20 duplicates is displayed with only 2 records in each duplicate group.

TableName is the name of the table containing duplicates. It can be any table name even using 3 or 4 part names. Square brackets are needed if the table name contains special characters.

The **UniqueColumnList** is the list is the list of columns whose values should be unique .Note that when using SETVAR, any values containing spaces must be surrounded by double quotes.

The **JoinCondition** is the UniqueColumnList translated into the form required to use in a self join between two aliases, T1 and T2. This is used when displaying a sample of duplicates.It is possible to derive the JoinCondition from the UniqueColumnList, but that would mean using dynamic SQL so it makes it harder to read and present.

The **SampleSize** and **MaxRowsPerGroup** parameters control how many duplicates are displayed - (in case you get thousands).

When you use SETVAR in Management Studio you need to use SQLCMD mode. In MS 2005 it is a toolbar button. In MS 2008 it is under the Query menu. If you don't do this you will get error messages because the :SETVAR and $(varname) syntax is not understood

Section 2: Count the Duplicates

```
SET NOCOUNT ON;
PRINT 'Count / show / delete duplicates records from
$(TableName) based on ($(UniqueColumnList))';
-- 1. Count the duplicated records

-- This is the number of records that will be deleted
-- For example if there are five records in a group with

-- the same values for $(UniqueColumnList) this counts four

WITH DupCounts AS
( SELECT _RowNum_ = row_number()
OVER (
PARTITION BY $(UniqueColumnList)
ORDER BY $(UniqueColumnList) ),*
FROM $(TableName)
)
SELECT CountOfDuplicateRows = count(*) FROM DupCounts WHERE
DupCounts._RowNum_ > 1;
```

Section 3: Show a Sample of the Duplicates

```
-- 3. Show a sample of the duplicated records
WITH DupCounts AS
( SELECT _RowNum_ = row_number()
OVER (
PARTITION BY $(UniqueColumnList)
ORDER BY $(UniqueColumnList) ),*
FROM $(TableName)
)
SELECT TOP ($(SampleSize)) T1.*
FROM DupCounts T1
WHERE
T1._RowNum_ <= $(MaxRowsPerGroup)
AND EXISTS
(SELECT *
FROM $(TableName) T2
WHERE $(JoinCondition)
GROUP BY $(UniqueColumnList)
HAVING COUNT(*) >1)
ORDER BY $(UniqueColumnList), T1._RowNum_;
```

Section 4: Delete the Duplicates

```
-- Delete duplicates if you need to:
-- I leave this commented to avoid disasters
WITH DupCounts AS
```

```
( SELECT _RowNum_ = row_number()
OVER (
PARTITION BY $(UniqueColumnList)
ORDER BY $(UniqueColumnList) )
FROM $(TableName)
)
DELETE FROM DupCounts WHERE DupCounts._RowNum_ > 1;
SELECT RowsDeleted = @@rowcount;
```

Note that the delete statement as presented does not control which of the duplicate records in a group are deleted. It will delete all but the first record in each group *(WHERE DupCounts._RowNum_ > 1)*. However, the row_number function is really returning a random ordering, because the ORDER BY columns are the same as the PARTITION BY columns. You would need to use another column in the ORDER BY clause if you needed to specify which records from the duplicate list to keep. For example, to ensure all but the lowest ContactID in each group is deleted, use this:

```
WITH DupCounts AS
( SELECT _RowNum_ = row_number()
OVER (
PARTITION BY $(UniqueColumnList)
ORDER BY ContactID )
FROM $(TableName)
)
DELETE FROM DupCounts WHERE DupCounts._RowNum_ > 1;
```

Automating Excel from SQL Server

By Wayne Sheffield

You get a new email & from your boss. It says: Hey Wayne. I get the data that's in the attached Excel spreadsheet from these 5 reports (which he then lists). Can you automate this so that this spreadsheet will be updated weekly with those values? Note that it needs to add new information to the end of the spreadsheet, not just replace the data. Oh yeah & can you have everything formatted like it currently is? When you look at the spreadsheet, there are many rows of data (one per week), and many columns. Some columns are text, some numbers, and some are calculations. Some of the text is left-justified, some center, some right-justified. Some numbers have no decimals, some have one or two. And some are percentages.

So, you get to work. You get a procedure together that gathers the information. But when you use the OpenRowset method to insert the data into the spreadsheet, there is no formatting. So you decide to investigate whether you can get T-SQL to perform Excel Automation to do all the work for you. (Note this is not to say that there aren't other, better ways to do this. It's just what you decided to do.)

So, what is Excel Automation? Simply put, it's having one application (in our case, SQL Server) essentially "drive" Excel, using built-in Excel properties and methods. In SQL Server, this is accomplished by use of the sp_OA stored procedures.

Obviously, if SQL Server is going to drive Excel, then Excel needs to be installed on the server that it's running from.

The first thing that SQL needs to do is to open up an instance of Excel. The code to do that is:

```
declare @xlApp integer, @rs integer
execute @rs = dbo.sp_OACreate 'Excel.Application', @xlApp
OUTPUT
```

So what we done is to start up the excel application. The variable @xlApp is a handle to the application. I have found it useful to set the Excel Properties "ScreenUpdating" and "DisplayAlerts" to false. ScreenUpdating turned off will speed up the code, and you won't be looking at it anyway. DisplayAlerts turned off will prevent prompts requiring a response from appearing; Excel will use the default response. These are set by:

```
execute @rs = master.dbo.sp_OASetProperty @xlApp,
'ScreenUpdating', 'False'
execute @rs = master.dbo.sp_OASetProperty @xlApp,
'DisplayAlerts', 'False'
```

Now we need to get a handle to the open workbooks. The code to do that is:

```
declare @xlWorkbooks integer
execute @rs = master.dbo.sp_OAMethod @xlApp, 'Workbooks',
@xlWorkbooks OUTPUT
```

Now we have a decision to make. Are we going to open an existing spreadsheet, or make a new one?

To open an existing one:

```
declare @xlWorkbook integer
execute @rs = master.dbo.sp_OAMethod @xlWorkbooks, 'Open',
@xlWorkBook OUTPUT, 'C:\Myspreadsheet.xls'
```

To add a new workbook:

```
declare @xlWorkBook integer
execute @rs = master.dbo.sp_OAMethod @xlWorkBooks, 'Add',
@xlWorkBook OUTPUT, -4167
```

(The 4167 is the value of the constant xlWBATWorksheet, which specifies to add a new worksheet).

Now that we have a handle to the workbook, we have to get a handle to the worksheet:

```
declare @xlWorkSheet integer
execute @rs = master.dbo.sp_OAMethod @xlWorkBook,
'ActiveSheet', @xlWorkSheet OUTPUT
```

Now we have to find out the last row. Thankfully, Excel can tell us that:

```
declare @xlLastRow integer
execute @rs = master.dbo.sp_OAGetProperty @xlWorkSheet,
'Cells.SpecialCells(11).Row', @xlLastRow OUTPUT
```

If you want to, you can also get the last column:

```
declare @xlLastColumn integer
execute @rs = master.dbo.sp_OAGetProperty @xlWorkSheet,
'Cells.SpecialCells(11).Column', @xlLastColumn OUTPUT
```

After all of this setup work, we're finally ready to start putting the data into the spreadsheet. First, you need to get a handle to the cell:

```
declare @xlCell integer
set @LastRow = @LastRow + 1
execute master.dbo.sp_OAGetProperty @xlWorkSheet, 'Cells',
@xlCell OUTPUT, @LastRow, 1
```

Now we put the data into that cell:

```
execute @rs = master.dbo.sp_OASetProperty @xlCell, 'Value',
@Value
```

If you want to format that cell:

```
Execute @rs = master.dbo.sp_OASetProperty @xlCell,
'NumberFormat', '0%'
```

- 0% sets it to be a percentage with no decimals.
- 0.0% sets it to be a percentage with one decimal.
- 'd-mmm' set it to be a character date in the format "10 Oct"
- 'mm-dd-yyyy' sets it to be a character date in this good old format.
- 'mm-dd-yyyy hh:mm:ss' sets it to be a character date in the date/time format.
- '$#,##0.00' sets it to be a number with the currency symbol, 2 decimal points, and at least one whole number. Numbers would be separated by comma at every third number.

Setting font settings are a little harder:

```
Declare @objProp varchar(200)
Set @objProp = 'Font.Bold'
Execute @rs = master.dbo.sp_OASetProperty @xlCell, @objProp,
'True'
```

(You can underline it by using Font.Underline)

One big note: everything that you have a pointer to needs to be destroyed at some point in time. So, before you move on to a new cell, you need to:

```
execute @rs = master.dbo.sp_OADestroy @xlCell
```

Now you need to save and close the file and close Excel:

```
Declare @FileName varchar(100)
Set @FileName = 'C:\MyNewExcelSpreadsheet.xls'
execute @rs = master.dbo.sp_OAMethod @xlWorkBook 'SaveAs',
null, @FileName, -4143
```

(The 4143 is the file format constant to save the file as.)

```
execute @rs = master.dbo.sp_OAMethod @xlWorkBook, 'Close'
execute @rs = master.dbo.sp_OAMethod @xlApp, 'Quit'
```

Several other things you can do:

To change the name of the workbook:

```
execute @rs = master.dbo.sp_OASetProperty @xlWorkBook, 'Title',
'My workbook name'
```

To change the name of the sheet:

```
execute @rs = master.dbo.sp_OASetProperty @xlWorkSheet, 'Name',
'My sheet name'
```

To get the format of an existing cell:

```
execute @rs = master.dbo.sp_OAGetProperty @xlCell,
'NumberFormat', @Value OUTPUT
```

To get the value of an existing cell:

```
execute @rs = master.dbo.sp_OAGetProperty @xlCell, 'Value',
@Value OUTPUT
```

If you want to automatically size all of the columns to be the width of the widest data:

```
execute @rs = master.dbo.sp_OAMethod @xlWorkSheet,
'Columns.AutoFit'
```

Finally, I did say earlier that all pointers need to be destroyed:

```
execute @rs = master.dbo.sp_OADestroy @xlWorkSheet
execute @rs = master.dbo.sp_OADestroy @xlWorkBook
execute @rs = master.dbo.sp_OADestroy @xlWorkBooks
execute @rs = master.dbo.sp_OADestroy @xlApp
```

If you want to use a formula, set the value of the cell to the formula, ie: '=sum(a4.a50)' or '=(+a4+a5)/a6'. Note that the equal sign must be the first character to signify a formula.

Notice that in all of the sp_OA procedure calls, I put the result of the call into the variable @rs. This can be evaluated to return many errors:

```
If @rs <> 0 execute master.dbo.sp_OAGetErrorInfo @Object,
@OA_Source OUTPUT, @OA_Descr OUTPUT, @HelpFile OUTPUT, @HelpID
OUTPUT
```

Note that you're not limited to working with spreadsheets you can work with charts also.

One last note: Excel's help file gives us most of this information. Just look under "Programming Information", and then under "Microsoft Excel Visual Basic Reference" for all of the objects, methods and properties that can be used. Occasionally I would have to look up the constant values on the Internet just do a search on the constant name.

Moving Indexes

By Thom Bolin

I have a client that was in need of moving all there indexes from the primary file group to an index file group. There were a total of 25 databases so the time needed to script each one individually would have been overwhelming not to mention the need to perform this across multiple environments.

I scoured the web and found some examples but many either didn't work the way I needed or were complex in their logic and difficult to understand. I took the best ideas of each of those and created the two attached scripts. After execution the results can be copied to a new query window and executed.

Unique constraints associated with indexes required using the alter table command where as the normal indexes only used the drop/create index command. Clustered indexes and foreign keys were excluded for ease of execution, and because I didn t want to move the data.

Lets breakdown the process and show how it all fits together. These scripts were written for SQL 2000 so system tables rather than management views were used. The scripts will execute on SQL2005 as written but could be modified to use the management views provided.

First we need to collect all the meta-data needed to drop and recreate the indexes, this is the same for both non-unique and unique indexes:

```
select dbo.sysobjects.id,            -- id of table
       dbo.sysobjects.name,          -- name of table
       dbo.sysindexes.indid,         -- id of index
       dbo.sysindexes.name indname,  -- name of index
       dbo.sysindexes.origfillfactor, -- fillfactor for index
       dbo.sysindexes.groupid        -- filegroup where
index is currently stored
```

The joins needed to gather the information is between sysindexes and sysobjects based on the object id:

```
from sysindexes inner join
        dbo.sysobjects on dbo.sysindexes.id = dbo.sysobjects.id
```

The following where clause removes clustered indexes from the selection. Clustered indexes need to be excluded based on the fact that moving a clustered index also moves the associated data. This would in effect nullify the moving of the other indexes since the data and index would once again be located in the same filegroup. All user indexes will be associated with objects of xtype 'U', user table. Only including index ids between 2 and 254 exclude entries associated with text and image data. indexproperty is a system function that display properties of an index. IsClustered is used to exclude the clstered indexes. The default filegroup, Primary, is 1. This can be changed if indexes are already stored in a different filegroup

```
where (dbo.sysobjects.xtype = 'U') and (sysindexes.indid
BETWEEN 2 and 254
and (indexproperty(sysindexes.id,sysindexes.name,'IsClustered')
= 0)
and sysindexes.groupid = 1
```

By using a subquery all the indexes that are being used as a constraint are excluded. sysconstraints contains a row for each constraint in the current database. Where constid is the object id of the constraint and the name is the index name. A colid of 0 indicates it is a table level constraint as opposed to column level. sysconstraints.id is equal to the sysobject id for the table.

```
and not exists (select 1 from sysconstraints
                      join dbo.sysobjects so2
                        on so2.id = sysconstraints.constid
                      and so2.name = sysindexes.name
                    where colid = 0 and sysconstraints.id =
dbo.sysobjects.id)
```

The order by clause sorts the output by table name and index id.

This data is stored in a cursor that is then processed and the appropriate create and drop statements are generated. Once the cursor is opened and a record fetched the columns that make up the index are needed in the correct order. A select statement with much of the same logic as above is used. Lets take a look at how this is done.

```
SELECT @list=@list +'['+dbo.syscolumns.name+']' +
       (case
indexkey_property(@id,@indid,sysindexkeys.colid,'IsDescending')
         when 1 then ' DESC ,'
         else ' ASC , '
       end )
```

The select appends to variable @list all the columns that make up the index as well as the sort order of the column. Indexkey_property is used to find this value and then either DESC or ASC is added to the column definition.

```
FROM dbo.sysindexes
       INNER JOIN dbo.sysobjects on dbo.sysindexes.id =
dbo.sysobjects.id
       INNER JOIN dbo.sysindexkeys on dbo.sysindexes.id =
dbo.sysindexkeys.id
              and dbo.sysindexes.indid = dbo.sysindexkeys.indid
       INNER JOIN dbo.syscolumns on dbo.sysindexes.id =
dbo.syscolumns.id
              AND dbo.sysindexkeys.colid = dbo.syscolumns.colid
       WHERE (dbo.sysobjects.xtype = 'U') and
(dbo.sysindexes.indid = @indid)
          and (dbo.sysobjects.id = @id)
```

The select if very similar to the one above with the some of the filters removed since we are working with only the subset of indexes we need to script.

```
ORDER BY dbo.sysindexes.indid, dbo.sysindexkeys.keyno
```

The Order BY clause is used to keep the columns in the original order. Once @list is populated it is time to script the drop and create statements.

```
set @strsql = 'drop index ['+@tbname+'].['+@indname+']'
   print @strsql
```

The drop index statements only needs the table name and index name. the print statement sends the statement to the results pane of Query Analyzer.

```
IF @fill = 0
   SET @fill = 90
```

@fill will be returned as zero for system created statistics and possibly for some indexes, but a value of 0 is invalid in the create statement.

```
IF (indexproperty(@id,@indname,'IsUnique') = 0)
   set @strsql = 'create unique index '
   else
   set @strsql = 'create index '
```

Use correct create index statement by including the unique keyword if original index was unique.

```
set @strsql = @strsql + '['+@indname+'] on
[dbo].['+@tbname+']('+@list+') with fillfactor = '+cast(@fill
as nvarchar(3)) + ' on [' + @newgroup +']'
print @strsql
```

Prepend the create statement to the remaining command needed for the create. The tablename, indexname, list of columns, and fill factor are all needed along with the new filegroup name. @newgroup is set at the top of the script.

Once the script has completed executing the output should look similar to what it below:

```
drop index [Order Details].[OrdersOrder_Details]
create index [OrdersOrder_Details] on [dbo].[Order
Details]([OrderID] ASC ) with fillfactor = 90 on [INDEX]

drop index [Order Details].[ProductID]
create index [ProductID] on [dbo].[Order Details]([ProductID]
ASC ) with fillfactor = 90 on [INDEX]

drop index [Order Details].[ProductsOrder_Details]  create
index [ProductsOrder_Details] on
[dbo].[Order Details]([ProductID] ASC ) with fillfactor = 90 on
[INDEX]

drop index [Orders].[CustomerID]
create index [CustomerID] on [dbo].[Orders]([CustomerID] ASC )
with fillfactor = 90 on [INDEX]
```

In order to move the indexes associated with unique constraints the code was modified as detailed below.

```
from sysindexes
   inner join dbo.sysobjects
     on dbo.sysindexes.id = dbo.sysobjects.id
   inner join dbo.sysconstraints
     on dbo.sysconstraints.id = dbo.sysobjects.id
    and dbo.sysconstraints.colid = 0
   inner join dbo.sysobjects so2
     on so2.id = dbo.sysconstraints.constid
    and so2.name = sysindexes.name
   where (dbo.sysobjects.xtype = 'U') and (sysindexes.indid
BETWEEN 2 and 254)
   and
(indexproperty(sysindexes.id,sysindexes.name,'IsClustered') =
0)
   and (indexproperty(sysindexes.id,sysindexes.name,'IsUnique')
= 1)
   and sysindexes.groupid = 1
```

Join the sysindexes table to the sysconstraints table where sysconstraints.colid = 0, signifying this is a table level constrainst, and the constraint is an index as represented by the join to sysobjects so2. This will include all unique index constraints on the table.

```
and not exists (select 1 from sysreferences fk
  where fk.rkeyid = sysindexes.id
  and fk.rkeyindid = sysindexes.indid)
```

Exclude any constraints that are associated with foreign keys. These objects reside in the sysreferences table using the table id and index id.

Cut and paste this output to a new query analyzer window and execute it to move the indexes.

When generating the output for these type of indexes the drop constraint and add constraint clause of the alter table is required as shown below.

```
set @strsql = 'alter table ['+@tbname+'] drop constraint
['+@indname+']'
```

Drop the constraint by using the tablename and indexname from the cursor fetch.

```
set @strsql = 'alter table [dbo].['+@tbname+'] add constraint
['+@indname+']  '
set @strsql = @strsql + ' Unique NonClustered ('+@list+') '
set @strsql = @strsql + 'with (fillfactor = '+cast(@fill as
nvarchar(3)) + ') on [' +@newgroup +']'
```

Issue the alter table with add constraint to create the new constraint. @list, @fill and @newgroup are populated the same here as in the normal index move logic.

Using the system tables to create transact sql statements as shown above an entire databases worth of indexes can be moved very small amount of time. SQLServer uses similar methods to return the alter statements that are generated out of Enterprise Manager when a script is saved after altering an object.

The output scripts can be used in a variety of methods to provide a higher quality of life. A couple of examples are that the scripts can be generated during the day and then scheduled for execution during off hours, saved for reuse in different environments involving the same schema.

Improvements could be made to the scripts to include the dropping and recreation of associated foreign keys, using management views for execution on SQLServer 2005 instance.

I hope that by sharing the method used above it will open a door to scripting that may not have been used before.

On Indexes and Views

By Timothy Wiseman

Used properly, indexed views can be a magnificent way of improving performance and providing greater ease for both users and developers while still maintaining a fully normalized and constrained database. However, to fully realize the benefits of the indexed view, the execution plan must actually make use of it.

When a nonindexed view or a view whose index will not be used in the execution plan is referenced in a query, the optimizer considers the select statement the view represents the same way it would consider a subquery. In a way, this is very much like using the view as a macro. It saves the user or developer from having to type, or even be fully aware of, the exact contents of the view, but the optimizer looks at it as though the developer had typed it in.

When dealing with a view with an index that will be used, the optimizer can go to materialized data the view represents instead. In most cases, this is can be much more efficient than expanding the view, especially when the view includes multiple joins or complex where statements within it. So, while some exceptions do exist, it is generally desirable to ensure that the index is used.

According to Books Online, the optimizer for SQL Server 2005 Enterprise Edition will intelligently decide when it is best to use or ignore indexes on views. Not only that, it has the ability to consider using the indexes on views if they would by applicable to the base tables as well. That only applies to Enterprise Edition, to quote directly from the Resolving Indexes on Views article on MSDN:

To use an indexed view in all other editions, the NOEXPAND table hint must be used.

In short, indexed views in every version but Enterprise will only be used to their full potential if the developers and users carefully ensure that they appropriately use the NOEXPAND hint. Also, applying the NOEXPAND hint to a view which does not have an index will generate an error. It can be illuminative to see an example. First, some test data is needed:

Note: This code is at www.sqlservercentral.com

Then, run the select statements and compare:

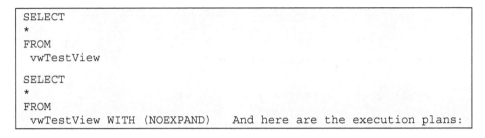

```
SELECT
*
FROM
 vwTestView

SELECT
*
FROM
 vwTestView WITH (NOEXPAND)     And here are the execution plans:
```

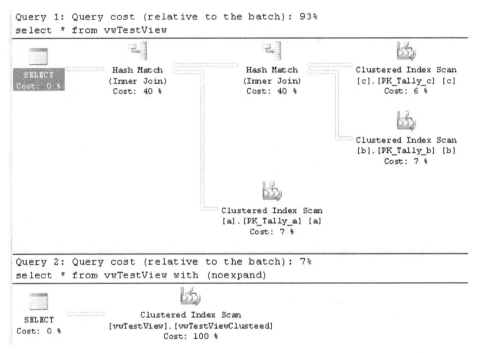

```
Query 1: Query cost (relative to the batch): 93%
select * from vwTestView
```

SELECT Cost: 0 %	Hash Match (Inner Join) Cost: 40 %	Hash Match (Inner Join) Cost: 40 %	Clustered Index Scan [c].[PK_Tally_c] [c] Cost: 6 %

Clustered Index Scan
[b].[PK_Tally_b] [b]
Cost: 7 %

Clustered Index Scan
[a].[PK_Tally_a] [a]
Cost: 7 %

```
Query 2: Query cost (relative to the batch): 7%
select * from vwTestView with (noexpand)
```

SELECT Cost: 0 %	Clustered Index Scan [vwTestView].[vwTestViewClusteed] Cost: 100 %

The second plan generated with the NOEXPAND query hint is vastly more efficient than the one without because of the way they are processed. This particular execution plan was generated by SQL Server 2005 Express, but the same results come from Standard Edition as well.

One way to simplify this for developers and users is to use another view to hide the query hint. For instance:

```
CREATE VIEW vwTestViewX
AS
SELECT
```

```
*
FROM
   dbo.vwTestView WITH (NOEXPAND)
```

Then a query against this view will include the NOEXPAND against the other and generate an appropriate execution plan like:

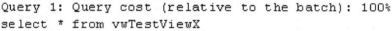

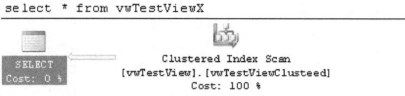

One thing to note with embedding the NOEXPAND hint is that the query will return an error if NOEXPAND is specified and no indexes exist on the view. This should rarely be an issue, but it is worth noting. This is especially true since if a change is made to one of the base tables using SSMS Designer, the Designer will display a confirmation message that the table is referenced with Schemabinding but then readily destroy the index if the confirmation is given. This can lead to indexes being destroyed in development environments very easily.

As long as the optimizer knows to use them, indexed views can provide enormous performance benefits. In the more powerful Enterprise Edition, the optimizer will handle this and there is rarely a reason to explicitly force their use. In other versions, though, the optimized must be explicitly told if they are needed. But, like other query hints, this explicit instruction can be made just once in a view on the indexed view if that is desirable.

REFERENCES

- Creating Indexed Views by MSDN (***http://msdn.microsoft.com/en-us/library/ms191432.aspx***)

- Resolving Indexes on Views by MSDN (***http://msdn.microsoft.com/en-us/library/ms181151.aspx***)

- View Resolution by MSDN (***http://msdn.microsoft.com/en-us/library/ms190237.aspx***)

- The "Numbers" or "Tally" Table by Jeff Moden
  (*http://www.sqlservercentral.com/articles/TSQL/62867/*)

RELATED ARTICLES

- What is Denormalization? By Chris Kempster
  (*http://www.sqlservercentral.com/articles/Advanced/whatisdenormali zation/1204/*)
- The Myth of Over-Normalization by Tony Davis
  (*http://www.simple-talk.com/community/blogs/tony_davis/ archive/2008/07/21/63094.aspx*)

Missing Indexes in SQL Server 2005

By Ranga Narasimhan

There are several new features in SQL Server 2005. There are a few features to help find missing indexes, which are some of the very good ones. How great it will be if you know what indexes you need to create based on your workload? In SQL Server 2000, we had to use SQL Profiler trace files and Index tuning wizard. But with SQL Server 2005 DMVs, we can easily figure out what indexes we need to create which would benefit our application.

The following are the missing index DMVs (From SQL Server 2005 BOL)

sys.dm_db_missing_index_group_stats	Returns summary information about missing index groups, for example, the performance improvements that could be gained by implementing a specific group of missing indexes.
sys.dm_db_missing_index_groups	Returns information about a specific group of missing indexes, such as the group identifier and the identifiers of all missing indexes that are contained in that group.
sys.dm_db_missing_index_details	Returns detailed information about a missing index; for example, it returns the name and identifier of the table where the index is missing, and the columns and column types that should make up the missing index.
sys.dm_db_missing_index_columns	Returns information about the database table columns that are missing an index.

Let's see what indexes are there for table [Person.Address] table in AdventureWorks database by running this code:

```
use AdventureWorks;
exec sp_helpindex [Person.Address]   Fig:1
```

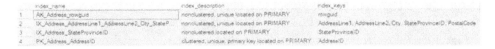

Note: This image is at www.sqlservercentral.com

I don t see an index for **ModifiedDate** column for [Person.Address] table. So, to get a entry in the sys.dm_db_missing_index_details DMV, let's run a query like this:

Query: 1

```
select * from Person.Address where ModifiedDate = '01/01/2008'
```

You may not see any results for the query above, but SQL Server internally recorded that a query was run and a index on ModifiedDate column would have been very useful.

Query: 2

```
select * from sys.dm_db_missing_index_details:
```

Fig: 2

In Fig: 2, see the equality_columns field, which implies that a index on the [Modified Date] column is missing (or might be helpful)

Query: 3:

```
select db_name(d.database_id) dbname, object_name(d.object_id)
tablename, d.index_handle,
d.equality_columns, d.inequality_columns, d.included_columns,
d.statement as fully_qualified_object, gs.*
from  sys.dm_db_missing_index_groups g
      join sys.dm_db_missing_index_group_stats gs on
gs.group_handle = g.index_group_handle
      join sys.dm_db_missing_index_details d on g.index_handle
= d.index_handle
where  d.database_id =  d.database_id and d.object_id =
d.object_id
   and object_name(d.object_id) = 'Address'
```

Run Query 1 several times. Now, run Query: 3,

Fig: 3

dbname	tablename	index_handle	equality_columns	inequality_columns	included_columns	fully_qualified_object	group_handle	unique_compiles	user_seeks
AdventureWorks	Address	1	[ModifiedDate]	NULL	NULL	[AdventureWorks].[Person].[Address]	2	1	6

Note: This image is at www.sqlservercentral.com

In Fig 3, notice the user_seeks column. So every time a query is run, for which an index might be useful, SQL Server keeps updating the missing index DMVs. This is very valuable information, based on this you can create indexes to support those queries. Isn t this cool! Yes, SQL Server 2005 rocks!

The DMVs for missing indexes are great new features. I work with a Siebel CRM database where queries are built dynamically. So it is hard to design indexes in advance. The missing index feature helps to me create indexes for those queries that have high user_seeks for a particular column in a table.

For more information see About the Missing Indexes Feature in SQL Server 2005 Books Online.

Using the Script Component with Multiple Outputs

By Tim Mitchell

One of the more common questions I find in SQL Server SSIS forums is how to split apart a single text file into multiple outputs. Files extracted from foreign sources often arrive in nonstandard formats, and are too often unchangeable at the source and must be dealt with during the import process. For unconventional custom transformations such as this, the script component is a highly flexible and almost infinitely configurable tool that is quite useful for getting things done.

In this article, I will demonstrate a relatively simple way to address single files with multiple output types using the SQL Server Integration Services (SSIS) script component.

The example we'll use demonstrates what I refer to as the "record type" format. A single file may contain many different record types, and each is identified by the first element in each record (line of text) in the file. You may find other formats, including those that are identified by their position in the file, a particular string of text, or number of elements; this example could be easily modified to handle these types of nonstandard formats. In the healthcare industry where I spent most of my time, the record type layout is quite common in EDI (electronic data interchange) situations. As you can see in the example below, there are varying numbers of elements within this file source, which would pose significant problems if you simply use the off-the-shelf transformations provided within SSIS.

```
1|202|Scott,Michael|District Manager|Scranton PA
2|241|202|Halpert,Jim|Sales
3|241|3348|Lackawanna County
3|241|9582|Bob Vance Refrigeration
2|189|202|Dwight Schrute|Sales
3|189|1102|Smith Machinery
3|189|2792|State of Pennsylvania
3|189|4929|Office Systems of America
1|339|Filipelli,Karen|Management|Utica NY
2|493|339|Smith,Marshall|Sales
3|493|2555|Ace Printing Center
```

In the snippet for this demonstration, record type 1 contains manager details, record type 2 lists the employee information, and record type 3 shows the list of clients. Since the number of columns and their respective data types differ from one record to the next, we can't simply use a conditional split to create multiple paths for data flow; this is a case for the script component.

To get started, we will create a single Data Flow task in our SSIS package. Go to the Data Flow tab and drag over a Script Component from the Toolbox. You will be prompted for the usage type of the script component; click the radio button beside Source and click OK (Figure 1). Using this component as a source creates only the Output without configuring any Inputs, which is appropriate in our case since we will be creating our own data rows.

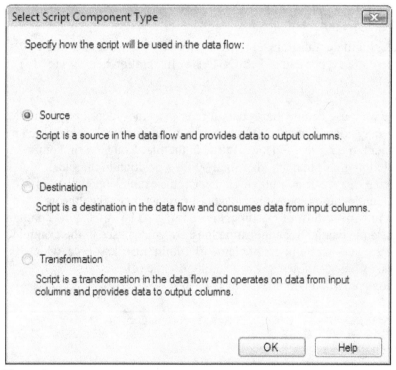

Figure 1

Double click your new instance of the script component in your Data Flow pane to open the editor for that component. Under the Inputs and Outputs pane, you can see that there is a single output created by default (Figure 2).

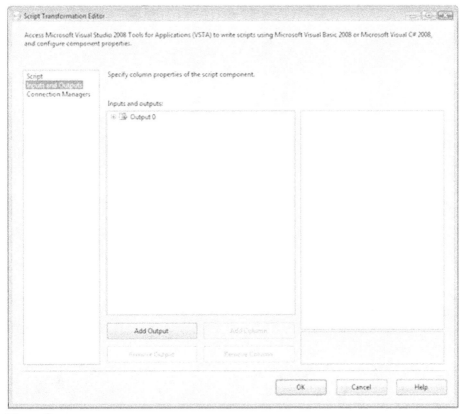

Figure 2

For our example, we actually need three outputs, one each for Managers, Employees, and Clients. To create the additional outputs, click on the Add Output button twice to create two more outputs. For each output, highlight the Output Columns folder and add the appropriate number of data columns by clicking the Add Column button. Configure the data types for each column in the Data Type Properties (Figure 3). You can see that I have changed the names of the outputs, as well as the columns within each, so that they have meaningful names - this will come in handy when we start scripting in a moment.

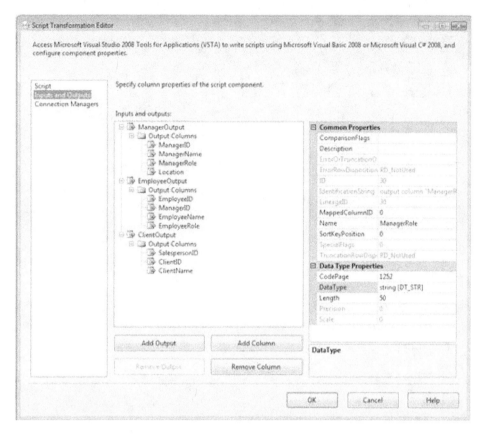

Figure 3

Now, I'll open up the script editor by clicking the Edit Script button near the bottom of the window in the Script tab. For this example, we are leveraging the addition of the C# language to the SSIS scripting tools; this is new to SQL Server 2008, as the previous version required you to use VB.NET for most scripting situations.

In this script, the first thing we'll do is set up a connection to the source file by creating a a System.IO.StreamReader object. The file name we use is defined in our SSIS package as the variable named Filename, which has already been populated with the path to the source file. Using the while loop, we read each line of the file into a variable and process each line in turn. Our test data is pipe-delimited, so I use the C# string function Split() to break apart each line into atomic elements, and I'll evaluate the first element on each line (referred to as items[0], as a zero-based index) to send each row of data to the correct output.

```
public override void CreateNewOutputRows()
{
// Create the StreamReader object to read the input file
System.IO.StreamReader reader = new
System.IO.StreamReader(this.Variables.Filename);
// Loop through the file to read each line
while(!reader.EndOfStream)
{
// Read one line
string line = reader.ReadLine();
// Break the file apart into atomic elements
string[] items = line.Split('|');
// Record type 1 is Manager
if (items[0] == "1")
{
ManagerOutputBuffer.AddRow();
ManagerOutputBuffer.ManagerID = int.Parse(items[1]);
ManagerOutputBuffer.ManagerName = items[2];
ManagerOutputBuffer.ManagerRole = items[3];
ManagerOutputBuffer.Location = items[4];
}
// Record type 2 is Employee
elseif (items[0] == "2")
{
EmployeeOutputBuffer.AddRow();
EmployeeOutputBuffer.EmployeeID = int.Parse(items[1]);
EmployeeOutputBuffer.ManagerID = int.Parse(items[2]);
EmployeeOutputBuffer.EmployeeName = items[3];
EmployeeOutputBuffer.EmployeeRole = items[4];
}
// Record type 3 is Client
elseif (items[0] == "3")
{
ClientOutputBuffer.AddRow();
ClientOutputBuffer.SalespersonID = int.Parse(items[1]);
ClientOutputBuffer.ClientID = int.Parse(items[2]);
ClientOutputBuffer.ClientName = items[3];
```

You'll see that our program will follow one of three paths depending on the first element of the row, with each path leading to one of the buffers to be wired up to one of our intended destinations. The buffer objects, which follow the Buffer naming convention, are objects that are automagically created for each output we've defined in the editor in the previous step. In each of the paths, we must create a new output row to send to the data stream by calling the Buffer.AddRow() method. Note that you must call the AddRow() method before attempting to assign values to any of the output variables for that row. After adding the new output row for the appropriate path, we assign the corresponding value from the data file to each of the output variables.

When the script is complete, we'll exit out of the script editor, and click OK on the Script Transformation Editor to save changes to this component.nt.

Next, we'll add a data destination for each output you defined in your script component. In our case, we will use a Flat File Destination to send each of the three data streams to a delimited file. After creating the output destinations, we connect the output (green arrow) from the script to each of the 3 outputs. You'll notice that, when you are dealing with components with multiple outputs, you'll be prompted to select the output you wish to use, as shown in Figure 4. Be sure to match the output from the script component to the corresponding destination.

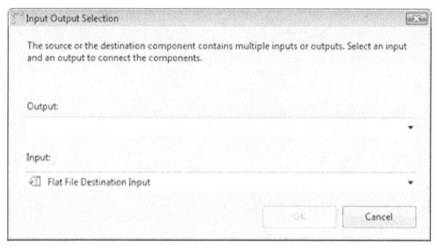

Figure 4

After all three of our destinations are configured and properly connected to the Script Component, our package is ready to execute (see Figure 5). The output paths are labeled by default with the name of the output we created in the script component; you can see now why it's essential to create meaningful names rather than using the default names Output0, Output1, etc.

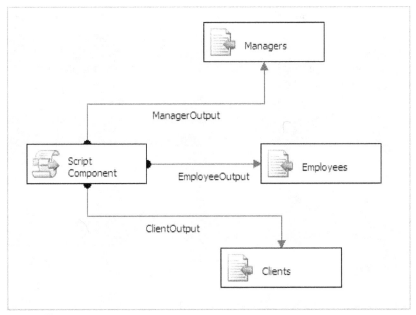

Figure 5

After we execute the package, you can see in the Data Flow pane that we have rows flowing to all 3 of our outputs, consistent with the data in our sample file.

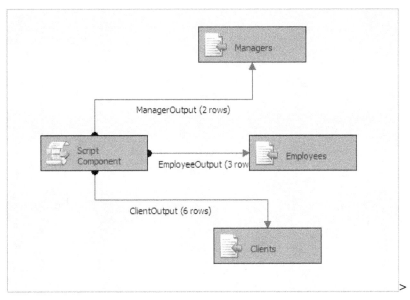

Figure 6

A final review of the 3 output files confirms that the rows were directed to the correct destinations.

In this brief demonstration, we have reviewed how the script component in SSIS can be used to extract data from source files that have varying metadata. The record type format is just one example of such files, but you can see the methodology I've used here and hopefully can adapt it for your own needs.

SSIS and Stored procedures using temp tables

By Michael Cape

In SSIS, have you ever tried to use a store procedure which uses a temp table to generate its output. When you try to use a procedure like this in SSIS's OLE DB Source data flow source, there won't be any columns listed. Consider this simple stored procedure which outputs some data from AdventureWorks' Contact table. The procedure simply dumps some columns into a temporary table, and then selects rows from the temp table.

```
CREATE PROC dbo.TestSSISTempTable AS
SET NOCOUNT ON
SELECT ContactID, FirstName, MiddleName,
LastName, Suffix, EmailAddress

INTO #Contact
FROM Person.Contact

SELECT ContactID, FirstName, MiddleName,
LastName, Suffix, EmailAddress
FROM #Contact
```

When I try us this proc in an SSIS data flow I don't get any columns listed, which means I can't complete the mapping of source columns to destination columns.

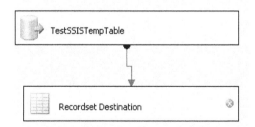

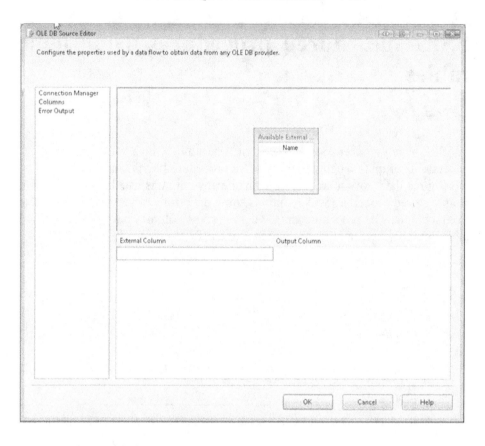

There are three techniques which can be implemented to work around this issue. One is good (sorta), one is bad, and one is downright wacky.

The Bad

The easiest way to fix this is to add a simple SET statement at the beginning of the stored procedure. Adding the statement SET FMTONLY OFF at the start of the original procedure will allow the column information to come through in the column listing of the OLE DB Source control.

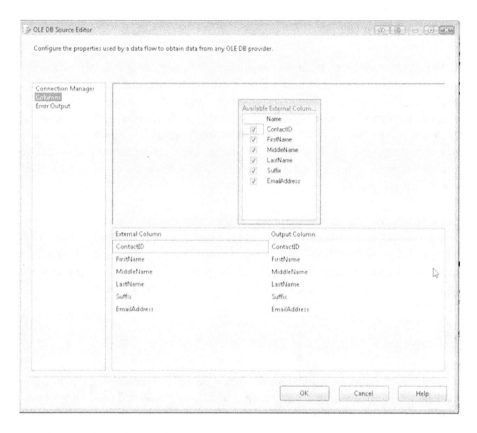

So, what's so bad about this technique? In a word, bad performance. This was the first technique I tried, when I was working with an SSIS package that was part of a daily job run. The problem I encountered was that my stored procedure didn't perform very well, sometimes running for hours. However, every time I ran the procedure with Query Analyzer it would never take more than 5 minutes. And most times, it ran in less than 1 minute.

As I was researching this, I found the explanation for this in the article "Coping with No Column Names in the SSIS OLEDB Data Source Editor"[11] By Paul Ibison. According to this article this technique will cause the procedure to execute 5 times! Yikes! After, reading this, I too verified this. Indeed, my stored procedure ran 5 times. Well, as you can image this definitely has a negative impact on performance. Furthermore, a more potentially dangerous issue is if the stored procedure did any updating or inserting into a table. Those would be done 5 times!

---

[11]http://www.sqlservercentral.com/articles/Integration+Services/61824/

The Good (Sorta)

The next technique that I tried was to convert the temp table to a table variable. This too worked, although it was a little harder to implement than the first technique. However, it avoided the issue with running the procedure 5 times. However, performance can be an issue with this technique as well. Sometimes, table variable perform as well or better than temp tables. However, sometimes temp tables are better performers. SQL Server doesn't maintain any statistics for table variables. This means that every time they are used in a query they are always table-scanned.

Another problem with this is that apparently all temp tables have to be converted into table variables. Suppose your stored procedure has 3 temp tables, and only one of them provides the output. Simply converting that one temp table to a table variable doesn't seem to work. When I tried implementing this technique, I couldn't get it to work unless I converted all temp tables to table variables.

The Wacky

This last technique is definitely weird. Again, as I was researching this issue, I found Jamie Thomson's blog entry called SSIS: 'Using stored procedures inside an OLE DB Source component'.[12]

Here, Jamie states that a stored procedure doesn't have any metadata for the OLE DB provider to retrieve. He further states that the OLE DB provider has to make a "best guess" by taking the metadata of the first select statement in the stored procedure. However, if the stored procedure doesn't have a good query for the OLE DB provider to use then it can't guess. Furthermore, Jamie goes on to reference Adam Machanic's blog entry, 'Stored procedures are not parameterized views'.[13]

Here Adam states that stored procedures don't provide an output contract. However, I started to wonder if I couldn't trick the OLE DB provider into inferring an output contract for a stored procedure. The idea is pretty simple. I put a "no-op" select statement at the top of my procedure which structurally

---

[12]http://blogs.conchango.com/jamiethomson/archive/2006/12/20/SSIS_3A00_-Using-stored-procedures-inside-an-OLE-DB-Source-component.aspx
[13] http://sqlblog.com/blogs/adam_machanic/archive/2006/07/12/109.aspx

mimicked the output of the stored procedure. Therefore, revisiting the previous stored procedure, I added the IF 1 = 2 code block in the following example.

```
CREATE PROC dbo.TestSSISTempTable AS
SET NOCOUNT ON
IF 1 = 2
BEGIN
SELECT CAST(NULL AS INT) AS ContactID,CAST(NULL AS
NVARCHAR(50)) AS FirstName,
CAST(NULL AS NVARCHAR(50)) AS MiddleName, CAST(NULL AS
NVARCHAR(50)) AS LastName,
CAST(NULL AS NVARCHAR(10)) AS Suffix, CAST(NULL AS
NVARCHAR(50)) AS EmailAddress
END

SELECT ContactID, FirstName, MiddleName,
LastName, Suffix, EmailAddress

INTO #Contact
FROM Person.Contact

SELECT ContactID, FirstName, MiddleName,
LastName, Suffix, EmailAddress
FROM #Contact
```

Sure enough, this worked! There are a few issues you have to keep in mind when using this technique. You have to make sure that every column in the output query is accounted for in the "contract" query. You also have to make sure that the columns have the right data type as the output columns. Any columns which are in the output query and not in the "contract" query won't be available in SSIS. Furthermore, any column in the "contract" query but not in the output query WILL be available in SSIS, but the SSIS package will fail when you run the package, and you have mapped a column which doesn't really exist in the output.

All in all, I like this technique because it doesn't impose the unnecessary overhead of repetitive executions that the SET FMTONLY OFF technique did. I also didn't have to convert all my temp tables to table variables, thereby exposing the procedure to a potential performance bottleneck. Creating the "contract" query required a little more work than simply adding a SET statement, and required a little less work than converting temp tables to table variables. The result was a stored procedure which still performed well and didn't require any reworking of the core components.

SSIS Custom Error Handling

By Zach Mattson

If you have ever worked on a data integration project "in the old days" of pre-SSIS, you know how much custom work has to be done to deal with data that comes from systems with bad source data and a severe lack of constraints. With SSIS, you can easily direct rows that cause errors to a different destination for saving.

After working on some basic packages, it was becoming cumbersome to set up custom data destinations for each transformation where I wanted to redirect bad data. Having all these different tables or files would make it difficult to aggregate into a report that was meaningful or make it easy to search for patterns. With a central logging table for these various pieces of bad data, anyone could setup reports that are automatically emailed to the source data owners as a kind of "rub it in your face" report of their data quality. My initial intention was for my own use, but immediately it became clear this could be used to arm project managers with enough information to call meetings with other project managers and let everyone else work. There would be little need for them to call you into the meeting if they had all the information (in theory it sounded good). Whatever your interests might be, this article offers a quick step by step way to aggregate a variety of data source's information into a single source to be queried as needed.

I started by doing what we all do when faced with a new problem, search to see who has come across this same problem, and solved it already. My search ended up here on www.SQLServerCentral.com reading Jack Corbett's article 'Error Handling in SSIS'[14] . I downloaded his component (link in the article discussion) and began converting it for use in Business Intelligence Development Studio(BIDS) 2008. Once it was working, I noticed that I wanted to add a few things to the logged output like package name and the user who invoked it.

1. To get started, we need a table to house the error rows in. This is the schema I use, it lets the component auto map the columns from the component to the table - saving a little time on each use.

---

[14] http://www.sqlservercentral.com/articles/Integration+Services/62662

```
CREATE TABLE [dbo].[SSIS_ERROR_LOG](
 [ErrorLogId] [int] IDENTITY(1,1) NOT NULL,
 [ErrorCode] [int] NULL,
 [ErrorColumn] [nvarchar](128) NULL,
 [ErrorDetails] [xml] NULL,
 [ErrorDesc] [nvarchar](256) NULL,
 [ErrorStep] [nvarchar](256) NULL,
 [ErrorTask] [nvarchar](256) NULL,
 [PackageTime] [smalldatetime] NULL,
 [PackageName] [nvarchar](256) NULL,
 [UserName] [nvarchar](128) NULL,
 CONSTRAINT [PK_SSIS_ERROR_LOG] PRIMARY KEY NONCLUSTERED
(
 [ErrorLogId] ASC
)WITH (PAD_INDEX = OFF, STATISTICS_NORECOMPUTE = OFF,
IGNORE_DUP_KEY = OFF, ALLOW_ROW_LOCKS = ON, ALLOW_PAGE_LOCKS =
ON) ON [PRIMARY]
) ON [PRIMARY]
```

2. Using the SSIS.Logging.dll (download at the end of the article), you will need to use gacutil.exe to register the custom component before adding to the BIDS toolbox. I setup a batch script in my bin folder to help with quick deployment as I modify the component.

```
copy "C:\myfolder\SSIS.Logging\bin\SSIS.Logging.dll"
"C:\Program Files\Microsoft SQL
Server\100\DTS\PipelineComponents\"
"C:\ETL\gacutil.exe"
   /if "C:\Program Files\Microsoft SQL
Server\100\DTS\PipelineComponents\SSIS.Logging.dll"
```

3. Now that you have the component registered, you can add it to your toolbox. Right-click in the Data Flow Transformations pane and click "Choose Items".

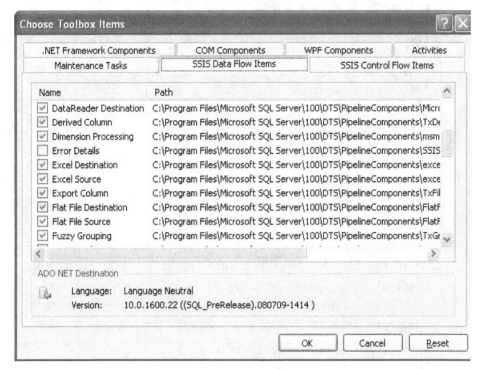

Once added, you can now utilize the component for error handling. I setup a simple csv of a few baseball players from Milwaukee (note JJ Hardy is missing a number),

```
21,Alcides Escobar,12/16/86
28,Prince Fielder,05/09/84
24,Mat Gamel,07/26/85
,J.J. Hardy,08/19/82
9,Hernan Iribarren,06/29/84
8,Ryan Braun,11/17/83
25,Mike Cameron,01/08/73
22,Tony Gwynn,10/04/82
1,Corey Hart,03/24/82
```

4. I want to load this into a table on my database server. I setup a Data Flow task and connections to the file and database. I map the tranform and then add the Error Output from the database destination component to redirect the row to the Error Details component. Here is what the package looks like after I ran it.

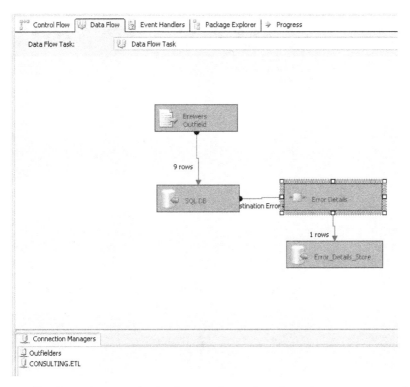

5. I won't cover the basic transformation, but what we want to do is redirect the rows in error to the "Error Details" component.

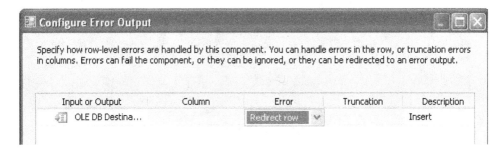

6. Next, open the Error Details component and go to the Input Columns tab. Add the columns that you want to track to the input buffer of the component.

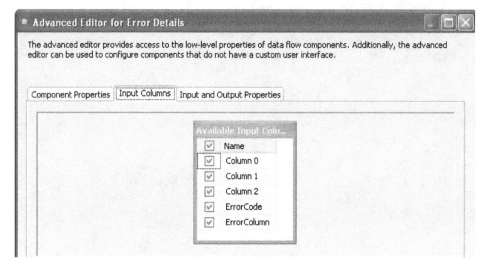

7. After setting up your database connection, map the columns from the Error Details component to the OLEDB destination.

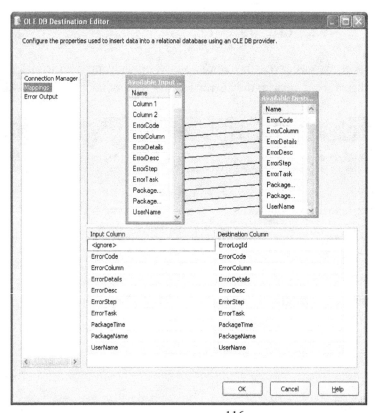

That is it, you can execute your test package and query the bad data. Here is a query that I have come up with to find what baseball player has no number. (Column 0 has no value in this case)

```
SELECT * FROM ETL.dbo.SSIS_ERROR_LOG
WHERE ErrorDetails.exist ('/fields/field[@name = "Column 0" and
@value = ""]') = 1
```

That is it! If you have any enhancements or thoughts on improving the component, post to the article discussion so everyone can benefit. Thanks to Jack for doing all the initial hard work in his article!

Simple Steps to Creating SSIS Package Configuration File

By Lanre Famuyide

After putting so much effort into creating an Integration Services (SSIS) package to provide a structured solution to a set of daily routine tasks or a daunting business problem, the next thing that comes to mind is how to ensure that the solution you have implemented in the development environment is successfully deployed into the production environment. In this article we will be considering one of the steps to ensure successful deployment of SSIS packages: the use of a package configuration file.

Creating a package configuration file for SSIS solutions makes package deployment in the production environment less error prone, portable, and very easy to modify input parameters. In order to demonstrate this concept, I have created an SSIS package using Microsoft's Business Intelligence Development Studio to export contacts list from the contacts table in the Person schema of the Adventure Works database in SQL Server 2005. The contacts list is exported into a text file.

To make the package robust, I created package level variables as input parameters for the data source, export data dump directory, and the exported data file which are included in the configuration file. I have assumed prior knowledge of creating variables in SSIS packages and that they are used to supply values at runtime. The next section outlines one approach to create a configuration file for our export package.

Procedure:

Open the completed SSIS package and click on the Control flow tab if not already selected.

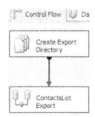

Right-click on a blank area in the control flow work area, then click on Package configurations.

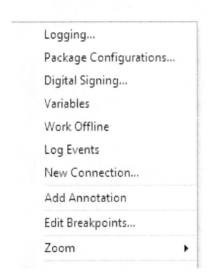

Click on the Add button to start creating a configuration file.

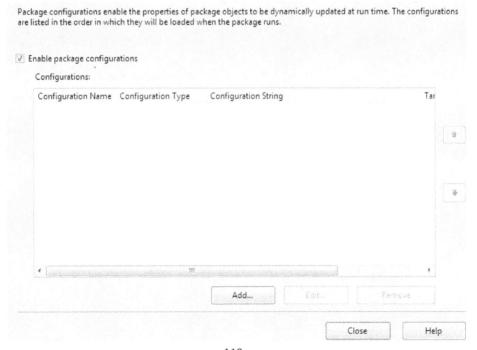

Select a configuration type, and then specify configuration settings and a file name. In this example, we will use the XML configuration file type in order to make the configuration file settings format independent and editable using any text editor outside the BIDS development environment. Click the Next button to continue.

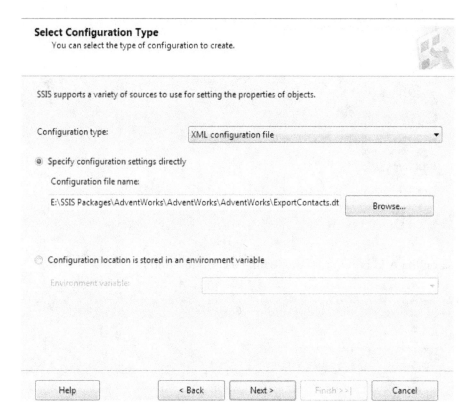

Check the configurable properties of objects in the package that are to be included in the configuration file. For simplicity, we will select the value property of the data source; the dump directory and the export file name variables. Click the Next button to continue.

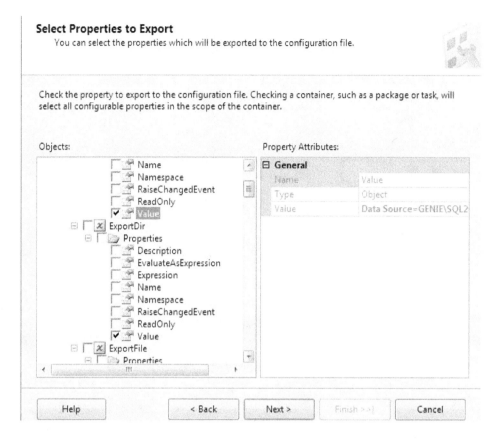

Give the configuration settings a name, and review the settings. Click the Finish button to complete the configuration process.

Completing the Wizard
Specify the configuration name and review settings.

Configuration name:

ExportContacts

Preview:

Name:
    ExportContacts

Type:
    Configuration File

New configuration file will be created.

File name:
    E:\SSIS Packages\AdventWorks\AdventWorks\AdventWorks\ExportContacts.dtsConfig

Properties:
    \Package.Variables[User::ExportFile].Properties[Value]
    \Package.Variables[User::ExportDir].Properties[Value]
    \Package.Variables[User::ExpDS].Properties[Value]

| Help | | < Back | Next > | Finish | Cancel |

Click on the Close button to close the configuration wizard.

Package configurations enable the properties of package objects to be dynamically updated at run time. The configurations are listed in the order in which they will be loaded when the package runs.

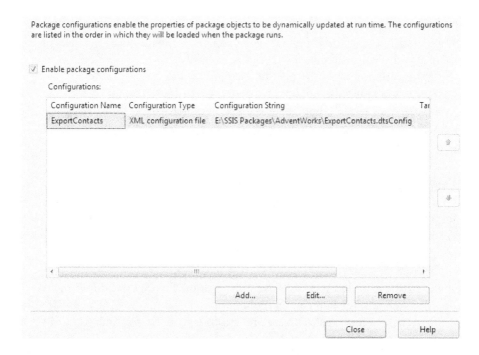

Now that the configuration file for the package has been created, navigate to the location where the file is stored and make a copy. Open the original configuration file with any text or XML file editor and change the values of variables to values suitable for the target deployment environment. This is the configuration file that will be used to deploy the SSIS package. Below is a copy of the generated XML of the configuration file.

```xml
<?xml version="1.0" ?>
- <DTSConfiguration>
  - <DTSConfigurationHeading>
    <DTSConfigurationFileInfo GeneratedBy="Domain\Username"
    GeneratedFromPackageName="ExportContacts" GeneratedFromPackageID="{DA368823-
    EBA4-4065-A09B-C24E0013A50C}" GeneratedDate="11/11/2006 11:55 am" />
    </DTSConfigurationHeading>
  - <Configuration ConfiguredType="Property" Path="\Package.Variables[User::ExpDS].Properties
    [Value]" ValueType="String">
    <ConfiguredValue>Data Source=GENIE\SQL2005DEV;Initial
    Catalog=AdventureWorks;Provider=SQLNCLI.1;Integrated
    Security=SSPI;</ConfiguredValue>
    </Configuration>
  - <Configuration ConfiguredType="Property" Path="\Package.Variables
    [User::ExportDir].Properties[Value]" ValueType="String">
    <ConfiguredValue>E:\SSIS Packages\Data</ConfiguredValue>
    </Configuration>
  - <Configuration ConfiguredType="Property" Path="\Package.Variables
    [User::ExportFile].Properties[Value]" ValueType="String">
    <ConfiguredValue>E:\SSIS Packages\Data\ExportContacts.txt</ConfiguredValue>
    </Configuration>
  </DTSConfiguration>
```

It is important to ensure that you create the configuration file after the SSIS package development is completed. Any changes to the application package that changes the value of any of the package variables will require editing the configuration file to reflect the update; else the package may not run successfully and may raise an error similar to this "Error: 0xC0017004. The expression was evaluated, but cannot be set on the property".

Conclusion

The importance of configuration files to SSIS packages cannot be over emphasized. Package configuration files make deployment of SSIS packages easier, more manageable, and less error prone compared to the process of deploying DTS packages where you might have to create one package for the development environment and one for the production environment.

As mentioned earlier in the article, we only created a basic configuration file. There are other settings that can be included in configuration files to fulfill your package needs. So feel free to create and explore more on configuration file settings.

Using Checkpoints in SSIS (Part 1)

By Aaron Akin

This is the first part of a series on using checkpoints in SSIS. In this article, I'll look at the basics of checkpoints, including enabling and configuring them in their simplest form. Future articles will cover more advanced usages of checkpoints.

Note: this article applies to SQL Server 2005.

What are checkpoints?

SQL Server Integrated Services (SSIS) offers the ability to restart failed packages from the point of failure without having to rerun the entire package. When checkpoints are configured, the values of package variables as well as a list of tasks that have completed successfully are written to the checkpoint file as XML. When the package is restarted, this file is used to restore the state of the package to what it was when the package failed.

Enabling checkpoints

There are 3 package-level properties that need to be set in order to enable checkpoints.

- **CheckpointFileName** Specify the full path to the checkpoint XML file. This file will be automatically created when checkpoints are enabled.
- **CheckpointUsage** Indicates whether checkpoints are used. *IfExists* indicates that the checkpoint file should be used if it exists and is the most common setting used. *Always* indicates that the checkpoint file must always exist or the package will fail.
- **SaveCheckpoints** Indicates whether the package saves checkpoints. This value must be set to *True* in order for packages to restart from the point of failure.

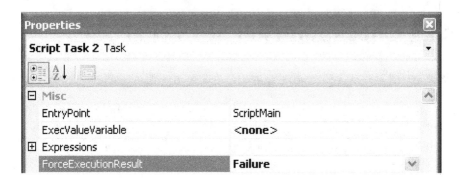

Setting these 3 package-level properties will enable checkpoint functionality in a package, but by default, no tasks are setup to log checkpoints. For each task and container in the package that you want to identify as a restart point, you must set the FailPackageOnFailure property True. By default, this property is set to False, so you ll need to remember to change it after adding new tasks to the package.

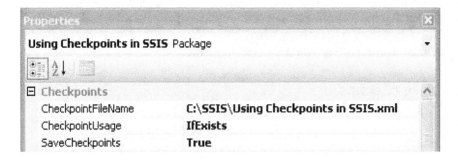

Verifying checkpoints

I added two Script Task objects to my package and set the FailPackageOnFailure property on each task to True. In order to verify that the checkpoints are setup properly and working as expected, I have set the ForceExecutionResult property on Task 2 to Failure.

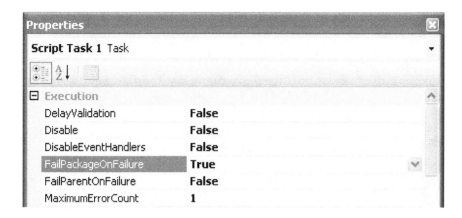

This is a fast and easy way to force a task to fail so that you can verify checkpoints. Don t forget to change this property back to its default value of None once you have verified checkpoints are working as expected, unless, for some reason, you have a need for a task to fail once it goes to production.

When the package is executed, Task 1 will succeed and a checkpoint will be written with its task identifier, whereas Task 2 will fail and no checkpoint will be written to the file.

You ll now need to determine what caused the task to fail. It could be that there is an issue with the underlying data that s referenced by the task and you just need to clean up the data. There might also be a problem with the task itself, in which case you ll need to resolve the problem by opening the package and making changes to the task. Once the cause of the failure has been resolved, the package can restart.

In my case, I know that the task failed because I forced it to, so I just need to change the ForceExecutionResult property on Task 2 back to the default value of None.

Since a checkpoint was written for Task 1, this step will be skipped and the package will restart on Task 2.

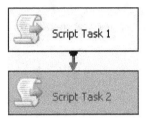

If the cause of the failure was resolved, Task 2 will now succeed and the checkpoint file will be updated.

Since all tasks in the package have now completed successfully, the checkpoint file will automatically be deleted. The next time the package is executed, SSIS will look for the checkpoint file to determine whether it needs to start from the beginning of the package or at a particular task. Since the file was deleted upon successful completion of the package, a new file is created and execution starts from the beginning of the package.

Conclusion

This article is intended to show you the basics of checkpoints in SSIS. Here are some of the key points from this article.

- Checkpoints files do not track the status of parallel tasks/containers.
- Checkpoints are only available within the control flow, not the data flow.
- The most common value for the CheckpointUsage property is IfExists. Rarely, if ever, will you set this property to Always.
- The easiest way to verify checkpoints are working properly is to add a script task and set the ForceExecutionResult property to Failure.

Reporting Services: Read Data from SSAS and SQL Server in One Dataset

By Martin Cremer

Introduction

In my last article, 'Reporting Services: Adding extra columns / rows to a matrix'[15] I showed you how to add an extra column to a matrix. The basic idea was to write a stored function that retrieves the data in the way it is needed. This allows you to expand the standard functionality of a matrix which only supports subtotals and totals.

You can use a similar method to solve another common problem: Reporting Services cannot join 2 data sets. If you want to build a table or a matrix which holds data from two different SELECT-statements, you have two options:

1. You could use sub reports which suffer from poor performance and limited export functionality (Excel).

2. You could develop a stored function to bring together all the relevant data. Then, you have only one SELECT-statement - from Reporting Services' perspective.

In this article, I want to show how to use the second method to retrieve data from Analysis Services and a SQL Server relational database in one dataset. As you can imagine, this leads to many new possibilities.

I will reuse the example I had in my previous article. I want to create the following report.

---

[15] http://www.sqlservercentral.com/articles/Reporting+Services/63415/

	Jan 2008	Feb 2008	Mar 2008	Apr 2008	May 2008	Total	Target	Delta
Franz Beckenbauer	10		7	12		29	20	9
Toni Schumacher	3	5	7	9	2	26	10	16
Diego Maradora			4			4	8	4
Pele					12	12	12	0
Michel Platini	8				16	24		24
Jear-Marie Pfaff							13	-13
Total	21	5	18	21	30	95	63	32

For this article, we assume that the actual values Jan 2008-May 2008 come from an Analysis Services cube and the target values come from SQL Server tables. (Of course, this is not realistic, but I think, it's a good example). If you want, you can download a backup of my (tiny little) cube at the end of that article.

The approach is quite straight-forward, but there are a lot of obstacles to overcome. Therefore I will describe the process step by step. We have to manage 2 main parts:

1. get data from Analysis Services from T-SQL

2. get the collected data to Reporting Services:

Get data from Analysis Services from T-SQL

Since we want to use the idea of a SQL-Server-Stored function to collect the data, we must be able to retrieve data from the cube within T-SQL.

For this, we are going to use a linked server to the cube and OPENQUERY to execute an MDX-Statement which reads the cube data.

Linked Server to Analysis Services

You can add a "linked server" to an Analysis Services cube within SQL Server Management Studio (when connected to the SQL Server relational database):

1. Go to Server Objects > Linked Servers

2. Right click and choose "New linked server ..."

3. Fill in the fields in the popup:

- Linked Server: The name you want to use for the linked server - in our example "MYCUBE"

- Provider: Select Microsoft OLE DB Provider for Analysis Services 9.0 from the drop-down-list

- Product name: put any name here. It is not needed, but it is not allowed to stay empty. I use "empty" in my example.

- Data Source: the Analysis Services server - in my example "localhost"

- Catalog: the database of Analysis Services you want to use - in my example "Article_Sales"

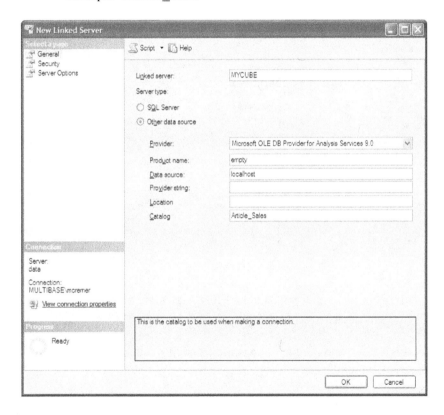

On the tab "Security" you should set the radio button to "Be made using the login's current security context". This will only work if you connect to SQL Server with Windows Security. Then this user will also be used to connect to Analysis Services. (Of course, you can change the settings according to your needs. However, be careful, not to open a security hole)

Build the appropriate MDX-statement

Now we need an MDX query to get the data. I assume you are familiar with MDX. If not, you can use Reporting Services to create the appropriate MDX-statement. You can use the Dataset-Designer to create the statement with drag-and-drop:

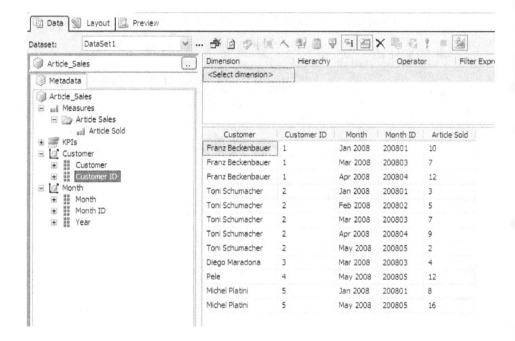

When you click on you will see the MDX-statement corresponding to that query.

Of course, this MDX statement is not optimized, so it's better to write a good MDX statement manually:

We start with the MDX statement giving us the customers, months and the amount of sold articles:

```
select [Measures].[Article Sold] on columns,
non empty [Customer].[Customer].[Customer].members *
  [Month].[Month].[Month].members on rows
from [Article_Sales]
```

Since we need the IDs (we used them for ordering in my last article), we have to add the IDs as well. We could do that the same way Reporting Services' Dataset Designer does it by adding the ID-attributes. Since this is a cross join it is not efficient (in our example we will not see a difference since there is so little data, of course). Therefore we add "dimension Properties MEMBER_CAPTION, MEMBER_KEY" to our query which will give us the desired result - the name and the ID of the dimension element:

```
select [Measures].[Article Sold] on columns,
non empty [Customer].[Customer].[Customer].members *
  [Month].[Month].[Month].members
  dimension Properties MEMBER_CAPTION, MEMBER_KEY on rows
from [Article_Sales]
```

If you run these two MDX-statements in SQL Server Management Studio as an MDX-query, you will not see any difference in the result set, but click on any dimension member in a row and you will see two more entries in the popup:

Execute this MDX-Statement with OPENQUERY

Now we can execute the MDX-Statement with OPENQUERY within T-SQL:

```
select * from
OPENQUERY(MyCube, 'select [Measures].[Article Sold] on columns,
non empty [Customer].[Customer].[Customer].members *
  [Month].[Month].[Month].members
  dimension Properties MEMBER_CAPTION, MEMBER_KEY on rows
from [Article_Sales]')
```

The result will contain the following columns:

- [Customer].[Customer].[Customer].[MEMBER_CAPTION]
- [Customer].[Customer].[Customer].[MEMBER_KEY]
- [Month].[Month].[Month].[MEMBER_CAPTION]
- [Month].[Month].[Month].[MEMBER_KEY]
- [Measures].[Article Sold]

We will need these column names later when we access the columns in a SQL-statement such as

```
select "[Customer].[Customer].[Customer].[MEMBER_CAPTION]" from
OPENQUERY(MyCube, 'select [Measures].[Article Sold] on columns,
non empty [Customer].[Customer].[Customer].members *
  [Month].[Month].[Month].members
  dimension Properties MEMBER_CAPTION, MEMBER_KEY on rows
from [Article_Sales]')
```

As you can see we used the column name with quotation marks to access the appropriate column.

This works fine, but it has one limitation: OPENQUERY only accepts a hard-coded string as the second parameter - neither a variable nor an expression is allowed. In our case, this is sufficient, but in real life, it is not: You will want to build your MDX-Statement dynamically, because your statement probably includes parameters. Then you should build the SQL-String (as shown above) dynamically and execute it with sp_executesql.

Let's assume the year is passed to the stored function parameter @year. Then, our SQL-Statement would look like:

```
declare @year as nvarchar(4)
set @year = '2008' -- this simulates a passed parameter
declare @mdx as nvarchar(4000)
set @mdx = 'select [Measures].[Article Sold] on columns,
non empty [Customer].[Customer].[Customer].members
  * [Month].[Year_Month_Hierarchy].[' + @year + '].children
  dimension Properties MEMBER_CAPTION, MEMBER_KEY on rows
from [Article_Sales]'
declare @sql as nvarchar (4000)
set @sql = 'select * from OPENQUERY(MyCube, ''' + @mdx + ''')'
exec sp_executesql @sql
```

[Be careful not to forget the '" before and after @mdx.]

Side remark "allow inprocess"

Sometimes the above shown OPENQUERY-statement gives an access denied-error. For my case it did on 2 production servers. However, on my local machine it worked perfectly fine.

This error can be fixed by allowing inprocess for the MSOLAP-Provider for Linked Servers.

You can set this property with the following steps:

1. Go to Server Objects > Linked Servers > Providers > MSOLAP

2. Right click and choose "Properties"

3. Enable "Allow inprocess"

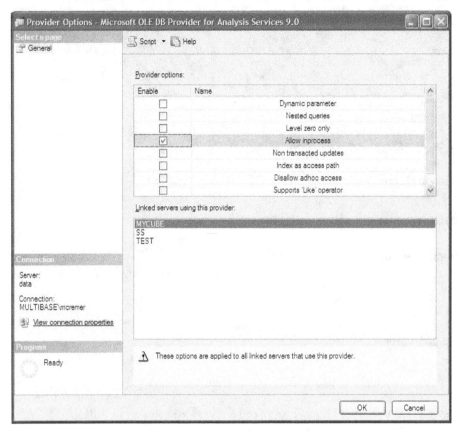

Microsoft advises to set this property for performance issues anyway.

Now we've finished the first task of accessing the Analysis Services cube. It's now time to address the second task of bringing this data into Reporting Services.

Reporting Services gets the desired data

Replace the SQL statement of the last article's example by the OPENQUERY-SQL

The SQL statement of my last article, which reads the actual data, was

```
SELECT ArticleSales.CustomerID, Customers.CustomerName,
ArticleSales.MonthID,
Months.Monthname, ArticleSales.ArticleSold
```

```
FROM ArticleSales INNER JOIN
 Customers ON ArticleSales.CustomerID = Customers.CustomerID
INNER JOIN
 Months ON ArticleSales.MonthID = Months.MonthID
```

In order to use the OPENQUERY-statement the same way as the old statement, the OPENQUERY-statement should return the 5 needed columns in the appropriate order. This is easy with what we have learned above. I added the @columns-variable into my script:

```
declare @mdx as nvarchar(4000)
set @mdx = 'select [Measures].[Article Sold] on columns,
non empty [Customer].[Customer].[Customer].members
 * [Month].[Month].[Month].members
 dimension Properties MEMBER_CAPTION, MEMBER_KEY on rows
from [Article_Sales]'
declare @columns as nvarchar(4000)
set @columns =
'"[Customer].[Customer].[Customer].[MEMBER_KEY]",
"[Customer].[Customer].[Customer].[MEMBER_CAPTION]",
"[Month].[Month].[Month].[MEMBER_KEY]",
"[Month].[Month].[Month].[MEMBER_CAPTION]",
"[Measures].[Article Sold]"'
declare @sql as nvarchar (4000)
set @sql = 'select ' + @columns + ' from OPENQUERY(MyCube, '''
+ @mdx + ''')'
exec sp_executesql @sql
```

Actually we should convert the columns to the appropriate data types, since OPENQUERY returns ntext for all the column results. In order to convert them to int, we first need to convert them to nvarchar(...). Therefore, the @columns-variable should finally read like the following:

```
set @columns = 'convert(int, convert(nvarchar(10),
"[Customer].[Customer].[Customer].[MEMBER_KEY]")) as
CustomerID,
convert(nvarchar(50),
"[Customer].[Customer].[Customer].[MEMBER_CAPTION]") as
CustomerName,
convert(int, convert(nvarchar(10),
"[Month].[Month].[Month].[MEMBER_KEY]")) as
MonthID,
convert(nvarchar(50),
"[Month].[Month].[Month].[MEMBER_CAPTION]") as MonthName,
convert(int, convert(nvarchar(10), "[Measures].[Article
Sold]")) as ArticlesSold'
```

Stored Procedure

Since we need to use sp_executesql in our SQL-statement, we cannot use a stored function any more. If you try, SQL Server produces the following error:

```
Only functions and extended stored procedures can be executed
from within a function.
```

Ok, so now we have a problem.

We now need to change the stored function to a stored procedure.

The first idea is to use a @CrossTab-table-variable, then the changes will be minor. This will not work, however, since this variable will not be accessible within sp_executesql. Therefore, we must use a temporary table, #CrossTab. The changes in detail:

- In the beginning we create the #CrossTab manually
- We replace all the references of @CrossTab to #CrossTab
- In the end we return all the entries of the #CrossTab
- In Reporting Services, we execute the Stored Procedure instead of the Stored Function

The changes in Detail:

	Old text	New text
Start	CREATE FUNCTION [dbo].[createReportExample3] () RETURNS @CrossTab TABLE (rowSort int, rowDesc nvarchar(50), colSort int, colDesc nvarchar(50), value int	CREATE PROCEDURE [dbo].[createReportExampleWithAS2] as BEGIN CREATE TABLE #CrossTab (rowSort int, rowDesc nvarchar(50), colSort int, colDesc nvarchar(50),

	Old text	New text
	) AS BEGIN	value int)
References	INSERT INTO @CrossTab (rowSort, rowDesc, colSort, colDesc, value)	INSERT INTO #CrossTab (rowSort, rowDesc, colSort, colDesc, value)
Return values	RETURN	SELECT * FROM #CrossTab
Reporting Services	SELECT * FROM dbo.createReportExample3()	exec dbo.[createReportExampleWithAS2]

Missing fields in Reporting Services

So far, our approach was simple and straight-forward. There is only one problem: it is not going to work:

Reporting Services cannot detect the fields of the temporary table correctly. There will not be any fields contained in this dataset and, henceforth, we cannot build our report :-(

You could try to add the fields manually, either in the datasets-window when right-clicking on the appropriate dataset or when editing the selected dataset (button ... in tab "Data") in the "Fields" tab.

I managed to enter the numeric fields (rowSort, colSort, value), but failed to enter the string fields (rowDesc, colDesc). As soon as I enter them I get an error when executing the reports, even if this field is not shown on the report:

```
Index was outside the bounds of the array.
```

(I think this is a bug in Reporting Services or the OLE DB driver, but - any way we have to live with it.)Therefore we have to find another solution.

Non-temporary tables

Since temporary tables do not work, the next option is to create a real table (In my example, I will call it ExampleReport-table).

Of course, you could use global temporary tables like ##CrossTab. These tables vanish when the last connection is closed which uses this table. If two users accessed the report at the same time, we would need to check the existence of the ##CrossTab-table which would not make the solution simpler.

When we use real tables, we must make them "multi-session-proof". This means, the solution must work in circumstances as well, when 2 (or more) users call the report the same time. Therefore, our stored procedure cannot simply empty and fill the table.

The most straight-forward method is to have a column in the real table which holds the session information. This means some changes for the stored procedure:

- The table does not need to be created inside the stored procedure any more.
- At the beginning of the stored procedure, a session-identifier is created. The best data type for the session-identifier is a uniqueidentifier (Guid), because this is unique for every stored procedure call by default. From now on I will call it session-guid
- All inserts into the table need to insert the session-guid as well.
- Even more important, all selects from the table must have an extra WHERE-condition to make sure we only retrieve the data of the current session.
- In the end, you can delete the records in the table belonging to this session.

There is one crucial point: You must double check that you added the WHERE SessionGuid = @sesGuid condition to every SELECT-statement. You will not receive an error message as you do when you forget it in the INSERT-statement, but you will retrieve wrong data.

Therefore, I encourage you to omit the delete-statement first and check whether or not you're getting the correct data. In this test, the table is filled with lots of data rows, which simulates the simultaneous execution of the stored procedure.

Now we have succeeded, and our changed code generates the result shown at the very beginning. (I did not speak about the layout of the report since this did not change from the last article).

Here is the SQL-statement for the table ... and the stored procedure in our example:

Note: This code is at www.sqlservercentral.com

Some final remarks

When you want to put this solution into production, you have to consider error robustness. We need to add this to our solution:

Try - Catch when reading data from Analysis Services

I do not want to talk about problems arising if the SQL Server or Analysis Services are down, because you will need to have a solution for this anyway (or the decision you don't need it).

Often, with solutions such as this one, errors can occur, which need to be handled:

Assume the MDX-statement does not return any data. We can force this situation by adding a filter on the year 2007:

```
select [Measures].[Article Sold] on columns,
 non empty [Customer].[Customer].[Customer].members
  * [Month].[Month].[Month].members
  dimension Properties MEMBER_CAPTION, MEMBER_KEY on rows
 from [Article_Sales] where (Month.Year.[2007])
```

Then we will get a result set with 1 column "Article Sold" but no row.

Therefore, our OPENQUERY does not return the columns which we expected. This means the SELECT * FROM OPENQUERY(.. would work fine, but the SELECT

```
"[Customer].[Customer].[Customer].[MEMBER_CAPTION]", ...
```
FROM OPENQUERY(... will lead to an error:

```
Invalid column name
'[Customer].[Customer].[Customer].[MEMBER_KEY]'.
```

Since this error can occur, so we need to take care of that error.

The best method is to wrap the SELECT OPENQUERY part into a try-catch- ▸
block.

Now the error is caught and we have to decide what needs to be done. In our
example, it is quite easy. Since there is no actual data, there should not be any
columns in our matrix. Therefore, we do not do any inserts. This means our
Catch-Block does not do anything. Depending on your situation, this may vary.

In our example, the part of the code looks like:

```
declare @sql as nvarchar (4000)
 set @sql = 'INSERT INTO ExampleReport (sessionGuid, rowSort,
rowDesc,
 colSort, colDesc, value)
 select ''' + convert(nvarchar(100), @sesGuid) + ''', '
 + @columns + ' from OPENQUERY(MyCube, ''' + @mdx + ''')'
BEGIN TRY
   exec sp_executesql @sql
END TRY
BEGIN CATCH
   /* An error would arise if the MDX does not return any rows
*/
   /* In this case we do not need to do anything */
END CATCH
```

Of course, the error handling could be more sophisticated. You could check
whether the MDX works but does not return a row. With this, you could
distinguish between "Server unavailable" and "no data". For my example, this
is not necessary.

Next steps

Now you have a method which allows you to gather data from different data
source types (ORACLE, SQL Server, Analysis Services ...) or different cubes,
for example.

In one of my productive reports, I used it for getting information from two different cubes. This solution was superior (in terms of performance) to building a bigger cube and having a complex MDX-statement gather the data in one statement.

In real-life scenarios, you will naturally have parameters for the stored procedure, but this is not a problem to implement, so I did not cover this subject.

Example data

You can download the example here. This includes

- The SQL scripts for the demo data
- The SQL scripts for the stored procedure and the table
- The solution which holds the Reporting Services and Analysis Services example
- A backup of the Analysis Services database.

Acknowledgements

I want to thank bteague for reading my draft of this article and his valuable comments.

SQL Server 2008 Mirroring Testing

By Jason Shadonix

Overview

One of the areas improved for SQL 2008 is database mirroring. Two of the improvements listed in Books Online that caught my eye are compression of data sent across the network (at least 12.5 % compression ratio according to books online), and "Write-ahead on the incoming log stream" on the mirror server. I decided to do some simple testing to see if these changes made a noticeable difference.

Setup

For testing purposes, I used basic workstation-class development machines. The machine that served as the principal was running XP-Pro, and the machine serving as the mirror was running Server 2003 standard. For both machines I installed SQL 2005 Developer Edition (SP2) and SQL 2008 Developer Edition (RTM). I installed both instances as named instances, and while testing only started the instance that I was using for the test.

For the test database, I used a copy of one of our production databases (about 4GB in size) and configured the mirroring for high-safety with no automatic failover. To simulate a load, I wrote a simple script that inserted records at a steady pace, and a script that randomly updates records at a steady pace. Mirroring sessions were set up as high safety (synchronous) without automatic failover.

I found that the scripts I had developed for configuring database mirroring in SQL 2005 worked for SQL 2008 without modification. In fact from what I can tell by scanning Books Online, there are no obvious changes to configuring and administering database mirroring in 2008. All of the changes are under the hood.

I tested mirroring from a 2005 principal to a 2005 mirror, a 2005 principal to a 2008 mirror, and from a 2008 principal to a 2008 mirror, and ran each test for about 7 min, using perfmon counters to collect data every 15 seconds.

I found it interesting that SQL allowed a 2005 principal to mirror to a 2008 server. While I was playing around I observed that the mirroring seemed to work fine with this setup, but it did not allow you to take snapshots (from what I can tell, this is because the 2005 database isn't actually upgraded to 2008's file structure until the recovery process in a database restore runs). If you manually fail over to the mirror server, it prints out messages saying it is upgrading the database to 2008. I didn't test it, but I assume this means you can't put that database back on a 2005 SQL server. I don't know how much support you will get mirroring like this for long periods of time, but Books Online briefly mentions a rolling upgrade strategy to upgrade mirrored servers from 2005 to 2008 that involves upgrading the mirror server first, so I think all of the behavior I observed is by design. Just something to keep in mind.

Results

The amount of data writes to disk increased slightly (about 10%) when using SQL server 2008. I assume this is a result of the way 2008 is simultaneously writing log records to disk and processing log records. Unless the disks on your mirror server are stressed to begin with, this is probably insignificant.

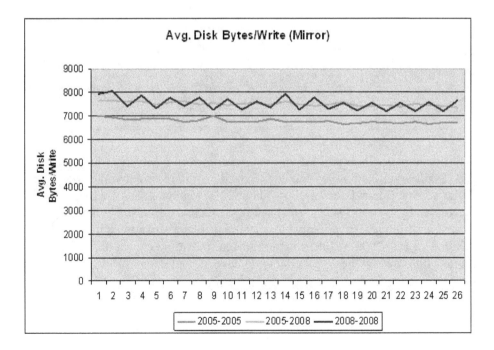

CPU usage on the principal server when mirroring from a 2008 principal to a 2008 mirror was significantly higher for a few minutes, then settled down to be roughly the same as 2005 mirroring for the remainder of the test. I'm not sure how to account for this. I was expecting a slight increase in CPU usage due to overhead in compressing the log stream, but that is not what is observed. I would expect the CPU usage to vary a little bit based on the size of the data changes made, data types involved, etc.

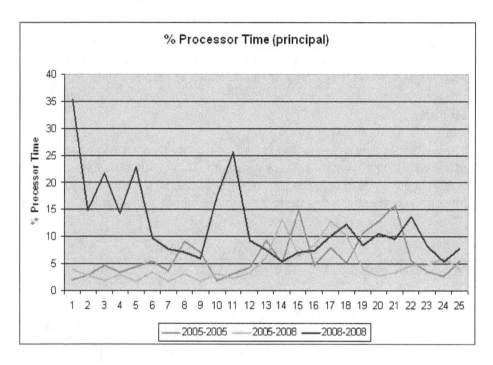

The counters perfmon provides for database mirroring network traffic indicate that SQL server 2008 mirroring does indeed result in less network traffic. Total bytes sent per second decreased by about 32%, log bytes sent per second decreased by about 15%, and total sends per second decreased by about 34%. Mirroring from a 2005 principal to a 2008 mirror server showed little if any difference than 2005 to 2005 mirroring. Again, I would expect this would vary quite a bit based on the type of data you have in your database.

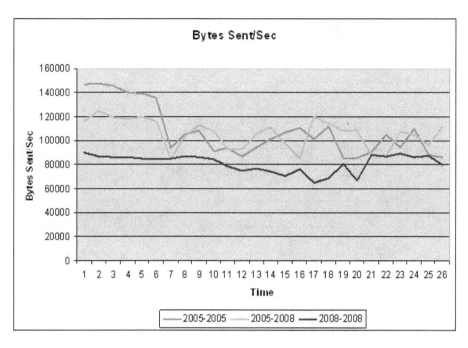

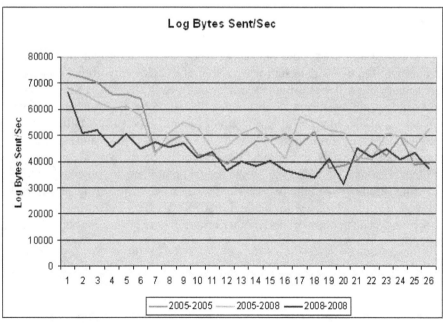

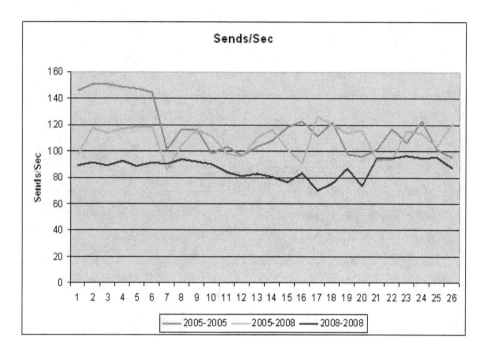

Conclusion

For the test setup I used, I did indeed see a potentially significant decrease in the amount of network data sent when using SQL 2008 mirroring. With the exception of the disk performance, mirroring from SQL 2005 to SQL 2008 shows little if any performance difference than 2005 to 2005 mirroring. If your network capability in your mirroring environment is currently a bottleneck, then SQL 2008 mirroring may help you out a little bit. This feature alone probably doesn't justify an upgrade, but it's a nice bonus if you are upgrading for other reasons also. I also really like the fact that there are no changes to the mirroring setup between the two versions so all of your mirroring scripts will still work. (I did not play with the GUI that SSMS offers for setting up mirroring, so can't comment on whether or not they are different between 2005 and 2008).

Disclaimer

These results are what I happened to achieve today while running tests. Actual results may vary based on database characteristics, network characteristics, server characteristics and the alignment of Saturn's moons. Do your own testing rather than relying on this article to make important upgrade decisions

On-Call Duties

By TJay Belt

It's Monday morning, and your calendar reminder just popped up and let you know that you are on call. Since its Monday morning, and you got in before anyone else, to have some alone time with your systems, this is the perfect time to start in on your on-call duties. Where to begin? Which task do you perform first? What tasks were performed last by the preceding on-call rotation individual? I hope to stimulate some thought on this process and get you ready to better satisfy the time you have to monitor your systems and ensure their availability and uptime.

I would first like to suggest that you keep a diary or record of tasks, and their results. This record will allow others to see what has and has not been done previously. It will allow you to start a baseline and gather metrics. See trends and patterns. We have chosen a simple spreadsheet that keeps track of tasks, results and other gathered data. A template tab exists to copy from, to a new tab. Each day a new tab is created and populated. As you complete tasks, the results are filled in. Those tasks that do not get completed simply have no results associated with them. This way others can look back on specific days and see what results were, or which items were not done. The need to completely fill in all tasks will be determined in your individual companies and teams. Each server that we are responsible for has a column in this spreadsheet, where individual data can be collected, on a per server basis.

Some of the items that we have on our task list are as follows.

Scan OS error events.

In Computer Management, in the Event Viewer, we perform a review of the errors that appear in the Application, Security, and System sections. Filter each of these sections by errors and look for anything that has occurred since the last time this process was completed. Anything that appears in these sections, detail it in your record keeping, and you may even have to dig in and find out the reasons for it, and mediate it. This task can be quick, or occur over a few days, depending on the events that you encounter.

Check on Backups

We all have maintenance plans, 3rd party solutions, or whatever to ensure we have backups of our systems. Whatever the solution you have, make it a habit to check it as often as you can while on call. Ensure that backups are being processed properly. If you do this on a daily basis, while on-call, odds of you going a couple days without a backup will diminish greatly. Unfortunately, most shops that implement this task usually do so after finding no exhausting backups for a period. Don't let this happen to you.

System specific output files

You may have reports, text files, dumps, snapshots, etc. that are output from your system. These will be for a variety of reasons. Identify them, document them, and then monitor them. Ensure that they are occurring on a regular basis, and that you have the means to prove so.

Log and data file sizes

To keep a handle on the growth of your systems, you should devise a way to monitor and keep tabs on the sizes of your database files. A simple solution is to run a query that gathers all this info, and paste it into a spreadsheet. More complex solutions could be implemented. The end result needs to be that you know the sizes of these files, and be able to have metrics over time to help you plan and monitor those systems. Doing this task on a daily basis, while on-call, will help keep tabs on growth and expected results.

Space available/Free space on drives

We could have other processes that take up space on our servers. Maybe these reside on your drives with your data files. If this is the case, you need to monitor the free space to ensure that your databases don't run up against a wall. This has occurred to me on simple database servers, and the results are often wild and unpredictable. This task may not be relevant in all of your systems or database servers. However, I think it's worth noting, and thinking about, at least to discount it as a necessary task. If it is necessary, add this into your on-call duties.

Replication health check

If you have replication executing on your systems, how do you monitor it? How do you know that it is functioning properly? What about latency? Can you tell what latency is during peak times, compared to non-peak times? You may have third party replication or native replication. Determine the best way to monitor it, and document it. Gathering the data associated with it and creating a baseline will help solve future issues as well.

Scan SQL Server Logs

Something that is often missed is simply looking into the SQL Server Logs. Make it a habit to scan these logs and you will soon become more knowledgeable about the logs and what they can teach us. Make it a habit to peruse them on a repeatable basis, and document what you see.

Other Notes of Interest

During your on-call rotation, you may encounter odd things that need to be noted. Make sure you comment on these and document them. If you resolve them, document this as well. Other individuals will greatly appreciate your notes and observations of these odd occurrences. If persistent, you may want to add them into the above rotation.

Specific Needs

Since your shop will have specific needs, you will need to come up with more of these tasks. You may have items that do not appear on this list that you need to add to your on-call duties. Share these with the rest of us, as well as your fellow DBA's at your shop.

If we can take the time, when we are not head-long into problems of the day, we can better gather our wits about us, and devise solutions to make our jobs easier, more automated, and successful. This is an important hump to get over, so that you are not fire-fighting all the time, but have a plan of action to solve issues as they arise. Keeping a record of these tasks, and results is a sure-fire way to see patterns and way to fix those pesky problems that always seem to get placed on the back burner. By creating metrics to measure yourself by, you can spend more time on the important tasks, and not just fix things as they appear. There's nothing like 'knowing' that your systems are healthy, and being able to prove it.

Configuring Replication for Partitioned Tables Using T-SQL

By Michelle Ufford

By default, partitioning schemes are not persisted when replicating partitioned tables to a subscriber. This can be nice if you want to replicate partitioned data from SQL 2005 Enterprise to SQL 2005 Standard (where partitioning is not supported), but most of the time, you probably want the replicated table to be partitioned, too. This post will walk you through the basics of creating transactional replication for a partitioned table to ensure the subscription table is also partitioned.

First, let's set up our test databases and data:

Note: This code is available at www.sqlservercentral.com

Up until now, this has been pretty straight forward. This next step is where we specify the bitwise product for article options. We're going to specify that we want to copy partitioning schemes for tables and indexes, and we also want to copy nonclustered indexes.

Personally, I prefer to cheat and let SQL Server tell me what the appropriate bitwise product should be for a given article. To do this, I walk through the process of creating a new article using the GUI, then I script it out and snag the @schema_option value.

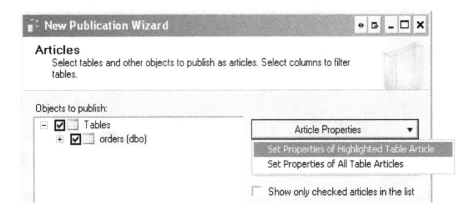

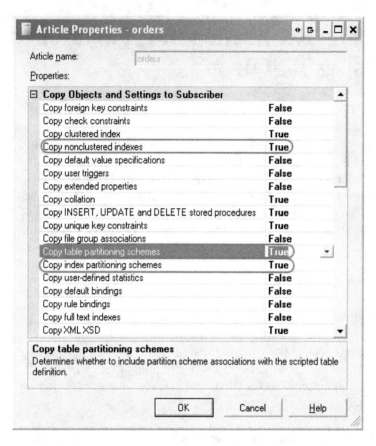

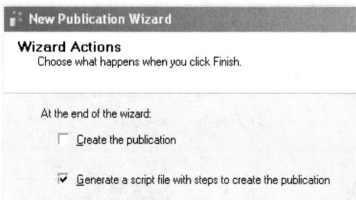

```
use [sandbox_publisher]
exec sp_addarticle @publication = N'myTestPublication', @article = N
'orders', @source_owner = N'dbo', @source_object = N'orders', @type = N
'logbased', @description = null, @creation_script = null, @
pre_creation_cmd = N'drop', @schema_option = 0x00000000081B50DB, @
```

Using the @schema_option above let s now create our article.

Note: this code is available at www.sqlservercentral.com

You can find more about the @schema_option under sp_addarticle on Books Online (*http://msdn.microsoft.com/*
en-us/library/ms173857.aspx)

Now let's finish up with our script to create the snapshot and add a subscription,

Note: this code is available at www.sqlservercentral.com

When everything is done, check your subscriber and ensure your table has been created. Also verify that the table is partitioned. If you do not see it right away, wait a minute and try again... SQL Server just may not have caught up yet.

```
USE sandbox_subscriber;
GO
/* You should now have a partitioned table with a partitioned
   nonclustered index in your subscription database... */
EXECUTE sp_help N'dbo.orders';
```

Results | Messages

	Name	Owner	Type	Created_datetime
1	orders	dbo	user table	2008-11-29 19:57:11.470

	Column_name	Type	Computed	Length	Prec	Scale	Nullable	TrimTrailingBlanks	FixedLenNu
1	order_id	int	no	4	10	0	no	(n/a)	(n/a)
2	orderDate	datetime	no	8			no	(n/a)	(n/a)

	Identity	Seed	Increment	Not For Replication
1	No identity column defined.	NULL	NULL	NULL

	RowGuidCol
1	No rowguidcol column defined.

	Data_located_on_filegroup
1	test_monthlyDateRange_ps

	index_name	index_description	index_keys
1	IX_orders_aligned	nonclustered located on test_monthlyDateRange_ps	order_id
2	PK_orders	clustered, unique, primary key located on test_monthlyDateRange_ps	order_id, orderDate

It may sometimes be beneficial to use a different partitioning scheme on the subscription table. In that case, create the table on the subscriber in advance using the desired partitioning scheme; then specify that, during initialization, the objects should be retained if they already exist.

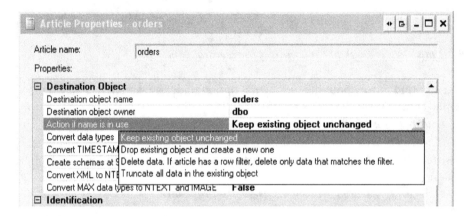

I hope that helps get you started with replicating partitioned tables. In my next post, we'll walk through the process of swapping out a partition on a replicated table (SQL 2008 only). For more information on partitioning, please check out the following resources:

- SQLFool - Partitioning posts - *http://sqlfool.com/tag/partitioning/*

- Partitioned Tables and Indexes in SQL Server 2005 - *http://msdn.microsoft.com/en-us/library/ ms345146.aspx*

- Querying Data and Metadata from Partitioned Tables and Indexes - *http://msdn.microsoft.com/en-us/library/ms187924.aspx*

Performance Implications of Database Snapshots

By Gail Shaw

Database snapshots are a new feature of SQL Server 2005. They offer a read-only, point-in-time view of a database. There have been some articles published here explaining what they are and discussing possible uses for them, but not about the performance impact of multiple snapshots, so I thought I'd take a look at that.

All examples shown here were done on a Windows XP, service pack 2 machine, running SQL Server 2005 Developer edition, RTM.

Statistics

The SQL Books Online states that performance may be decreased due to increased I/O on database snapshots. After running into a performance problem involving snapshots I decided to do some tests to see exactly how the performance of some typical operations degraded when using snapshots.

I set up a database with a sample table with 40 000 rows in it. The table had an int and a char(3000) column, ensuring that only two rows would fit onto a page. The int column was an identity and the clustered index.

For the first test, I inserted four sets of 5000 rows, taking care that each set affected different rows, and hence different pages. The database was restored from backup after each set. The first sets of tests were done with no snapshots on the database. I then ran tests with one, two, three, four and five snapshots. For each, I measured how long the data modification would take and how long a subsequent checkpoint operation would take.

Likewise, I did tests where I deleted four sets of 5000 rows and updated four sets of 5000 rows, again with the database restored after each set of tests and the tests were done with differing numbers of snapshots in place

As the graphs show, the duration of the operations increases significantly as the number of snapshots that needs to be updated increases.

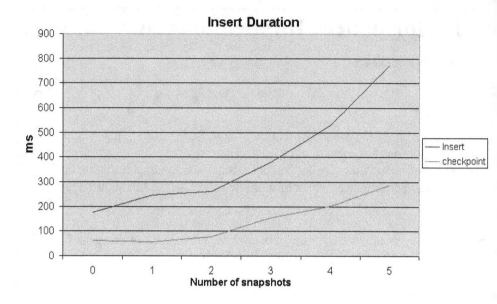

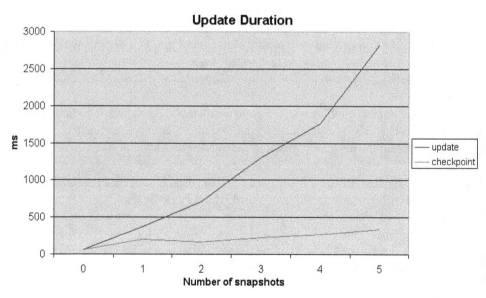

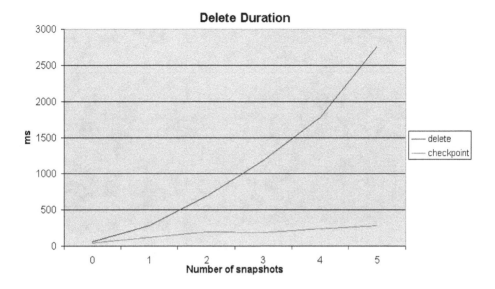

From the results, it would seem as though large numbers of snapshots can seriously degrade database performance. The tests were done on a workstation, with all the files on a single drive, so the effects won't be so pronounced on a properly configured server with multiple properly configured drives, but it is still something to be watched.

While I was expecting an increase in the durations, I was not expecting a increase of this magnitude. In the case of deletes and updates, the difference in time to affect 5000 rows with no snapshots and with five snapshots is a factor of fifty!

I also did a quick test on a server (16 processor, 64 GB memory, SAN storage, SQL 2005 Enterprise SP2) to see how a number of snapshots affected delete speed on a high-powered machine. I wasn't being as careful as with the earlier experiments, but this does go to show that the performance degradation affects well-configured servers as well as desktop PCs.

I had a table with several million rows in and I was deleting 5000 at a time. 8 tests were done with each number of snapshots and the resulting times were averaged. The graph below shows how the delete time varied with the number of snapshots present.

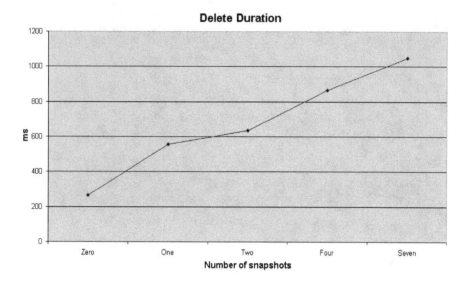

A recent post[16] by the PSS Engineers described in detail how IOs work in a snapshot, and the reason for the increase in duration.

Normally, when SQL modifies a data page, the data page is changed in memory and only the log record is hardened to disk before the transaction is considered complete.

Since snapshots do not have a transaction log, changes to the snapshot cannot be written to the log, but must be written directly to the data file. Hence, when a transaction modifies a page that must be written to a snapshot, to ensure durability the write of that page must be completed to disk before the transaction that modified the page is considered complete. This increases the number of physical disk writes that must be done during the transaction.

If the IO system that the snapshot is stored on is slow (as in my case with the initial experiment, since I was using a workstation PC), these additional writes (1 per snapshot file) can cause quite substantial slow downs in the source database.

This also explains why the checkpoint process does not show any appreciable increase in duration as the number of snapshots increases. Since the copy-on-

---

[16] http://blogs.msdn.com/psssql/archive/2008/02/07/how-it-works-sql-server-2005-database-snapshots-replica.aspx

write is done as part of the data modification statement, the checkpoint has no extra work to do.

Conclusion

While database snapshots have their uses, they are not without side-effect. Planning should be carefully done when using snapshots, especially if large numbers of snapshots are needed, or they are needed for long periods of time.

Depending on the capacities of the IO system, the extra load that the snapshots impose may be unnoticed, or it may drag the system down completely. Careful testing should be done before using them in production environments, especially in systems where fast transactions are essential.

Filtering Unneeded Dimension Members in PerformancePoint Filters

By Boyan Penev

Sometimes we need to utilise dynamic dimension security in an Analysis Services solution and we also need to display dynamically the allowed members in a PerformancePoint filter.

In case our hierarchy is multi-level and in case we can expect to have security on multiple levels, PerformancePoint will display the full path upwards to the root member of the dimension. So, in the case where in a Business Unit hierarchy we have access to some third level members, in PerformancePoint we will see all their parents. In example if our hierarchy looks like this:

```
  All Business Units
 - Europe
   - UK
   - France
   - Bulgaria
 - North America
   - USA
   - Canada
```

And we give someone access to France, they will in fact see:

```
  All Business Units
 - Europe
   - France
```

Indeed, when they select All Business Units or Europe they will still see only France data but this may be confusing. To eliminate the top levels we need to change the way we create our PerformancePoint filter.

To achieve this, first we need to create a MDX Query filter. For more information about PerformancePoint filters and dynamic dimension security you can read the following brilliant post on Nick Barclay's blog: PPS Data Connection Security with CustomData. Nick explains how to set up PerformancePoint to work with Analysis Services dynamic dimension security and related topics. I will now concentrate on actually filtering the members of the already set-up MDX Query filter.

Instead of requesting all dimension members with a simple statement like:

```
DESCENDANTS([Business].[Business Hierarchy].Members,,
SELF_AND_AFTER)
```

We can write some fairly simple MDX which means:

Get me the descendants of all dimension members whose ascendants (excluding themselves) have no more than one child.

And the MDX code is:

```
DESCENDANTS(
  FILTER([Business].[Business Hierarchy].Members AS a,
  ((FILTER(ASCENDANTS(a.CurrentMember) AS a_asc,
  a_asc.CurrentMember.CHILDREN.Count > 1).Count = 1)
  And
  a.CurrentMember.Children.Count > 1)
  Or
  ((FILTER(ASCENDANTS(a.CurrentMember) AS a_asc,
  a_asc.CurrentMember.CHILDREN.Count > 1).Count = 0)
  And
  a.CurrentMember.Children.Count = 0))
  ,,SELF_AND_AFTER)
```

The result will be France being displayed as the only available member in the PerformancePoint drop-down. Also, if we had two different allowed members, the code above would show us the top common parent of the two. Therefore, if we had France and Canada as the allowed set of dimension members, the drop-down would consist of the following hierarchy:

```
All Business Units
  Europe
    France
  North America
    Canada
```

Thus satisfying our requirements.

Powering up DTS with PerlDTS

By Alceu Rodrigues de Feitas Junior

Introduction

When implemented together with MS SQL Server 2000, DTS offers several features to help managing ETL processes, including process automation, scheduling and notification. While DTS is considered a RAD tool, the true capabilities of DTS are only unrevealed when its exposed API is used.

While the documentation includes steps for Visual Basic or Visual C++ to use or extend DTS, such programming languages are not the ideal ones for developing applications quickly (considering that they will run in the background). Interpreted languages are much more suited to doing jobs like executing DTS packages outside Enterprise Manager or scheduling a task, for example.

Any interpreted programming language that supports COM can deal with DTS API, like Vbscript or Perl. With several years being part of system administrator and programmers tools, Perl is a natural choice for being used as a glue language for DTS ETL tasks, specially if one considers the amount of several read-to-use modules available in CPAN, dealing with the most different problems that a programming language can solve.

Being a Perl programmer for a couple of years and inspired by the article "Flexible DTS Packages with Perl"[17] of Jeremy Brown (published in this very website!), I decided to give a try to write Perl code to deal with DTS API when some tasks became too boring to solve with click-and-drag procedures in DTS designer.

Enter PerlDTS

PerlDTS is the name of the project I created to hold several Perl classes that represents DTS classes in a more natural way (for a Perl programmer perspective).

---

[17] http://www.sqlservercentral.com/articles/DTS/flexibledtspackageswithperl/1818/

In the article mentioned, the author teaches how to use the module Win32::OLE to connect to DTS API. While Win32::OLE is the backbone of PerlDTS project, using it can be cumbersome for a Perl programmer because it deals with details of MS Windows operational system (like converting variable types) that brings complexity into the problem a programmer is trying to solve. Talking about DTS API this is even worse, because documentation expects that the programmer will use Visual Basic, Vbscript or Visual C++. I had to improve a fair amount of my Vbscript skill just to understand the examples.

PerlDTS is different. I implemented a lot of DTS API classes (and there is still a lot of other ones to implement) using an interface that is pure Perl code with added syntactic sugar for convenience. Since I did this, my job got much easier when I was in a project dealing with hundreds of DTS packages to implement batch integration with Oracle Siebel CRM.

What can Perldts do?

The nowadays implementation of Perldts allows a programmer to:

- Search and query information of DTS packages.
- Execute DTS packages and retrieve execution information.

Differently of the article of Jeremy Brown, I did not implemented anything related to the capability of creating DTS packages on the fly, keep them only in memory, executing and ceasing to exists as soon the program job is over. I'll comment those implementations decisions latter in the article.

Right now, instead of telling all features of PerlDTS, I invite the reader to check some program examples that I'll comment here to get a grasp of the project and, maybe latter, check the online documentation and UML diagrams for more details in the project website.

Why took you so long to release this?

Maybe you're asking yourself that question since MS SQL Server 2008 is already available and version 2000 is quite outdated. It's a fair question.

Well, the answer is "I was quite busy". I started working with DTS packages in 2006 and took me a while before releasing something more than a distribution tarball in CPAN. Anyway, I wanted at least to document the distribution before releasing it and here it is, as free software.

Examples of using

Let's start with a very simple example: connect to a SQL Server database and search for DTS packages with a name that matches a regular expression. Here is the code:

Note: this code is available at www.sqlservercentral.com

The program starts with the usual lines expected for a Perl program and loads the modules DTS::Application and XML::Simple. All modules of PerlDTS project starts with the package name "DTS". This will change very soon to the registered name I got in CPAN called Win32::SqlServer::DTS. DTS::Application is, in most cases, the unique module will need to load, since from it you can fetch all other classes and methods.

For all examples, we will use a XML file with the details of connecting into the SQL Server and that's why we are using XML::Simple, that will read a XML file and return an hash reference with the keys the method new of DTS::Application expects.

Once connected to a SQL Server database, DTS::Application got its method regex_pkgs_names, expects a regular expression to match the DTS package name and returns a list in a form of an array reference. This one was easy!

What about implementing a simple script to backup the DTS packages in a zip file?

Note: this code is available at www.sqlservercentral.com

Here we load the DTS::Application class to connect to the server and retrieve DTS packages for us.

There is a list of DTS packages to save in the modify.xml XML file. The DTS::Application object will them loop over the package names list and try to fetch them as DTS::Package objects, which is returned by invoking the method get_db_package.

A DTS::Package object is capable of saving itself to a structured file with the save_to_file method, but there is a price when doing that: all design made in the DTS designer will be lost. That means that beautiful diagram you made, with comments and everything will be lost. Every time the Enterprise Manager opens a DTS package saved as a structured file, it will try to recreate the design automatically. The result is usually ugly (and sometimes very ugly) to see and understand what's going on. Looks like Microsoft engineers didn't want to implement design persistence, because this a problem with the DTS API itself, with no workaround documented.

To make a job with better quality, I decide to load the modules Archive::Zip and DateTime to create zip files with the date of the backup in the filename (thanks CPAN!).

In the next example, we will fetch a DTS package, retrieve one of it's dynamic property task and change a assignment of it, saving the package after that. Modifying properties of a DTS package is a detail that deserves some comments about because it's not all properties that can be modified and used latter.

Note: this code is available at www.sqlservercentral.com

DTS::Assignment::Destination is a few of the classes that has set methods that allow changes to a object. Most of the classes are "read only" in this aspect because the absence of set methods in the DTS distribution but it is still possible to execute the method get_sibling available in almost all of the classes and fetch the original object from the original DTS API and change the value there.

Of course, any change made in the inner objects of a package will change their state if the method save of the package object is not invoked.

A real case of use

During development of the DTS packages, me and the other guys of development team were caught in a situation that we need to do unit tests with the DTS packages before moving them to environments of QA and production. Whenever we try to move a package, we find out that we forgot to activate a property or set the correct value to it, and those problems were repetitive.

I implemented some automated unit tests to verify those know problems and caught them even before trying to move a DTS package to other environment. These let us know to concentrate in the real problems we had to solve instead of looking for tiny details.

After defining the tests conditions and writing them using the module Test::More, I created a web application using CGI::Application and a modified version of Test::Harness to be able to execute tests without forking a new process. This allows the application to execute tests concurrent in different DTS packages and generating a HTML result of the tests.

The application is a bit too longer to mentioned every details of implementation of it here, but if the reader take some time of checking all methods calls, it's a very instructive way to learn how to move from one object to another till getting the desired property.

These are the set of test executed with any DTS package passed as an argument:

- check if the package it is not logging in the database server;
- check if the logging to a flat file is enabled;
- check if write completion status to Event Log is disable;
- check if Global variable are explicit declared;
- check if the package has at least two connections;
- check if the package has at least one datapump;
- check if the connections are setup automatically by using a Dynamic Property task;
- check if the Execute Package tasks have the Package ID property empty;
- check several properties of flat file connections;
- check several properties of datapumps.

Since the web application is MVC based, it's possible to modify the tests executed without worrying about modifying the other components.

The complete web application is included in the article and I intend to include it also in the PerlDTS project website. Be sure to read the README file to get the details about installing the web application in Apache 2.x and IIS. The web application has POD included when you install the available Perl modules with it.

Performance

With all this connect-to-server-and-fetch operations, it's valid to mention that a good practice is avoid using more than one DTS::Application in your program. Run the script benchmark.pl in the examples directory in the PerlDTS tarball to get an idea of speed difference.

Documentation and project website

PerlDTS project includes documentation in form of POD (exported to HTML as well) and UML diagrams. This documentation is complementary to the one provided by Microsoft SQL Server, not a substitute. It's necessary to use both for better understanding.

The PerlDTS project website is located at ***http://code.google.com/p/perldts/***.

Implementation decisions and future of PerDTS

Quoting the CAVEATS of DTS.pm module:

"All objects under DTS distribution cannot be created without a reference to the original DTS object they mimic: at the current development state, object can only be recovered from a MS SQL Server database. Some classes may have methods to change their inner attributes, other classes don't. Check the POD for each class to be sure, but future releases should have write methods for all classes implemented".

This means that each object instantiated will have a attribute called _sibling that holds a reference to a Win32::OLE object that is the exactly counterpart of the original DTS class it mimics. The PerlDTS project was initially developed to work as a "reporting" tool, not as a new way to create DTS packages. Since only the properties values are necessary for reporting, usually it's a good idea to execute the method kill_sibling to remove the reference to the original object and release computer resources during the process.

That said, if you want to create DTS packages in memory and on the fly, PerlDTS is not the project you're looking for.

I would argue the need to do it anyway. Some tasks are done much easier in the DTS designer (like creating new connections) than using programming languages. On the other side, executing a package through Perl has lots of advantages, including for using better scheduling tools and better reports for errors during execution (check out DTS::Package::Step and DTS::Package::Step::Result classes). It is better to use what is good in DTS packages created in the DTS designer and leave the rest for your Perl scripting skills. Perl, for example, is much more powerful to execute any data transformation than DTS (just check out CPAN for ready to use code).

There are a lot of work still be done in PerlDTS project (especially classes that don't have a Perl counterpart implemented). Any comment, suggestion or patches are much welcome!

Loading Data with PowerShell

By Chad Miller

From PowerShell you will inevitably want to load command and script output into a database. Let's look at three methods to you can use to load data into SQL Server from PowerShell.

Getting Started

The examples in this article use the following PowerShell script to extract disk space information. Save the PowerShell code below to a file as Get-DiskUsage.ps1:

Note: this code is available at www.sqlservercentral.com

You'll need to create the following table in your database to store the output:

Note: this code is available at www.sqlservercentral.com

Note: This article uses *C:\Users\u00\bin* as the file path, *Z002* as the computer name, *Z002\SQLEXPRESS* as the SQL instance and *dbautility* as the database. You'll need to change each item to suite your environment. Also note in PowerShell. / denotes the current directory, the examples presented assume both script and output are saved to the current directory from which you are executing the commands.

Method 1: Export-CSV/BULK INSERT

PowerShell makes it very easy to create CSV files from any PowerShell command/script by using the built-in cmdlet Export-CSV. For example, the following code executes the Get-DiskUsage.ps1 script against the computer named *Z002*, exports the results to a CSV using Export-CSV and as a result of -noTypeInformation switch, omits the type information as part of the output :

```
./get-diskusage.ps1 Z002 | export-CSV -path  ./diskusage.csv -
noTypeInformat
```

Let's look at the of the diskusage.csv file . The output includes a header row with the property names and a row for each drive:

```
UsageDT,SystemName,DeviceID,VolumeName,SizeGB,FreeGB,PercentFre
e
2008-10-25,Z002,C:,LOCAL_120,111.79,24.95,22.32
```

The output of Export-CSV can almost be imported as-is into SQL Server using the T-SQL command BUIK INSERT with one minor edit. Since a header row is included you will need to remove the first line which has the property names but not the actual data. The first line is removed in order to use the T-SQL BULK INSERT command without specifying a format file to skip the first line. Removing the first line is easy to do with PowerShell. For example, the following command will read in the contents of the diskusag.csv file skipping the first line and write the output back to the diskusage.csv file:

```
(Get-Content ./diskusage.csv) | where {$_.readcount -gt 1} |
Set-Content ./diskusage.csv
```

The CSV file is ready to be imported into the SQL Server table created during setup. The following code uses the SQL Server command-line utility SQLCMD from PowerShell to execute the BULK INSERT command against the diskusage.csv file:

```
sqlcmd -S "Z002\SqlExpress" -E -Q "BULK INSERT
dbautility.dbo.DiskUsage FROM 'C:\Users\u00\bin\diskusage.csv'
  WITH (FIELDTERMINATOR = ',', ROWTERMINATOR = '\n')"
```

Pros: Export-CSV/BULK INSERT is the simplest method and uses natively available cmdlets and utilities. This method is the fastest method in terms of load speed when dealing with large data sets.

Cons: Requires file management when the solution may not require staging the data. Some editing of the CSV file produced by Export-CSV is required. Depending on the data you may need to perform additional edits including removing extra quote marks around strings and converting Boolean values from true/false to 0 or 1 representations. Some data may have commas in the output which can wreak havoc on any load routines.

Recommendation: Use this method if your load process will benefit from staging the data in CSV files, when you are dealing with large data sets and when you know the data does not contain extra commas.

Method 2: XML/XMLBulkLoad

An additional setup task is required for this method, you'll need to download and install SQLXML. SQLXML 3.0 or 4.0 will work. It is difficult to find SQLXML on the Microsoft site so here is a link[18] which will take you to the x86 SQLXML 4.0 SP1 install package download at the time of this writing. Note: SQLXML 4.0 is also available on the SQL 2005 installation CD, but is not installed by default.

The XML/SQLXMLBulkLoad method requires we convert the output to XML and generate an XSD schema file with SQLXML annotations[19]. Both of these tasks can be accomplished using a the New-XML and New-XSD PowerShell scripts. The PowerShell Team blog[20] posted a function called New-XML in this blog entry entitled Using PowerShell to Generate XML Documents[21]. Copy the function to a text file called XML.ps1, save and source the function from PowerShell as follows:

```
. ./XML.ps1
```

Note: When you source a function you are simply loading the definition of the function into your current PowerShell session, but not executing the function. The notation is dot space dot forward slash. The New-Xsd script is available in the Resources section below. Save the file as New.Xsd.ps1. Now you are ready to create XML and XSD files. The following creates an XML file of the disk space information called diskusge.xml:

```
./get-diskusage.ps1 Z002 | ./New-Xml -ItemTag DiskUsage -
Attribute
UsageDT,SystemName,DeviceID -ChildItems Volu
meName,SizeGB,FreeGB,PercentFree >
diskusage.xml
```

To create the XSD file you first need to assign our disk usage information to a the variable $du as shown below::

---

[18] http://www.microsoft.com/downloads/details.aspx?familyid=228de03f-3b5a-428a-923f-58a033d316e1&displaylang=en&tm

[19] http://msdn.microsoft.com/en-us/library/ms172649(SQL.90).aspx

[20] http://blogs.msdn.com/PowerShell/default.aspx

[21] http://blogs.msdn.com/PowerShell/archive/2007/05/29/using-PowerShell-to-generate-xml-documents.aspx

```
$du = ./get-diskusage.ps1 Z002
```

Next run the following command from PowerShell to create the XSD file diskusage.xsd:

```
./New-Xsd.ps1 -Object $du -ItemTag DiskUsage -Attribute
UsageDT,SystemName,DeviceID -ChildItems VolumeName,SizeGB,F
reeGB,PercentFree >
./diskusage.xsd
```

Examine the XSD file produced by New-Xsd. Some properties may not be mapped to the desired SQL data type. For example UsageDT should be a datetime rather than a varchar(255). You'll need to manually change the data type in the XSD file to datetime as follows:

```
  <xs:attribute name="UsageDT" sql:field="UsageDT"
sql:datatype="datetime"/>
```

Because the XSD file can be reused for importing data in the same format, the file only needs to be generated and manually edited once and finally to import the data into your SQL Server table. Run the following set of commands from PowerShell:

```
$sqlxml = new-object -comobject "SQLXMLBulkLoad.SQLXMLBulkLoad"
$sqlxml.ConnectionString =
"provider=sqloledb;server=Z002\SQLEXPRESS;database=dbautility;I
ntegrated Security=SSPI"
$sqlxml.SchemaGen = $true
$sqlxml.Bulkload = $true
$sqlxml.Execute("C:\Users\u00\bin\diskusage.xsd","C:\Users\u00\
bin\diskusage.xml")
```

One of the benefits unique to this method of importing data is the option to automatically create the table if the table does not already exist by setting the SchemaGen property to true.

Pros: The data is well-formed XML. No need to worry about editing data produced as long as the schema file is correct. Bulk loading of the XML file is very fast. The biggest benefit is the automatic creation of the table from the XSD schema definition.

Cons: Some manual editing of the XSD schema file may be required. Does not validate input for possible escaping of invalid XML. The slowest of the three methods in terms of generating the XML file. Like the CSV method requires storing the data in an intermediate XML file when the solution may not need to be staged to a file.

Recommendation: Use this method if the data is already in an XML format, or when your process will benefit from XML file storage or when you need to automatically create the tables.

Method 3: DataTable/SQLBulkCopy

ADO.NET and the various wrappers around ADO.NET including the SMO ExecuteWithResults method, SQLPSX[22] Get-SqlData and Microsoft SQL Server PowerShell cmdlet Invoke-Sqlcmd will return a DataTable. But what about the times when the output of a PowerShell command isn't a DataTable such as the DiskUsage.ps1 script? Well, not surprisingly it is fairly easy to take the output of any PowerShell command and convert to a DataTable. Marc van Orsouw (/\/\o\/\/) in his 'ThePowerShellGuy'[23] blog posted a function called Out-DataTable[24] which will convert the output of any PowerShell command to a DataTable. This method will use the function to convert the disk usage information into a data table. Copy the function to a text file called DataTable.ps1, save and source the function from PowerShell as follows:

```
. ./DataTable.ps1
```

Note: As stated in Method 2, when you source a function you are simply loading the definition of the function into your current PowerShell session, but not executing the function. The notation is dot space dot forward slash. Now you can use the Out-DataTable function with the DiskUsage.ps1 saving the output to a new variable called $dataTable:

```
$dataTable = ./DiskUsage.ps1 Z002 | Out-DataTable
```

---

[22] http://www.codeplex.com/SQLPSX
[23] http://thePowerShellguy.com/blogs/posh/default.aspx
[24] http://thePowerShellguy.com/blogs/posh/archive/2007/01/21/PowerShell-gui-scripblock-monitor-script.aspx

Since the output of the PowerShell command is saved as a DataTable you can use the .NET 2.0 class, SqlBulkCopy with a few simple lines of code to load the data into a SQL Server table:

```
$connectionString = "Data Source=Z002\SqlExpress;Integrated
Security=true;Initial
Catalog=dbautility;"
$bulkCopy = new-object ("Data.SqlClient.SqlBulkCopy")
$connectionString  $bulkCopy.DestinationTableName = "DiskUsage"
$bulkCopy.WriteToServer($dataTable)
```

Pros: No intermediate file storage is required since everything is done in memory. Fastest when the data is already in a DataTable format. Not as complex as the XML method. For this example of loading disk space information, this method is the best solution.

Cons: Some solutions may require an intermediate file storage. Slower than CSV method on very large data sets.

Recommendation: This method is ideal for dealing with smaller result sets or when the data is already in DataTable format

Conclusion

This article demonstrated three methods you can use to import data from PowerShell into SQL Server. These methods produce a CSV file, an XML/XSD file or DataTable from PowerShell which can be imported into SQL Server. Using these techniques you can load any PowerShell output into a SQL Server table.

Add Styles to Your Reporting Services Reports

By Adam Aspin

As a seasoned BI developer I am used to producing reports using many different tools, and have been a delighted user of Reporting Services for several years now. However, I must admit that I am not a design guru, and that I prefer spending my time on the queries and code rather than the presentation of the reports that I produce. So I inevitably find it both frustrating and pointlessly time-consuming when I am asked to reformat a report for the umpteenth time, as the new boss (or new analyst or helpful staff member) suggests a complete makeover of the reports that I have just worked half the night to produce to an already tight deadline.

Sound familiar? Many of the BI people that I know have stories echoing these sentiments, and it got me thinking why are there no stylesheets in Reporting Services? Or at least why is there no easy way of reapplying style elements to a report or better still to a set of reports - without hours of painstaking effort? After all, HTML developers have CSS stylesheets, and ASP.NET developers have themes and skins, so what about us poor report developers?

After some time reflecting on this question, I came up with a style-based approach that I hope will give other developers the tools to help them increase their productivity, while avoiding repetitive and laborious report refactoring. The techniques described in these three articles apply equally well to SQL Server 2005 as to SQL Server 2008.

Let's be clear about this. It is impossible to duplicate in Reporting Services the functionality of ASP.Net themes or even Cascading Style Sheets. So what we are looking at is a simple and efficient way of changing the colour of cells, text and lines, as well as changing the thickness and type of borders instantly and globally for one or more reports, using a tagged, or named style approach.

The first question is is it worth the effort to create an abstraction layer like this?

Yes is the resounding answer for the following reasons:

- Reformatting reports is extremely time-consuming.

- The BIDS report designer is extremely clunky, and will only let you reformat cells which are identical so you spend an unreasonable amount of time selecting individual cells to reformat.

- Remembering and recognising colour codes (especially if you are using Hexadecimal or numeric codes like #990099) can be difficult.

- Abstracting style definitions to a set of user-defined names is not only easier to apply, but forces the designer and creator to be more rational and organised in their approach.

Assuming, then, that the effort of defining styles is worth the investment, let's begin with basic definitions. Firstly. by "Styles" I mean a synonym for a specific report attribute like colour or line weight; by "Stylesheet" I mean an organised collection of styles and their definitions.

I will presume that the reader has basic knowledge of Reporting Services, and can create and format reports. Indeed, this article will not explain how to create reports, as the techniques described can be applied to any report.

Using Reporting Services Embedded Code

Let's start with the fastest way to apply styles to a Reporting Services report, using embedded code. For this example we will only set colour styles, in order to make the example simpler.

The objective is to map the following styles to the following colours

Style Name	Colour
Header	Blue
Footer	Green
BodyText	Black
Subtitle	Dark Blue

This is how you do it:

Defining Styles

1. Open an existing report, or create a new report

2. Access the embedded code of a report by clicking Report/Report Properties in the BIDS menu (you need to have selected either the Data or Layout tabs for this menu option to be available). You can then select the Code tab from the Report Properties dialog and paste or enter the following code.

```
Function StyleColor(ByVal Style As String) As String
        Select Case UCase(Style)
            Case "HEADER"
                Return "LightBlue"
            Case "FOOTER"
                Return "SkyBlue"
            Case "MAINTITLE"
                Return "Purple"
            Case "SUBTITLE"
                Return "DarkBlue"
            Case Else
                Return "White"
        End Select
    End Function
```

You should have the following:

3. Click OK to close the dialog.

As you can see, the code snippet consists of a single function, which rakes an input parameter (imaginatively named "Style") and returns the selected colour.

The code itself is extremely simple, but what you have to grasp firmly is the concept here we are giving pseudonyms to colours, and consequently the naming convention that you use is important. After all the idea is to make life easier, not more complicated! The function that you create will use the style (the "pseudonym" used as an input parameter) to select and apply the correct colour.

Applying Styles

So how do you apply the styles? Simply replace the hard-coded reference to a colour (let's say to the title in our sample report) with the function you created in the Custom Code not forgetting to pass in the input parameter. This means:

1. Click to select the object whose colour you wish to modify.

2. Open or select the properties window (press F4 if necessary) and replace the current colour with the following:
   =code.StyleColor("Header")

The result should be something like this:

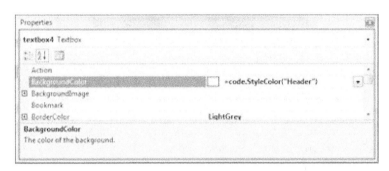

That is all. Simple, isn't it? All you need to do is prefix the function that you created with "code" (which tells Reporting Services to use the embedded code in the report), and pass in an appropriate style name. Note that the variable name is rendered case-insensitive through the UCase function if you do not use this function, you will need to make all style names case-sensitive.

You will then need to apply these steps to all elements to which you wish to apply a colour. This can be fonts, cell backgrounds or borders. It is worth noting that the code used to reference a colour can also be embedded in code so you can use it inside IIF or SWITCH structures also.

When you next preview or run the report, the object's colour will switch to the colour defined by the style.

"OK" you may be saying but isn't this harder work than just applying a hard-coded colour? Well, yes it is until you need to change all the colours in a report. Then all you need to do is change the colour reference of a style in your custom code and the entire report will be altered when you next run it. You can try this by opening the at the Custom Code tab, and (for instance) altering the colour defined by the style you used. If you now preview the report, you will see the colour change wherever it has been applied.

Of course, once you have a tried and tested style sheet in custom code, the code can be copied to all the reports you wish to standardize. This will ensure that the same colour scheme is applied to all the reports you format in this way.

So what are the drawbacks to this approach?

- Firstly, the main drawback is the limits of custom code creation and editing in BIDS. The custom code tab is a text box, there are no debugging tools, and it is not easy to read! You may find it easier to create the code in Visual Studio, or even in a text editor, and then copy and paste the code into BIDS.

- Secondly, the custom code is limited to the report which contains it so any changes to the code have to be carried over to all reports using this code as a stylesheet. Admittedly this extremely "self-contained" aspect of custom code can also be perceived as an advantage there is nothing special that you have to do to deploy reports for this technique to work.

- Thirdly, the difficulty of successfully creating multiple styles without bugs limits the number of styles that can be managed using this technique.

- Fourthly it is not possible to define a style which encompasses all the attributes of an object. For instance a font has a font family, colour, size and weight (and this list is not exhaustive). You will have to define a style for each individual element, unfortunately, as this is a limitation of BIDS. However, as there is no limit to the number of functions that you can add to the code tab in the Report properties dialog, there is nothing to stop you having different functions for each type of property that you wish to set dynamically.

Tips

One tip that you might find useful if, when updating an existing report to use styles, you want to replace all the occurrences of a colour in an existing report with the expression which uses the custom code, you can:

1. Close the report in BIDS if it is already open.

2. Right-click on the report in the Solution Explorer, and select "View Code"

3. Click Edit/Find and Replace/Quick Replace.

4. In the Search and Replace dialog enter "your colour" (the colour reference you wish to replace) in the Find field, and=code.StyleColor("Header")in the replace field (don't forget the equals sign).

5. Click Replace All.

6. Close the dialog.

7. Save the file

8. Reopen normally, in BIDS.

This saves an immense amount of selecting and pasting.

Another tip is always to use the Case Else in a Select Case possibly adding a peculiar colour completely outside your chosen colour palette for testing, as this will allow you to isolate elements to which you have erroneously attempted to apply stylesheet formatting more easily. By this I mean that if the colour that is used when an erroneous style parameter is passed into the code is violent purple, then you will see any styling errors far faster when building a report, than if you leave this as white! Of course, remember to reset this "default" colour to something innocuous before deploying reports to production.

Conclusion

So now you know how to gain time and also standardise report presentation when developing Reporting Services reports using custom code stylesheets. The next article will explain how to extend the stylesheet paradigm to centralised style definitions using Custom Assemblies and interactive style definitions stored in SQL Server tables.

Configuring Kerberos Authentication

By Brian Kelley

In my experience, configuring a SQL Server for Kerberos authentication, especially a SQL Server named instance, can be one of the most confusing things to do for a DBA or system administrator the first time around. The reason it can be so confusing is there are several "moving parts" that must all be in sync for Kerberos authentication to work. And what can make things all the more confusing is that in general, if we don't touch a thing, people and applications can connect to our database servers but as soon as we start down the road of configuring Kerberos authentication, they suddenly can't. And it can be rather frustrating to figure out why. In this article we'll look at both the hows and the whys.

If I Don't Do Anything, Why Does it Usually Work?

When it comes to authenticating a login (checking to see if you are who you say you are), SQL Server only does authentication when the login is a SQL Server based one. I've chosen my words carefully here, because it is important to understand that when it's a Windows-based login, SQL Server passes off the authentication to an operating system component, the Windows Security Support Provider Interface (SSPI). That's why when you have Kerberos authentication errors, you usually get some message about SSPI context. Basically, SQL Server realizes it's a Windows login, gets the information it'll need to pass on so SSPI can do it's checks, and then it waits to see what SSPI says. If SSPI says the login is good, SQL Server allows the login to complete the connection. If SSPI says the login is bad, SQL Server rejects the login and returns whatever error information SSPI provides. Now, there is one exception to SQL Server farming out Windows authentication to SSPI, but that occurs in Named Pipes and so we won't get into it because hopefully you're not using Named Pipes as your protocol.

Once we understand that SQL Server is handing off responsibility for authentication to SSPI, it's time to understand what SSPI is going to do. SSPI is going to first try and authenticate using Kerberos. This is the preferred protocol for Windows 2000 and above. In order to do this, there needs to be a Service Principal Name (SPN) in place. We'll talk more about that later. If there's no SPN, Kerberos can't happen. If Kerberos can't happen whether due to no SPN or another reason (across forests with no forest level trust), SSPI will drop back to the old security protocol, NT LAN Manager, or NTLM. So if we don't do anything, authentication will drop back to NTLM and everything tends to work. That is, until we have to do multiple "hops," like through SQL Server Reporting Services set up on a separate server or when we want to do Windows authentication across a linked server connection (see Figure 1).

Figure 1:

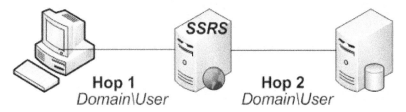

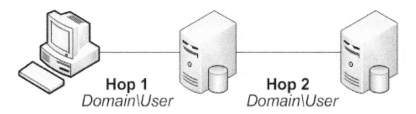

In Figure 1, the same set of credentials (Domain\User) is being passed from the client to a server and then from that server to a second server. Each time the credentials are passed, we call that a hop. Since we're not changing the credentials (for instance, we're not going to a second Windows account, such as a service account, or a SQL Server login, we say that there have been two hops, or what we call that a double hop situation. NTLM doesn't permit double hop situations (or triple or quadruple &); It is prevented by design. So in either of these particular scenarios, if we don't have Kerberos authentication set up, we can't make the second hop. We'll see errors logging in attributed to login (null) or NT AUTHORITY\ANONYMOUS LOGON. By default, Kerberos authentication only permits a single hop, but using a feature called Kerberos delegation, multiple hops can be configured and these double hop scenarios can be allowed. While Kerberos delegation is beyond the scope of this article, it is important to note that Kerberos delegation cannot happen without Kerberos authentication, and that's how DBAs usually get pulled into the fray.

What's So Bad About NTLM?

In general, NTLM (or at least, the revised versions) do a good job of authenticating the user and basically being secure. However, NTLM suffers from the following drawbacks:

- It is susceptible to "replay" attacks.

- It assumes the server is trustworthy.

- It requires more authentication traffic than Kerberos.

- It doesn't provide for a means of going past that first hop.

Let's look at each one of these to understand why they are drawbacks, starting with a replay attack. A replay attack is when an attacker is able to capture network traffic and re-use it. For instance, imagine I'm logging on to your SQL Server. An attacker has a packet sniffer and is able to capture that logon sequence. If, at a later point, that attacker could put that traffic back on the network and it work, that would be a replay attack. The classic example given is an attacker captures a bank transaction for some amount of money. Let's say you pay Mr. Attacker US$500 for services rendered. If the attacker can capture the network traffic and replay it multiple times, the bank will deduct US$500 from your account each time and deposit it into his. To the bank, the repeated transactions looked legitimate (although admittedly, with everyone worried about fraud nowadays, we would hope this kind of thing gets flagged and checked out). If this is the case, then the protocol for that transaction we're using is to blame because it provided us no protection from such an attack. Such is the case with NTLM. It provides no protection. Kerberos, on the other hand, includes a time stamp of when the network traffic was sent. If you're outside the window of the acceptable time range (by default this is 5 minutes), Kerberos rejects that network traffic. So in the case above, imagine if the bank put a timestamp on the transaction and had an acceptable time range within 10 seconds. If Mr. Attacker tried to replay the transaction after that 10 second window was up, the bank would know something was going on.

The second drawback with NTLM is that the server isn't verified. The client connects to MySQLServer. Or at least, it thinks it is connecting to MySQLServer. The NTLM protocol may have the ability to validate that Domain\User is connecting, but it doesn't allow Domain\User to verify that he or she is really talking to MySQLServer. This is where the Service Principal Name (SPN) comes into play. When the client attempts to connect via Kerberos, the SPN for the service being connected to is checked. In a Windows

2000 or higher domain, the SPN is stored within Active Directory, and the Active Directory domain controller is trusted by the client. Therefore, if the service, such as a SQL Server service, checks out based on the SPN the client finds for that service within Active Directory, it knows that it can trust the server is truly MySQLServer.

The third drawback is the amount of authentication traffic used by NTLM versus Kerberos. In NTLM, every time authentication happens, a check has to be made back to a domain controller (DC). With Kerberos, tickets are issued to both the client and the server containing the information each needs to validate the other. Therefore, the client and the server only have to check in with a domain controller once during the lifespan of those tickets (default is 600 minutes or 10 hours) to get the tickets in the first place. After that, they both have the information they need without checking back with a DC.

The final drawback is one we've already discussed, and that is situations where we want to make multiple hopes. Quite frankly, NTLM leaves us with no options. We have to make each hop different from the previous one, whether we like it or not. Kerberos delegation ensures we can pass the credentials through all the hops until we reach the final destination.

What Is an SPN, Why Do I Need to Configure It, and How Do I Do So?

A Service Principal Name (SPN) provides the information to the client about the service. Basically, each SPN consists of 3 or 4 pieces of information:

- The type of service (for SQL Server it is called MSSQLSvc)
- The name of the server
- The port (if this needs to be specified)
- The service account running the service.

All of these need to match up for the client to be able to validate the service. If any of these are wrong, Kerberos authentication won't happen. In some cases, we'll get that SSPI context error and in fact, SSPI won't even drop back to using NTLM, meaning we don't connect at all. Therefore, the key is to get everything correct when we set the SPN.

In order to set an SPN, you must either be a Domain Admin level user or you must be the computer System account (or an account that talks on the network as the System account, such as the Network Service account). Typically, we advise that SQL Server should be run as a local or domain user, so that rules out the second case. We also advise that SQL Server shouldn't be a domain admin level account, and that rules out the first case. What this means is a domain admin level account will need to set the SPN manually. Thankfully, Microsoft provides a nice utility called SETSPN in the Support Tools on the OS CD/DVD to do so. It can also be downloaded from the Microsoft site.

Using SETSPN

SETSPN has three flags we're interested in:

- -L : This lists the SPNs for a particular account
- -A : This adds a new SPN
- -D : This deletes an existing SPN

The key to understanding SPNs is to realize they are tied to an account, whether that be a user or computer account. If we want to see what SPNs are listed for a particular account, here is the syntax:

SETSPN -L <Account>

For instance, if I have a server called MyWebServer, I can list the SPNs assigned to that computer account by:

SETSPN -L MyWebServer

If, instead, I am running my SQL Server under the MyDomain\MyServiceAccount user account, I can check the SPNs listed for that account by:

SETSPN -L MyDomain\MyServiceAccount

To add an SPN, it's important that we know the service account SQL Server is running under. Also, it is important to know the TCP port SQL Server is listening on. If it's a default instance, the port by default is 1433, although this can be changed. If it's a named instance, unless we have gone in and manually set a static port, SQL Server could change the port at any time. Therefore, it's important to set a port statically. I've described how to do so in the a blog post[25]. Once we have those bits of information, we can add an SPN via the following syntax:

SETSPN -A MSSQLSvc/<SQL Server Name>:<port> <account>

If we're dealing with a default instance listening on port 1433, we can leave off the :<port> (but it is still a good idea to have an entry both with and without the port). One other thing to remember is it is important to specify SPNs for both the NetBIOS name (e.g. MySQLServer) as well as the fully qualified domain name (e.g. MySQLServer.mydomain.com). So applying this to a default instance on MyDBServer.mydomain.com running under the service account MyDomain\SQLServerService, we'd execute the following commands:

SETSPN -A MSSQLSvc/MyDBServer MyDomain\SQLServerService
SETSPN -A MSSQLSvc/MyDBServer:1433
MyDomain\SQLServerService
SETSPN -A MSSQLSvc/MyDBServer.mydomain.com
MyDomain\SQLServerService
SETSPN -A MSSQLSvc/MyDBServer.mydomain.com:1433
MyDomain\SQLServerService

For a named instance, we typically only require two commands, because there isn't a case where a client is just connecting to the name of the server. For instance, let's assume we have a named instance called Instance2 listening on port 4444 on that same server using that same service account. In that case we'd execute the following commands:

SETSPN -A MSSQLSvc/MyDBServer:4444
MyDomain\SQLServerService
SETSPN -A MSSQLSvc/MyDBServer.mydomain.com:4444
MyDomain\SQLServerService

And in those rare cases where we need to delete an SPN (for instance, we change the service account or switch ports), we can use the -D switch. It's syntax is parallel to the -A switch:

SETSPN -D MSSQLSvc/<SQL Server Name>:<port> <account>

---

[25] http://www.sqlservercentral.com/blogs/brian_kelley/archive/2008/05/17/setting-static-ports-when-dealing-with-named-instances-and-kerberos.aspx

I've Done All of That. How Can I Verify Logins Are Connecting Via Kerberos?

Within SQL Server there is a very simple query we can execute to determine what type of authentication was performed on each connection. Here's the query:

```
SELECT
    s.session_id
  , c.connect_time
  , s.login_time
  , s.login_name
  , c.protocol_type
  , c.auth_scheme
  , s.HOST_NAME
  , s.program_name
FROM sys.dm_exec_sessions s
  JOIN sys.dm_exec_connections c
    ON s.session_id = c.session_id
```

The query returns a lot of information to help you identify the connections. The connect_time and login_time should be pretty close together and it gives you a window of when the initial connection was made. The login_name, along with host_name and program_name, help you identify the exact login. From there the protocol_type helps you narrow down the connection if you have different endpoints for your SQL Server other than just TSQL (for instance, mirroring or HTTP). And finally, the auth_scheme will reveal, for a Windows account, what security protocol was used. If Kerberos authentication was successful, you should see the auth_scheme reflect Kerberos instead of NTLM.

Use Operations Manager to Monitor Your SQL Agent Jobs

By Thomas LaRock

I have long been an advocate of Operations Manager, having used MOM 2005 and now Operations Manager 2007. With both versions I have been content with the out-of-the-box functionality, and Operations Manager has plenty to be excited about. Some of the functionality is there but not enabled by default, so you have to hunt it down. One item of interest to most would be the ability to effectively monitor SQL Agent jobs.

I am not talking about simply getting an email notification when a job fails. No, I am talking about more in depth information such as job duration and last run status. Both of those items are included in the SQL Management Packs (both 2000 and 2005).

In the custom Database State view I created in a previous article, I had columns for the SQL Agent. If I clicked on one of them, the details view would be displayed as in Figure 1. I would see the Agent in a healthy state, and four open circles under the Availability, Configuration, Performance, and Security columns. I started to wonder about why the circles are empty, and then I noticed the words Not Monitored. So, I set about trying to find out how to get those items to be monitored.

Figure 1

The first step is to configure the object discovery for SQL Agent jobs. This can be done by going to the authoring tab and clicking on the Object Discoveries item as shown in Figure 2.

Figure 2

Your scope will need to include the SQL 2000 Agent Job and/or the SQL 2005 Agent Job targets. You should now see the following in Figure 3.

Name	Target	Management Pack	Enabled by default
■ Discovered Type: SQL 2000 Agent Job (1)			
Discover SQL 2000 Agent Jobs	SQL 2000 Agent	SQL Server 2000 (Discovery)	No
⊟ Discovered Type: SQL 2005 Agent Job (1)			
Discover SQL 2005 Agent Jobs	SQL 2005 Agent	SQL Server 2005 (Discovery)	No

Figure 3

These discoveries are disabled by default and you will need to manually override the discoveries. In our case, we did an override for our custom group of database servers. But what does this discovery do for us? Well, it gathers info about every job within SQL Agent by using the monitors already defined. You can see the monitors by clicking on the Monitors item on the Authoring tab, right above the Object Discoveries item as shown in Figure 2.

After selecting the Monitors item you should see Figure 4, where I have expanded the monitor for the SQL 2005 Agent Job target which is identical to the SQL 2000 Agent Job target. You will notice that there are only two monitors in total, one named Last Run Status as part of the Availability rollup and another named Job Duration as part of the Performance rollup.

Target	Type	Inherited from	Management Pack
⊞ SQL 2000 Agent Job			
⊟ SQL 2005 Agent Job			
⊟ Entity Health	Aggregate Rollup	Entity	Health Library
⊟ Availability	Aggregate Rollup	Entity	Health Library
◯ Last Run Status	SQL 2005 Agent Job...	(Not inherited)	SQL Server 2005 (Monitoring)
⊟ Configuration	Aggregate Rollup	Entity	Health Library
⊟ Performance	Aggregate Rollup	Entity	Health Library
◯ Job Duration	SQL 2005 Agent Lon...	(Not inherited)	SQL Server 2005 (Monitoring)
⊟ Security	Aggregate Rollup	Entity	Health Library

Figure 4

If you were to go back to your database state view and examine the details view for one of the SQL Agents you should see the following (Figure 5).

State	Instance	Availability	Configuration	Performance	Security	SQL 2005 Agent Job
✔ Healthy	SQLSERVERAGENT	✔ Healthy	⬤ Not monitored	✔ Healthy	⬤ Not monitored	✔ Healthy

Figure 5

So, we have gone from four unmonitored items to only two, as Security and Configuration do not have any monitors associated with them by default. Now, after all that work, what is the end result?

If you were to double click on the line item shown in the detail view in Figure 5, you would open up the Health monitor for the SQL Server Agent (Figure 6). You can then expand the Availability and/or the Performance monitors and quickly see all of the jobs in SQL Agent for that instance. So, if a job had failed, or if a job had run too long, then you would be able to quickly see which job had the issue.

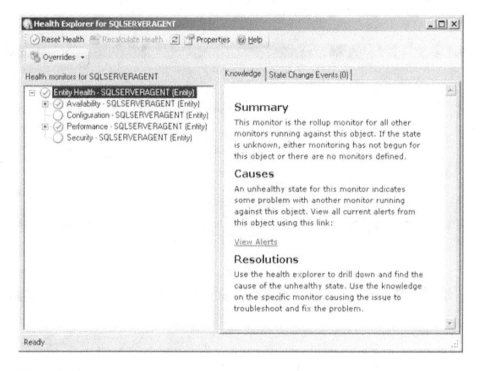

Figure 6

As good as this information may be I should point out the default settings for job duration is 60 seconds for a warning threshold and 120 seconds for an error. I am not certain about how your shop operates, but our shop uses SQL Agent jobs to do database dumps, and quite often those dumps take longer than two minutes. So, when I started enabling this functionality a while back I was alarmed to see a lot of jobs being flagged as critical. As a result, I set an override for the job duration monitor to have thresholds of 3600 and 5400 seconds as the lower and upper bounds for all jobs.

After some investigation I found that the override will not work for the SQL 2000 Agent Job Duration monitor, as that monitor does a compare to the duration taken from the msdb database, which is in the format of HHMMSS. This means that if your job runs for one hour, forty seven minutes and sixteen seconds, the msdb stores that as 14716. This number is converted to a proper format when you examine the job history through SSMS, but Operations Manager does a compare to the 14716 as if that was the duration in seconds. So, if you set an override to 7200 seconds (two hours) as an error threshold, you would be as surprised as I was that a job would be flagged as critical. But, 7200 is less than 14716, right? No, not exactly, so you will need to override your SQL 2000 Agent Jobs differently than your SQL 2005 Agent Jobs. For me, I used 10000 as the lower threshold and 13000 as the upper threshold of my SQL 2000 Agent Jobs, and eliminated a lot of false alarms.

Operations Manager has the ability to monitor additional details with regards to your SQL Agent jobs, you just need to take a few extra steps in order to start collecting some valuable information. And while it may not be perfect, it is still better overall than most in-house solutions. I find the console easy to use and by shifting our team to rely on the use of Operations Manager we are freeing up valuable time to spend on other projects.

Oracle for the SQL Server Guy - Instances and Databases

By Jagan Kumar

Introduction

It is quite common nowadays to see DBAs supporting databases from different vendors. Although much is common between database products, there are also many differences that can be a challenge for a DBA or a database developer who is new to a particular database product.

The purpose of this article series is to present Oracle 10g features from a SQL Server 2005 stand point.

In this article, I introduce you to the concept of Instance and Database which is a key term in understanding RDBMS architecture. Like anything you build, be it a nest of Taj Mahal, the foundation is the key.

Instance and Database

In Oracle, processes (background processes) and memory allocated make up an instance.

Database refers to the physical files(.dbf and .log etc). Having a database is not necessary to run an instance. If the instance is not part of parallel server configuration (Real Application Clusters) the relationship between an instance and a database is always 1:1. The main properties of an Oracle instance are specified using the initialization parameter file (pfile or spfile). When the instance is started, the parameter file is read and the instance is configured accordingly.

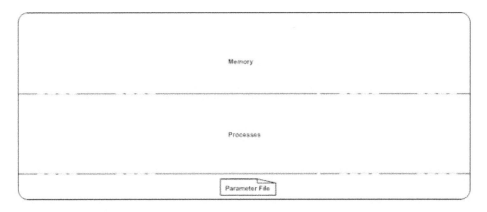

Oracle Instance without database

Having a database is not necessary to run an Oracle instance.

In SQL Server, an instance refers to processes, memory allocated and physical files associated with default system databases used by that particular installation. By default SQL server installation comes with a set of system databases (with its own hierarchy of objects and settings).

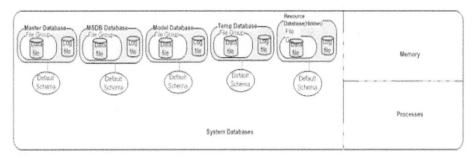

SQL Server Instance without user databases

In SQL Server, the settings for the instance are stored in the registry, master/resource database and msdb database.

To an Oracle DBA, creating a database means creating an entire database system that contains control files, redo logs and, data dictionary and tablespaces. In the coming section, we will discuss what these objects are and how they are mapped to the SQL Server equivalents.

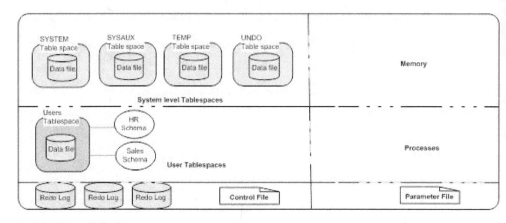

Oracle Instance with database

In SQL Server, these tasks are accomplished as part of the installation process. Hence creating a database in SQL Server implies adding a user database to the already existing system databases.

One SQL Server instance can hold more than one user defined database and the instance and database ratio is 1..32767.

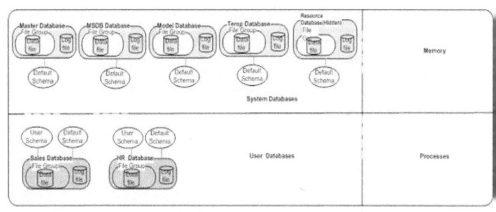

SQL Server Instance with user databases

Oracle storage architecture encompasses:

1. Data File: Similar to SQL Server, data file is an operating system file to store objects and data. One or more data files are logically grouped together to make a tablespace. One data file is associated with only one

tablespace. Unlike SQL Server, there are no Primary/Secondary data file types in Oracle.

2. Redo Log: The Redo Log is similar to Log File in SQL Server. Oracle writes all final changes made to data first to the redo log files before applying the changes to data files. The set of redo log files that are currently being used to record the changes to the database are called online redo log files. These logs can be archived or copied to a different location before being reused and the saved logs are called archived redo logs. Archive Log Mode setting similar to Recovery Model setting in SQL Server decides whether the Redo Logs need to be archived or overwritten for reuse.

3. Tablespace: A Tablespace is a set of one or more data files. The SQL Server equivalent of the tablespace is the filegroup. While filegroups are similar in function, their organization differs from that of tablespaces. Oracle tablespaces are at the instance level. SQL Server filegroups come under and are associated with the individual databases. There are three types of tablespaces:

      a)Permanent tablespaces
      b)Undo tablespaces
      c)Temporary tablespaces

In SQL Server, file groups are of two types, primary and secondary. System wide tablespaces in Oracle include,

      System Tablespace (Permanent): The System tablespace stores the data dictionary for the instance/database, which is some what equivalent to the master/resource database in SQL Server.

      Sysaux Tablespace (Permanent): The Sysaux tablespace stores all auxiliary database meta data related to options and features such as RMAN, Job Scheduling, AWR repository, etc. Sysaux tablespace can be roughly equated to the msdb database in SQL Server.

      Temp Tablespace (Temporary): The Temp tablespace contain data that persists only for the duration of a user's session. Oracle uses Temp tablespace as a sort work area and for join operations involving internal work tables. Similar to Tempdb database in SQL Server.

Undo Tablespace (Undo): An Oracle database has a method of managing information that is used to roll back, or undo, changes to the database. The information consists of records of the actions of transactions, primarily before they are committed. Undo records provide read consistency (avoiding reader-writer blocking scenarios) by maintaining the before image of the data for users who are accessing the data at the same time another user is changing it.

There are major differences in the way Undo is managed in SQL Server. UNDO management is implemented in SQL Server as part of the transaction logs of each database which handle both redo and undo related functions.

4. Control File - The Control file is a file that Oracle maintains to manage the state of the database. Every database has at least one control file or multiple identical copies. The control file contains the names and locations of the data files, redo log files, backup set details and SCN. In SQL Server, the master/resource database has some of the information that is stored in the control file of an Oracle database.

Oracle Schema

The objects that a user owns are collectively called schema. A schema is bound to exactly one user. A SQL Server database has the features of an Oracle scheme because objects are created inside the database.

In Oracle, the schema and tablespace have independent identities objects of a schema can be created in different tablespaces, and a single tablespace can contain objects from multiple schemas. In this context, SQL Server databases are similar to Oracle tablespaces an owner can create objects in different databases, and a database can contain objects from different schemas.

Summary

Oracle's functional equivalents in SQLServer

Oracle	SQL Server
System tablespace	Master/Resource database
Sysaux tablespace	MSDB database
Database template files(Data warehouse, General purpose, Transaction processing)	Model database
Undo tablespace	Tempdb Database/Transaction Log
Temp tablespace	Tempdb
Redo Log	Transaction Log
Schema/User	Schema, Not a User

Default trace - A Beginner's Guide

By Adam Haines

We have all been subject to or know someone who has been in a situation where an object has been altered/created/deleted, without our knowledge, and the application comes to a screeching halt. After fixing the problem, your boss asks you some questions, like what happened, why did it happen, and who did it. SQL Server 2005 introduced a new type of trigger called a DDL trigger that can provide all the answers we need; however, you did not get a chance to implement this functionality. So... what do you do?

Some would tell their boss "I do not know, but I can find out" and then search franticly for 3rd party tools to read the transaction log, hoping for instantaneous salvation. What these few do not know is an answer is silently running in the background. SQL Server 2005 has built in functionality that gives administrators the answers to all these questions.

The answers lie in a new background trace called the default trace. The default trace is exactly what the name specifies, a trace. Default trace is always running in the background of your instance capturing events that administrators can use to troubleshoot problems. The default trace is enabled by default and does not burden the system because it is fairly lightweight. Chances are you had not even noticed this trace running on your instance. To those concerned about overhead, yes there is overhead, but in my mind the benefits far outweigh the minimal overhead. The default trace is not intended to replace DDL trigger functionality and should be used as a means to monitor an SQL Instance, or quickly obtain detailed information about problematic events.

The default trace does not capture all trace events, but captures enough information to become a powerful tool in your toolkit. The default trace captures key information including auditing events, database events, error events, full text events, object creation, object deletion and object alteration. From my experiences and observations on forums, I will be focusing on object level events. It seems that a greater number of people want the "who done it" answer for object DDL events.

The first piece of code is to check the default trace to see if it is enabled.

```
SELECT * FROM sys.configurations WHERE configuration_id = 1568
```

If this feature is not available, you will have to configure the advanced option "default trace enabled". Below is the code to enable the trace. Note: you will need the ALTER SETTNGS permission or be in the sysadmin or serveradmin fixed server role to reconfigure.

```
sp_configure 'show advanced options', 1;
GO
RECONFIGURE;
GO
sp_configure 'default trace enabled', 1;
GO
RECONFIGURE;
GO
```

The next piece of information we need is the default trace file path, and the function below will return the current trace file. You can grab the initial trace file (log.trc) and rollup every trace file into a single table, but there is a higher overhead associated to bringing more data in. You should use the trace file that best represents the information you are looking for.

Note: the path is defaulted to the \MSSQL\LOG directory, but we can use the function below to get the path

```
--get the current trace rollover file
SELECT * FROM ::fn_trace_getinfo(0)
```

Now that we have all the information we need we can get into the trace data. Let's start by creating a new database call TraceDB.

```
USE [master]
GO
CREATE DATABASE TraceDB
```

Now open the trace file, as shown below. As you can see, we were able to gather some pretty significant information about who created the database and when the database was created. I have used category id of 5 and a trace_event_id of 46 to filter the data correctly. Event ID 46 represents Object:Created and category 5 is objects. I will provide queries that list all events and categories at the end of this article.

** Make sure to use your trace file path below. Yours may be different than mine.

```
SELECT
    loginname,
    loginsid,
    spid,
    hostname,
    applicationname,
    servername,
    databasename,
    objectName,
    e.category_id,
    cat.name as [CategoryName],
    textdata,
    starttime,
    eventclass,
    eventsubclass,--0=begin,1=commit
    e.name as EventName
FROM ::fn_trace_gettable('C:\Program Files\Microsoft SQL
Server\MSSQL.1\MSSQL\LOG\log.trc',0)
    INNER JOIN sys.trace_events e
        ON eventclass = trace_event_id
    INNER JOIN sys.trace_categories AS cat
        ON e.category_id = cat.category_id
WHERE databasename = 'TraceDB' AND
    objectname IS NULL AND --filter by objectname
    e.category_id = 5 AND --category 5 is objects
    e.trace_event_id = 46
    --trace_event_id: 46=Create Obj,47=Drop Obj,164=Alter Obj
```

- You will see more than one entry per object create because these objects have two event sub classes -begin and commit. Each subclass will have an entry.

- You can remove the databasename filter to get object creation events for all databases.

Results (Trimmed for Simplicity):

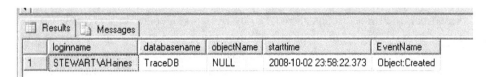

	loginname	databasename	objectName	starttime	EventName
1	STEWART\AHaines	TraceDB	NULL	2008-10-02 23:58:22.373	Object:Created

Now, we have seen what default trace is capable of. Let's create another object and repeat the query. This time around we are going to create a table called "MyTable". Use the following code to create the table.

```
USE [TraceDB]
GO  CREATE TABLE [dbo].[MyTable](
 [id] [int] IDENTITY(1,1) NOT NULL,
 [sometext] [char](3) NULL
) ON [PRIMARY]
```

Now query the default trace using the same query as above. Note you can use the ObjectName column to filter for the specific object you are looking for; otherwise all created database objects are returned.

```
WHERE databasename = 'TraceDB' AND
    objectname = 'MyTable' AND --filter by objectname
    e.category_id = 5 AND --category 5 is objects
    e.trace_event_id = 46
    --trace_event_id: 46=Create Obj,47=Drop Obj,164=Alter Obj
```

Results (Trimmed for Simplicity):

	loginname	databasename	objectName	starttime	EventName
1	STEWART\AHaines	TraceDB	MyTable	2008-10-03 00:26:05.717	Object:Created

Let's take the demo a step further by altering MyTable. Issue an alter table statement and add a new column to MyTable, as shown below.

```
USE [TraceDB]
GO
ALTER TABLE MyTable
ADD col INT
```

We can now search trace information on the alter event for MyTable. We can use the same query as before but need to make a small modification. You must change the trace_event_id to 164 because event 164 represents the object:Altered event.

```
WHERE databasename = 'TraceDB' AND
    objectname = 'MyTable' AND --filter by objectname
    e.category_id = 5 AND --category 5 is objects
    e.trace_event_id = 164
    --trace_event_id: 46=Create Obj,47=Drop Obj,164=Alter Obj
```

Results (Trimmed for Simplicity):

	loginname	databasename	objectName	starttime	EventName
1	STEWART\AHaines	TraceDB	MyTable	2008-10-03 00:33:06.623	Object:Altered

Now lets drop MyTable and view the trace details. You must change the trace_event_id to 47 because event 47 represents the object:Deleted event, as shown below.

```
USE [TraceDB]   GO     DROP TABLE MyTable
```

We can view trace data by changing the trace_event_id to 47.

```
WHERE databasename = 'TraceDB' AND
      objectname = 'MyTable' AND --filter by objectname
      e.category_id = 5 AND --category 5 is objects
      e.trace_event_id = 47
      --trace_event_id: 46=Create Obj,47=Drop Obj,164=Alter Obj
```

Results (Trimmed for Simplicity):

	loginname	databasename	objectName	starttime	EventName
1	STEWART\ahaines	TraceDB	MyTable	2008-10-03 08:27:02.270	Object:Deleted

As you can see, default trace gives an administrator the ability to find the history of any DDL transaction. I want to point out that default trace is not limited to object DDL history. Among other things, default trace captures log growth events, which can be invaluable to troubleshooting disk capacity problems.

For example, say your log file spontaneous grows enormous. It is important to understand why the log grew spontaneously. No one would argue that one of the first place to look may be SQL Jobs. There are many commands within a job that can potentially cause the log to grow enormous, like reindexing, bulk inserts, bulk deletes etc. By using the trace data you can more easily identify the problem because you can pin-point the exact time the log file began to grow. This greatly reduces the number of possible suspects, which reduces the amount of time required to find the culprit.

The query below will pull all trace data using the log auto growth event. Note: You will not have any log growth for TraceDb because we have not done in large inserts to make the log grow. You should apply this query to another database where you want to monitor log growth.

```
SELECT
      loginname,
      loginsid,
      spid,
      hostname,
      applicationname,
      servername,
      databasename,
      objectName,
      e.category_id,
      cat.name,
      textdata,
      starttime,
      endtime,
      duration,
      eventclass,
      eventsubclass,
      e.name as EventName
FROM ::fn_trace_gettable('C:\Program Files\Microsoft SQL
Server\MSSQL.1\MSSQL\LOG\log.trc',0)
      INNER JOIN sys.trace_events e
            ON eventclass = trace_event_id
      INNER JOIN sys.trace_categories AS cat
            ON e.category_id = cat.category_id
WHERE databasename = 'TraceDB' AND
      e.category_id = 2 AND --category 2 is database
      e.trace_event_id = 93 --93=Log File Auto Grow
```

Summary:

The default trace is a valuable tool for the modern DBA's tool belt. It offers a wealth of information, while minimally impacting the system. The default trace is not a widely publicized feature of SQL Server 2005, but is slowly gaining fame. The default trace gives administrators the ability to get detailed information about auditing events, database events, error events, full text events, object creation, object deletion and object alteration events. With this much information at their fingertips, administrators are more productive and can more easily identify problems in a production environment. My recommendations are to look through the events and see what information already exists for your instances. Default trace should not only be used reactively but proactively. A proactive mentality will reveal small problems before they escalate to bigger problems.

Event and Category Queries

```
  --list of events
SELECT *
FROM sys.trace_events
```

```
  --list of categories
SELECT *
FROM sys.trace_categories
```

```
  --list of subclass values
SELECT *
FROM sys.trace_subclass_values
```

```
--Get trace Event Columns
SELECT
     t.EventID,
     t.ColumnID,
     e.name AS Event_Descr,
     c.name AS Column_Descr
FROM ::fn_trace_geteventinfo(1) t
     INNER JOIN sys.trace_events e
          ON t.eventID = e.trace_event_id
     INNER JOIN sys.trace_columns c
          ON t.columnid = c.trace_column_id
```

References:

List of available events:

http://blogs.technet.com/vipulshah/archive/2007/04/16/default-trace-in-sql-server-2005.aspx

How to enable default trace:

http://msdn.microsoft.com/en-us/library/ms175513(SQL.90).aspx

Streaming Data into SQL Server 2008 from an Application

By Solomon Rutzky

Prelude to a Test

There are many new and coolio features in Microsoft SQL Server 2008 (such as FINALLY being able to initialize a variable when you declare it) and the term "streaming" has been thrown around quite a bit. Nearly all of the articles that include the word "streaming" are referring to the FILESTREAM feature of storing BLOB data on the filesystem. This article, however, is NOT about the FILESTREAM feature (which is fine because there are plenty of those already). Instead this article is about using Table-Valued Parameters (TVPs) to stream data from an application into the database.

Many articles have been written to cover the basic topic of what Table-Valued Parameters are and how to use them to pass data between Stored Procedures so I will not go into that here. What I am going to focus on is using TVPs to pass data from an application to the database. Now there are two ways of passing data to a TVP: sending the data all at once and streaming the data as you receive it. The first way -- sending all of the data at once -- is a topic that has been covered in a few articles but I will include it here for completeness and to compare it with the fully-streamed method. The streaming method is mentioned in a few places but I have not been able to find any articles about it, most likely due to it not being applicable as often as sending all of the data at once. In fact, the only example of it that I have seen -- and which I used as a reference for this article -- was a session at the SQL PASS 2008 conference presented by Himanshu Vasishth (see References section for details).

The Typical Method

Prior to SQL Server 2008 the only way to send data to the database was to send it in one row at a time. So we have all created the basic Insert, Update, and Delete Stored Procedures that accept a single row's data to work on. Of course for the Delete operations some people pass in a comma-separated list and split it out in the database using a User-Defined Function, but that doesn't work for Insert and Update. If there is only one row to operate on then there really is no issue of efficiency. But often enough we have a set of data that we want to work with at one time. Whether we are creating a matching set of data (e.g. creating a single Order Header record and several Order Detail records associated with it) or loading a set of data (e.g. data import or maybe persisting a .Net Grid View), we are forced to iterate over that set of data. And in the case of the Header / Detail situation, you have to create the Header record first and then create the Detail records based on the ID of the Header record. All of these calls add up in terms of network traffic and the length of time of the operation contributes to blocking if a transaction was opened by the application; if a transaction was not opened by the application then each statement is its own transaction which is a greater load on the server as compared to bulk / multi-statement operations. The only benefit here is that if you are importing a large dataset from disk or another source you can load each row into memory as you need it and hence consume a low amount of memory. But this benefit doesn't provide any efficiency in terms of time that it takes to perform the operation.

The Newer And Awesomer Method

Starting in SQL Server 2008 is the ability to pass real datasets to Stored Procedures using Table-Valued Parameters (TVPs). TVPs allow you to pass in a strongly-typed collection of data (i.e. a table). So now we can make a single call to the database to pass in all relevant records. This cuts down on network traffic and allows us to both combine operations such as the Order Header and Order Details into a single call as well as making use of multi-row DML operations which are much more efficient than iterative statements. In most cases this method will consume the same amount of memory as the iterative method since you will likely have the data collected to send to the database at that moment. The difference here is that you can make a single call to the database to send it all in which is both a cleaning programming model as well as an order of magnitude faster, especially as you work with larger sets of data. The only down-side here is that if you are importing a large dataset from disk or another source you do not have the ability to read that data in as you pass it to the database and hence an operation might consume too much memory before you get a chance to send it all at once to the database.

The Double-Plus Good Method

So the feature that is either not mentioned or is only alluded to but never shown (same as with this article so far ;-)) is the ability to not only send all of the data at once to a TVP (and gain the efficiency of a single network call with a multi-statement operation) but to also keep the memory footprint low. That's right, by doing a little extra work (not too much) you can stream an entire set of data to

SQL Server 2008 as it is being read into your application. To be fair, this method does not really offer any benefit over the standard TVP approach (using a DataTable) if you already have all of the data in memory and there is no way to get it in small chunks. However, for those operations that require loading large sets of data that are being read from disk, a Web Service call, a query result from another database, etc., this method allows you to start passing the data to SQL Server as you receive it. This allows you to get the low-memory benefit of the iterative method plus the network and database efficiency benefit of the basic TVP method.

But wait, there's more! Well, no there isn't. But now we can get to the technical details (i.e. the fun stuff).

Test Overview

The example code that is shown below (and attached to this article at the bottom in the "Resources" section) is a single C# file (a Console Application) that covers four different methods:

1. The "old school" (option = old) method of importing a text file iteratively by calling a Stored Procedure that accepts parameters for each of the columns,

2. The "standard TVP" (option = normal) method of importing the text file entirely and then calling the TVP-based Stored Procedure once to Insert the data by passing in a DataTable,

3. The "half-streaming" (option = half) method of reading all of the data into memory (same as the "standard TVP" method) but then calling the TVP-based Stored Procedure once while streaming the data from the DataTable using IEnumerable, and

4. The "full-streaming" (option = full) method of reading the data one record at a time from the text file and streaming each record to the TVP-based Stored Procedure in a single call by using IEnumerable

I have also attached the compiled .exe file of the code so that you don't need to compile this yourself if you want to run the same test. Just rename the file to end in .exe instead of .ex_ so that it runs.

Please note that I fully realize that the example code below is not 100% optimized in that there are a few places where I repeat blocks of code. This is by design since the purpose of this code is to be educational and I wanted to make it clear for people to see each of the four methods and the code required for each method without confusing the issue for people who might not be used to reading C#.

Note: this code is available at www.sqlservercentral.com

The sample data that I used was a 3 million row text file that consists of two columns: an INT that increments from 1 to 3,000,000 and a VARCHAR(50) which is just a GUID for the sake of simple variety. I generated the data (133 Megs of it) using two SQL# (*http://www.SQLsharp.com/*) functions in a single statement as follows (yes, there are two lines but the first is just setup):

EXEC SQL#.SQLsharp_SetSecurity 2 -- this is needed to write to the disk
EXEC SQL#.DB_BulkExport 'SELECT IntVal, NEWID() FROM
SQL#.Util_GenerateInts(1, 3000000, 1)', '', 0, 0, 'Word', 0, 0,
'C:\SampleData3M.txt', NULL, NULL, 'ASCII'

There are other ways to create sample data but this was easy and took 30 seconds but did require that the process running SQL Server had write access to C:\ (but on my laptop it was not an issue).

For the database side of things I did the following:

1. Created a new database called "Test"

2. Set the recovery model to: SIMPLE

3. Set the data file to 500 Megs and the Log file to 1.1 Gigs since we don't want the import time to be skewed by filegrowth operations which won't be consistent between tests

4. ran the following (also attached to this article):

Note: this code is available at www.sqlservercentral.com

Test Results

I ran my test in following environment:

- SQL Server 2008 (10.0.1600.22) Developer Edition
- Windows XP Professional, SP3
- Intel Core 2 Duo 2.4 Ghz with 2 Gigs RAM
- 5400 RPM SATA HD (it's a laptop)

Method	Time (avg.)	Memory (avg.)
Old School	34 minutes	Low (but still sucks at 34 minutes)
Normal / Standard TVP	41 seconds (22.8 to the DB)	660 megs
Half-Streaming	42 seconds (24.6 to the DB)	660 megs
Full-Streaming	23.3 seconds	40 megs
BCP	21 seconds	70 megs

Please note that the test result times are fully inclusive of reading the data from disk, which for all but the Full-Streaming method is typically 18 seconds. However, in the test code the number of seconds displayed after the Stored Proc is called is only showing what it takes to pass the data to the database and does not include any time needed to read the data from disk, except in the case of the Full Streaming method since you cannot separate the reading from the sending in that case. Also, the max CPU usage in all cases hovered between 65% and 75%.

From these results we can see that any usage of TVPs over the old method is an order of magnitude faster than doing things iteratively; about 50 times faster assuming 40 seconds for the TVP method. Deciding between the DataTable method and the IEnumerable method (fully streamed) depends on whether or not you have all of the data before calling the Stored Procedure or if you can manage to gather the data incrementally. The tests do show that if you have no choice but to collect all of the data first, then using the half-streamed method (IEnumerable) is actually a little slower than using the simpler DataTable method. However, there is no comparison for speed and efficiency (low memory usage) for the fully streamed method when you have the opportunity to get the data incrementally.

Also please note that one downside of using TVPs is the usage of the Log file. For these tests the log file grew to just over 1 Gig even though the data being imported was only 130 Megs. Hence my stating before the tests that I had set the Log File to 1.1 Gigs so that I would not have to worry about file growth. And when looking at the file usage (when doing a "shrink file" so that I could re-test with another method to see if it behaved similarly) only 40% of the log file was in use after each test was over and only 2% after doing a CHECKPOINT. This, however, is an acceptable situation given the speed and low memory usage.

Notes

- When using the DataTable method, the TVP parameter(s) need to have two options set:

  TypeName: this needs to be the name of the Table Type
  SqlDbType: this needs to be set to SqlDbType.Structured
  Value: this needs to be a variable of type DataTable

- Using the DataTable method (standard) grows the log file much larger than expected.

- In ADO.Net you can use a DbDataReader or an IEnumerable<SqlDataRecord> interface to stream the data directly to a Stored Procedure using a Table-Valued Parameter. Streaming outside of ADO.Net can be accomplished via ODBC using the data-at-execution paradigm or via OLE DB using a custom IRowset implementation.

- When using the IEnumerable<SqlDataRecord> method, you need to do the following:

  - Create a Class that implements IEnumerable<SqlDataRecord>
  - That Class needs to have at least three methods:
    - A constructor which is the Class name and any input parameters
    - The method that contains the logic to incrementally read in the data and that has the following signature: public IEnumerator<SqlDataRecord> GetEnumerator(). This method should have a loop that will pass back the data with the following statement: yield return DataRecordVariable;
    - And this one, exactly as it is here:
      IEnumerator IEnumerable.GetEnumerator()
      {

```
        return GetEnumerator();
      }
```
- o ProcParameter.TypeName: this needs to be the name of the Table Type
- o ProcParameter.SqlDbType: this needs to be set to SqlDbType.Structured
- o ProcParameter.Value: new instance of your IEnumerable Class name
- **Large datasets that are inserted directly (i.e. not transformed) will likely be faster via T-SQL BULK INSERT, bcp.exe, or the SqlBulkCopy object in .Net but otherwise this method would be faster. Small datasets would be similarly efficient between Bulk Insert and this streaming method even for straight inserts.**

Conclusion

As we have seen, the new Table-Valued Parameter feature of SQL Server 2008 allows us to pass in data to the database from an application in a much more efficient manner than iteratively calling a Stored Procedure to operate on one row at a time. The only draw-back to the basic / common implementation of using a TVP (i.e. using the DataTable method) is that you need to have all of the data in memory before you execute the Procedure. There is, however, a way to keep the memory footprint of your operation low by fully streaming the data to SQL Server 2008 by reading it incrementally and passing it to a Table-Valued Parameter via a Class that implements the IEnumerable interface. For situations that deal with large volumes of data, making use of the IEnumerable interface can get you both benefits of the blazing efficiency of a single call to a Stored Procedure with the low-memory utilization of the typical incremental method. And while BULK INSERT and/or BCP might be slightly faster with large volumes of data that are inserted as-is, an import doing any amount of transformation of the data would be much faster using the TVP / IEnumerable combination.

References

- SQL PASS 2008 in November, "Optimizing Bulk Operations Involving Data Cleansing and Merging with Table-Valued Parameters", Session AD-302-M (26:14 - 42:10), Himanshu Vasishth, Program Manager of ADO.NET

- Table-Valued Parameters (Database Engine):
  http://msdn.microsoft.com/en-us/library/bb510489.aspx

- Table-Valued Parameters in SQL Server 2008 (ADO.NET):
  http://msdn.microsoft.com/en-us/library/bb675163.aspx

SQL Server 2008 and Data Compression

By Nicholas Cain

One of the large advantages of migrating up to SQL Server 2008 is the ability to compress your data, reducing your disk overhead. It is a relatively simple process to compress your data.

Unfortunately from a production standpoint it is only available on the SQL Server 2008 Enterprise Edition (as per *http://msdn.microsoft.com/en-us/library/cc645993.aspx*), it can however also be used on the Developer Edition (*http://www.microsoft.com/sqlserver/2008/en/us/developer.aspx*)

The reduction in I/O required to pull data can lead to significant performance improvements, particularly in data warehouse and data mart environments where you are working with extremely large datasets.

What is Data Compression

Data compression is exactly what is says it is. It is a way of compressing the data within your database so that you can reduce greatly the amount of storage space required to host the data. There is a caveat with this, depending upon the amount of stored data within a table, the allocation unit size of your disk and the datatypes you could in fact end up using MORE storage

Note: Allocation Unit Size (AUS) is also known as the cluster or blocksize of your disk. This size is set when you format your disk and can range in size from 512 Bytes to 64 KB. The default AUS is based upon the size of the disk, see *http://support.microsoft.com/kb/140365* for more information. Larger file allocations will provide performance improvements for applications such as SQL Server, particularly the 64 KB AUS. The size of a SQL Server extent (8 pages) is 64 KB, and so optimizes performance. The downside of a larger AUS is that is takes a great deal more space to hold a file on the disk, so if you have a lot of smaller files you could end up using a far more disk space than you need to as the disk has to allocate 64 KB of space for even a 2 KB file. If you are curious about the existing AUS on your partitions Microsoft have published a technet article with a script to show the partition properties *http://www.microsoft.com/technet/scriptcenter/guide/sas_fsd_grsi.mspx?mfr=true*

There are two types of data compression:

- Row compression
- Page compression

Row level compression will provide savings by not storing blank characters within fixed character strings (such as a char(10) with a 5 character value). Null and 0 values are not stored and so do not incur additional storage overhead. For a list of data types that support row level compression see *http://msdn.microsoft.com/en-us/library/cc280576.aspx*.

Page compression uses a far more complex algorithm to minimize the storage space of data, known as dictionary compression. SQL Server looks at all of the data stored on a page and builds a dictionary based upon that data which can be referenced for repeated values, and only the dictionary id and changes of the dictionary value are stored. This provides great savings for similar patterned data. For full details on page level compression and how it works visit *http://msdn.microsoft.com/en-us/library/cc280464.aspx*. Page compression includesrow compression, so you get the benefit of both.

Potential Issues with Data Compression

Data compression is not for everybody. Depending upon the workload of your system, the performance requirements, and whether or not you use encryption this might not be the thing for you. There is a CPU overhead associated with using data compression, and this may adversely impact your system. High volume OLTP systems could be significantly impacted by attempting to implement data compression.

How Do I know if Data Compression is Right for Me?

- Estimate the potential storage savings that you could get by implementing (you could actually end up using MORE storage within certain circumstances)
- Complete a baseline performance analysis of your database server and reproduce this in a development or staging environment. Enable compression and evaluate the performance against that baseline.
- Look at which tables can provide you the biggest benefit. I have found that an audit table I have will actually use 75% savings in disk space with no impact to the application on top of the database. Tables which

have a lot of repetitive or numerical data or CHAR columns that are not fully populated are usually excellent candidates for compression.

- Check and recheck your analysis against the baseline, and seek feedback from the users if you do implement it in a production environment.

How Do I know if a Table is Worth Compressing?

There is a stored procedure in SQL Server 2008 called sp_estimate_data_compression_savings. This procedure accepts 5 parameters.

1. @schema_name
2. @object_name
3. @index_id
4. @partition_number
5. @data_compression

The two critical parameters are @object_name and @data_compression.

The object name refers to the table that you wish to evaluate and @data_compression can have one of three values (NONE, ROW, PAGE). Depending upon the value passed this will perform estimations for the two compression types and strangely for no compression.

The additional parameters provide some more advanced estimation options. @schema_name allows you to estimate the savings against tables on a different schema (by default the procedure only looks at tables within your own schema). @index_id will allow you to specify the estimated savings for a single index on a table based upon the index id, left with the default value of NULL it will assess all of the indexes on that table. @partition_number will allow you to define particular partitions on a table to evaluate potential savings. This can be very useful for estimating the savings on older data, rarely changed living on a partition, which you may want to compress as opposed to more volatile data within a different partition which may not be a good candidate for compression. Worth noting, you have to define an index id in order to evaluate a partition.

Estimating Savings for Entire Databases

It is obviously a time consuming task to go through each and every table an get an estimation of the potential savings you could find, which I why I created a procedure USP_Compression_Savings_By_DB (atttached to this article), which will go out and provide the estimated compression savings for all tables within a single database, or within all databases and load that information into a table for later analysis.

The procedure can be created in the database of your choice and the final analysis table located in another database of your choice. It accepts two parameters, both of which are optional.

- @checkdb this is the name of the database that we will be checking, if left null then all databases will be checked and the savings estimated
- @admindbname should you wish to put the results into a particular database you can put a value here, by default it will use the database in which the procedure resides

PLEASE NOTE: The sp_estimate_data_compression_savings procedure is a bit of a heavy hitter, and obviously with checking all tables in a database (or on an instance) using USP_Compression_Savings_By_DB, your system will be hit all the harder. I would recommend running this against a recent dump of your production databases restored on to another system. At the very least run it during the period of least activity on your system.

Final Thoughts

Compression can be a very useful tool and can provide huge benefits in not only storage but performance in heavy read applications.

Ensure to perform all of the analysis required to prevent your production systems from being negatively impacted by enabling data compression.

The code for usp_compression_savings_by_db is included in the Resource section below.

The FILESTREAM Data Type in SQL Server 2008

By Deepa Gheewala

Introduction

It has been a challenge to maintain files, documents along with the records in the database and gradually increasing the need of digitizing the data leads to the need for a more manageable system. Once a photographer asked me for a system that can manage all his customer data and the associated video clips, photos, etc. that go with each customer. Also he needed to maintain data for his associates and wanted a system that would be very efficient system to maintain and, more importantly, would allow the data to be easily backed up.

Much of the data that is created by the photographer above is unstructured data, such as text documents, images, and videos. This unstructured data is often stored outside the database, separate from its customer record which is structured data. Due to this separation it can lead to data management complexities in areas such as transactional consistency and database backups. Transactional consistency means if record gets updated, all parts of the record are updated. Backup for files and the database need to be done separately OR some external application has to manage the backup of both the storage systems. Well you might think if we can use the data type BOLB of SQL SERVER which allows us to store data upto 2 GB. But the problem with this is that file streaming becomes slow and performance of the database can be affected very badly.

SQL Server 2008 introduces a new data type: FILESTREAM. FILESTREAM allows large binary data (Documents, images, videos etc) to be stored directly in the Windows file system. This binary data remains an integral part of the database and maintains transactional consistency. FILESTREAM enables the storage of large binary data, traditionally managed by the database, to be stored outside the database as individual files that can be accessed using an NTFS streaming API. Using the NTFS streaming APIs allows efficient performance of common file operations while providing all of the rich database services, including security and backup.

What is FILESTREAM?

FILESTREAM is a new datatype in SQL SERVER 2008. To use FILESTREAM, a database needs to contain a FILESTREAM filegroup and a table which contains a varbinary(max) column with the FILESTREAM attribute set. This causes the Database Engine to store all data for that column in the file system, but not in the database file. A FILESTREAM filegroup is a special folder that contains file system directories known as data containers. These data containers are the interface between Database Engine storage and file system storage through which files in these data containers are maintained by Database Engine.

What FILESTREAM does?

By creating a FILESTREAM filegroup and setting a FILESTREAM attribute on the column of a table, a data container is created which will take care of DML statements.

FILESTREAM will use Windows API for streaming the files so that files can be accessed faster. Also instead of using SQL SERVER cache it will use Windows cache for caching the files accessed.

When you use FILESTREAM storage, consider the following:

- When a table contains a FILESTREAM column, each row must have a unique row ID.
- FILESTREAM data containers cannot be nested.
- When you are using failover clustering, the FILESTREAM filegroups must be on shared disk resources.
- FILESTREAM filegroups can be on compressed volumes.

How to use FILESTREAM

Step 1) Enabling FILESTREAM datatype

Before using FILESTREAM we need to enable it as FILESTREAM is by default disabled in SQL SERVER 2008. Enabling the instance for FILESTREAM is done by using the system store procedure *sp_FILESTREAM_configure* . The syntax is given as below:

```
   USE MASTER
GO
   EXEC sp_FILESTREAM_configure @enable_level = 3
```

There are various enable levels:

0 - Disable FILESTREAM

1 - Allow T-SQL only to access files

2 - Allow T-SQL as well File system access Locally

3 - Allow T-SQL as well File system access Locally as well as remotely

OR

Same thing can be done by setting the property of FILESTREAM i.e.
Configurable level = Transact-SQL and file system

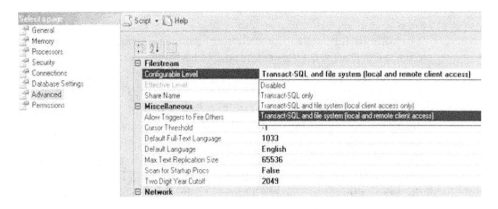

Fig 1: Configure FILESTREAM

STEP 2) Creating File Group

Now let us create a filegroup. As discussed earlier Filegroup is like a folder
which acts as an interface between Windows file system and SQL server.

```
USE MASTER
GO
```

```
CREATE DATABASE TEST_DB ON PRIMARY
( NAME = TEST_DB_data,
FILENAME = N C:\ TEST_DB_data.mdf ),
FILEGROUP FG_1
( NAME = TEST_DB_REGULAR,
FILENAME = N C:\ TEST_DB_data_1.ndf ),
FILEGROUP FG_2 CONTAINS FILESTREAM
( NAME = FS_FILESTREAM,
FILENAME = N C:\TEST_FS )
LOG ON
( NAME = FS_LOG,
FILENAME
= N C:\TEST_FS_log.ldf );
GO
```

The statement below means that a FileGroup of type FILESTREAM will be created i.e. a data container named TEST_FS is created, which will act as an interface between Database Engine and Windows file system. The Database Engine can manage the files through this folder. It is necessary to specify the CONTAINS FILEGROUP clause for least one filegroup.

FILEGROUP FG_2 CONTAINS FILESTREAM

Note:
The only difference in the statement above compared to a normal CREATE DATABASE statement is the filegroup creation for FILESTREAM objects.
There should not be any folder by the name TEST_FS as it will be created by SQL SERVER and permission will be granted. If the database is deleted then SQL SERVER will delete the related files and folders.
Please note that if you try to create this database by specifying a path for the FILESTREAM files that is not on NTFS, you will get the error message: The path specified by d:\TEST_FS cannot be used for FILESTREAM files because it is not on NTFS.

Below is the figure that shows the folder that is created after execution of above DDL statement

Fig 2: Special Filegroup folder created.

For the FILESTREAM filegroup, the FILENAME refers to the path and not to the actual file name. It creates that particular folder - from the example above, it created the C:\TEST_FS folder on the filesystem. And that folder now contains a FILESTREAM.hdr file and also a folder $FSLOG folder.

Important Note: The FILESTREAM.hdr file is an important system file. It contains FILESTREAM header information. Do not remove or modify this file.

Adding FILESTREAM filegroup to existing database

If you already have a database, you can add a FILESTREAM filegroup to it using ALTER DATABASE command.

```
ALTER DATABASE [TEST_DB]
        ADD FILEGROUP FG_2 CONTAINS FILESTREAM;
ALTER DATABASE [TEST_DB]
        ADD FILE
                (NAME = FS_FILESTREAM, FILENAME = N'
C:\TEST_FS
        ) TO FILEGROUP FG_2;
```

Step 3) Creating a Table

Once the database is ready we need a table having a column of Varbinary(max) with FILESTREAM attribute where the data will be stored. Let us create a table and add data into it.

```
USE TEST_DB
GO
CREATE TABLE FILETABLE
(
ID      INT IDENTITY,
GUID    UNIQUEIDENTIFIER ROWGUIDCOL NOTNULL UNIQUE,
DATA     VARBINARY(MAX) FILESTREAM
);
```

The table definition needs a ROWGUIDCOL column - this is required by FILESTREAM. The actual data is stored in the 3rd column DATA. Any data manipulation in this column will update the file stored in the Windows system.

```
INSERT INTO FILETABLE (GUID, DATA) VALUES (NEWID(),NULL);
INSERT INTO FILETABLE (GUID, DATA) VALUES (NEWID(),CAST( TEST
DATA  AS VARBINARY(MAX)));
```

Note: File will not be created for the data value NULL.

Execute select query on the table - FILETABLE, and you get the following output.

ID GUID DATA

1 78909DBF-7B26-4CA9-A840-4D45930F7523 NULL
2 0B0F5833-1997-4C9C-A9A7-F2536D68CFED
04D592044554D4D592054455354

As you can see on the file system, additional folders have been created under TEST_FS folder. The filename will be the GUID id. For eg. If you see the second record, the filename will be 0B0F5833-1997-4C9C-A9A7-F2536D68CFED and in the DATA column the contents of file are stored.

When to use FILESTREAM?

When applications need to store large files i.e. larger than 1 MB and also don t want to affect database performance in reading the data, the use of FILESTREAM will provide a better solution. Also one can use this for developing applications that use a middle tier for application logic.

For smaller files, still one can safely store in columns with datatype varbinary(max) BLOBs in the database which would provide better streaming performance for small files.

Advantages

FILESTREAM enables the database to store un-structured (files, documents, images, videos etc) data on the file systems and still use the SQL SERVER Engine.

It uses Windows API s for streaming the files.

When manipulating files, instead of using the SQL server cache, it uses Windows system cache.

SQL Server backup and recovery models support these files also along with the database. Only a single backup command is issued to back up the database and the FILESTREAM data.

All insert, update, delete, search queries will also work for this unstructured data.

FILESTREAM data is secured by granting permissions at the table or column level, similar to the manner in which any other data is secured. Only if you have permissions to the FILESTREAM column in a table, you can access its associated files.

In SQL Server, FILESTREAM data is secured just like other data is secured: by granting permissions at the table or column levels. If a user has permission to the FILESTREAM column in a table, the user can open the associated files.

Disadvantages

FILESTREAM does not currently support in-place updates. Therefore an update to a column with the FILESTREAM attribute is implemented by creating a new zero-byte file, which then has the entire new data value written to it. When the update is committed, the file pointer is then changed to point to the new file, leaving the old file to be deleted at garbage collection time. This happens at a checkpoint for simple recovery, and at a backup or log backup.

Limitations

Database mirroring cannot be configured on databases with FILESTEAM data.

Database snapshots are not supported for FILESTEAM data.

Native encryption is not possible by SQL SERVER for FILESTREAM data.

Conclusion

This article has explained about the new FILESTREAM datatype of SQL
SERVER 2008 which provides easy way to maintain unstructured data along
with the structured data as it uses Windows API to store files and manages the
data into SQL SERVER database. As explained in the article FILESTREAM is
easy to understand and implement in applications.

Investigating the new Spatial Types in SQL Server 2008 - Part 1

By Bennie Haelen

In this post we take a look at the new spatial data type support in SQL server 2008. First, I will make a case for why you would want to integrate spatial support in your applications. Next we will take a look at the two core spatial data types in SQL Server: the Geometry and Geography types. We will explain when to use each type, and we will take a look at the main application domains for the two types.

The spatial types are implemented as CLR types in the database engine. Since some database folks might be unfamiliar with CLR types, we will make a brief detour into SQL Server and CLR types. We will talk about the differences between static and instance methods, and explain the TSQL calling notation for each.

Both the Geometry and the Geography types are really just the top-level types of a rich object hierarchy. We will take a detailed look at the different classes in this hierarchy, and we will explore the methods and properties of each class by means of a number of TSQL scripts. A part of this exploration we will take a look at the three data formats that can be used to represent the spatial types: the SQL Server-native Well-Know-Binary (WKB) format, and the OGC[26] standard data types: the Well-Known-Text (WKT) and the Geography Markup Language (GML)[27] . We will use TSQL scripts for each object to illustrate the different notations.

As always, a picture is worth a thousand words, and nowhere this is more the case as for spatial information. Therefore, I will use both the "Spatial Results" tab in SQL server and a number of third-party rendering tools such as SpatialViewer[28] and GeoQuery[29] to present a spatial query result.

After we have a good understanding of the spatial data types, we will put them to some practical use. We will use Virtual Earth to create applications in which

---

[26] http://www.opengeospatial.org/
[27] http://en.wikipedia.org/wiki/Geography_Markup_Language
[28] http://www.codeplex.com/SpatialViewer
[29] http://www.conceptdevelopment.net/Database/Geoquery/

we create mashups of Spatial data with a variety of business data. A large volume of GIS data is available on the public domain (some good sources are the US Census[30] and USGS[31] Web sites), but the format of this data is typically not compatible with SQL Server. Therefore, as part of this series we will create a library that will enable us to convert the "traditional" formats into a SQL Server 2008-compatible format.

The above abstract covers a wide variety of formats, therefore I am planing to spread out this article over a number of different posts. This first post will cover the need for spatial support in our applications, the basics of the Geometry and Geography data types and a quick OO primer.

Why Spatial Data?

These days it is hard to find any data that DOES NOT have a spatial aspect. A number of applications attempt to answer questions like the following:

1. Where are my customers located?

2. What cities have the highest accident rates?

3. What Florida counties have the highest flood risk? (OK, that one's easy to answer: "All of them"!)

As GPS devices become more prevalent, more and more data is geo-tagged. For example, a lot of modern mobile phones have both a camera and a GPS chip build in.

While the above applications use spatial data only as part of their overall data set, there are a number of applications that use mapping and spatial data as their primary output:

1. Consumer products such as Microsoft's Virtual Earth or Google maps.

2. The government publishes the census results as spatial data.

3. Utilities use mapping tools such as ESRI Server to plot the layout of electrical grid lines or underground gas lines.

---

[30] http://www.census.gov/
[31] http://www.usgs.gov/

While the above examples are pretty self-evident, spatial data also plays an import role in applications that we might not think about right away:

- When a warehousing application generates a pallet "pick run", it will use geospatial information to calculate the most optimal route.

- When an interior architect uses a CAD tool such as AutoDesk to perform modeling of an interior space, he/she is using spatial data quite extensively.

- Computer-aided manufacturing tools use spatial data to layout out parts on a piece of sheet metal.

- The program in a municipal kiosk uses spatial data and geometric algorithms to predict the arrival times of buses and trains.

- A multi-player computer game use spatial coordinates to keep track of the current locations of all game participants.

From the above discussion it is clear that a large number of application have a need to work with spatial data. Some common requirements for spatial data support are:

- The ability to store spatial coordinates directly in the database, preferably in the same tables as its associated data.

- The data types used for this spatial data should go beyond simple point coordinates. Most geospatial data consists out of a mixture of points, lines (both single-segment and multi segment), and closed shapes (typically referred to as polygons in the literature).

- The ability to perform a multitude of operations on this geospatial data. For example, a chip design application might want to assure that certain routes on a chip do not cross, other applications will have a need to calculate the area of a complex polygon etc.

In the next section will take a look at how SQL Server 2008 addresses the above requirements.

Spatial Data Support in SQL Server 2008

Types of Spatial Data:

At the highest level, we recognize two major classes of spatial data:

- **Vector Data.** Vector data is data expressed by a set of vertices and their relationship to one another. Common spatial features represented by vector data include:

    Points.
    Lines (where a line can have one or more segments)
    Polygons. Polygons are typically used to represent areas and regions.

- **Raster Data.** Raster data is data expressed as a matrix of cells. We typically recognize raster data as images. Within a spatial or GIS context, we see raster data manifested as:

    Satellite images.
    The Virtual Earth bird's eye images.
    Google "street level" images.

An example of each type of spatial data is shown below

Sample Raster Image (a sample satellite heat map)

Sample Vector (in this case a simple line vector)

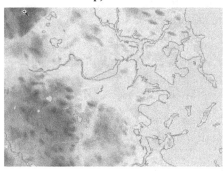
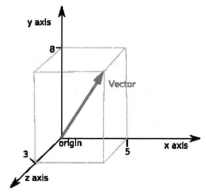

SQL Server 2008 does focus exclusively on Spatial Vector data.

The SQL Server 2008 Spatial Data Types

SQL Server 2008 introduces two new data types:

1. **Geometry.** The geometry data type is based on the Cartesian coordinate system, based upon a "flat earth" representation model. In this model, a point is represented by an X, Y and optionally a Z coordinate. This usage domain of this data type is either:

> The representation of simple coordinates in a two or three dimensional space. A example is the precise location of a pallet in a warehouse.
> The representation of map coordinates, where distances are limited enough so that they are not affected by the round earth model.

2. **Geography.** The geography data point can store points, lines, polygon and collections of each of these, using a "round earth" model as opposed to the "flat earth" model used by the Geometry data type. Instead of using X and Y coordinates, the geography data type will use a latitude/longitude combination to represent a single point. Most of the GIS data available on the Web is latitude/longitude based, so the Geography data type is the data type you should used in most of you GIS applications, especially when you are dealing with longer distances where the shape of the earth becomes relevant.

Geometry : Cartesian coordinate system, "flat earth" model

Geography: Latitude/longitude coordinates, "round earth" model

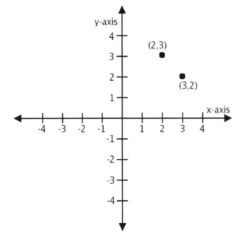

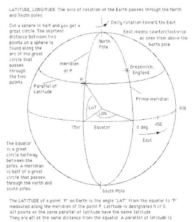

The geometry data type conforms to the Open Geospatial Consortium (OGC) Simple features for SQL specification version 1.1.0.[32] The OGC is a non-profit, voluntary consensus standards organization which is the leading consortium when it comes to the drafting and ratification of standards for geospatial and location based services. One of the standards published by the OGC is the Well-Know-Text specification (WKT[33]) for spatial data types. We will investigate this format in detail in part 2 of the series.

CLR Objects in the Database Engine and the Database Developer

Both the geometry and geography data types are implemented as user-defined types (UDT's) in the database engine. These UDT's are implemented as .NET Common Language Runtime (CLR) types. Before we take a more detailed look how to use these types, it is important that we make sure that the reader is familiar with some basic OO principles. If you are already familiar with object-orientation and .NET types, please feel free to skip ahead to the next part in this series.

The core abstraction in the object-oriented world is the class. A class can be seen as the blueprint for a particular type. From this blueprint, a client can create any number of actual object instances. A class hides away its implementation details behind a set of publicly accessible properties and methods. This principle is called encapsulation or information hiding. For example, a Car class will encapsulate the behavior of an automobile. It might expose methods such as Start, Stop, SlowDown and SpeedUp, and it might provide properties such as CurrentSpeed and DaysTillNextOilChange. The Car class will hide the details of how it executes these methods and exposes these properties, enabling the client to be "blissfully unaware" of the implementation details of the Car class.

Classes can be related to one another. At a high-level we can recognize the following types of relationships:

The "has-a" relationship. For example, a Car class might have a SteeringWheel and a GasTank. This type of relationship is sometimes referred to as a "uses" relationship, for example the Car class "uses" the SteeringWheel class and "uses" the GasTank class.

---

[32] http://www.opengeospatial.org/standards/sfa
[33] http://en.wikipedia.org/wiki/Well-known_text

The "is-a" relationship. To stay with our Car example, a SportsCar is a specialized type of Car, which is specially equipped. It might have a Spoiler, a HighPerformanceEngine etc.. When classes have such a relationship they will use an OOP concept called inheritance to implement this relationship. In an inheritance implementation, the class from which we inherit is called the base class and the more specialized class is called the sub class. The sub class gets all of the functionality of the base class "for free", so it only needs to worry about implementing it own specialized behavior on top of the functionality of the base class. For example, the SportsCar class only implements the additional functionality that makes it a sports car.

An example of a "uses" ("has a") and an inheritance ("is a") relationship is shown in the figure below:

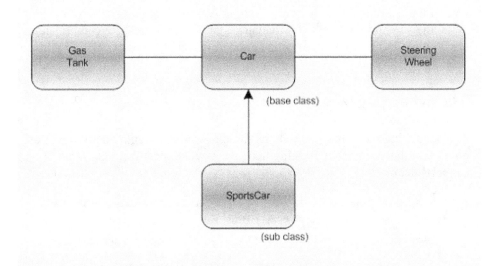

Some base classes only define a general abstract concepts or entities. These types of classes cannot be directly instantiated by the client, since they are not "feature complete". Such a class is called an abstract class. The features defined by an abstract class are implemented by a sub class of the abstract class. Such a sub class that can be instantiated is called a concrete class. We will see in the next section that the geometry and geography classes are indeed defined as abstract classes in the database engine.

In the next part of this series, we will take a look at the class diagrams for both the geography and geometry classes, and we'll start writing some TSQL code!

SQL Server 2008 SSMS Enhancements - Debugging Support

By Jacob Sebastian

Introduction

In the previous session[34] we discussed some of the enhancements/new-features added to SSMS 2008. This article and the previous[35] one are based on SQL Server 2008 RC0 release. Some of the features may change in the final release of the product.

One of the features that I find very exciting is the debugging support. SSMS 2008 allows you to debug TSQL batches, stored procedures, triggers, functions etc. We will have a quick look at the debugging capabilities of SSMS in this session.

The debugging menu

The debugging menu has menu items for almost all debugging activities. You could find there almost everything that you would expect from an IDE that supports debugging.

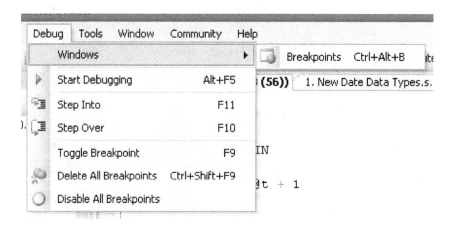

---

[34] http://www.sqlservercentral.com/articles/Management+Studio/63536/
[35] C:\Perl\eg\output.html

Debugging a Batch

You could debug database objects (Stored Procedures, Functions etc) as well as TSQL batches. If you wish to debug a specific portion of the code, you could select those lines and debug it.

```
DECLARE @t INT
  SELECT @t = 1

WHILE @t < 5 BEGIN
     PRINT @t
     SELECT @t = @t + 1
 END

 PRINT 'DONE'
```

You can add/remove breakpoints by pressing F9, selecting 'Toggle Breakpoint' menu item from the 'Debug' menu. You could also do this by clicking/right-clicking on the left margin of the IDE.

Debugging information

After you start debugging, you can open several debug windows to monitor different debugging information.

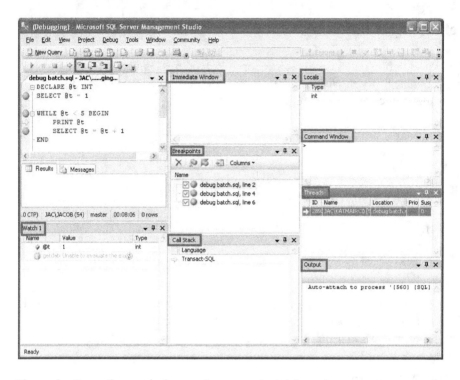

If you don't see those windows when you start debugging, you can open them from the "windows" submenu of the "debug" menu.

Using the debug windows

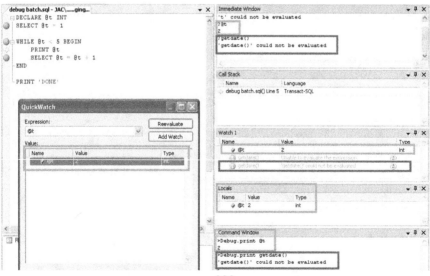

There are three windows that help to evaluate the value of expressions/variables: "immediate", "command" and "watch"/"QuickWatch". However, they do not seem to be able to evaluate functions. For example, the function "GETDATE()" returns an error.

Debugging stored procedures

Debugging stored procedures is pretty easy with SSMS. Just select the EXECUTE statement and click "Start Debugging" menu or press "ALT+F5".

```
debug stored procedure....(54))    debug batch.sql -
    EXECUTE Level3
   -PRINT 'Back at level 2'
    GO

  CREATE PROCEDURE Level1
    AS
    PRINT 'I am at level 1'
    EXECUTE Level2
   -PRINT 'Back at Level 1'
    GO

  EXECUTE Level1
```

You can drill down to other child stored procedures, functions etc being called from your stored procedure.

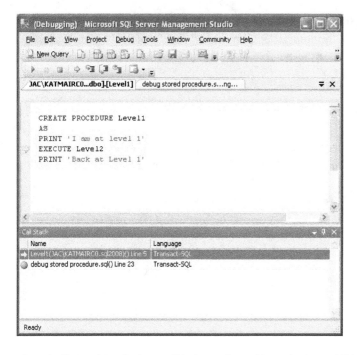

The "Call Stack" window will show the call stack that will help you to keep track of the execution path.

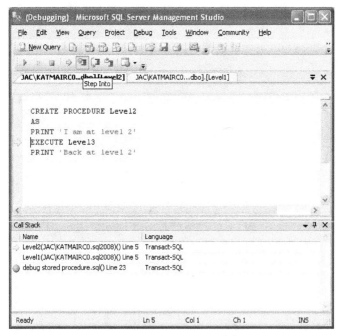

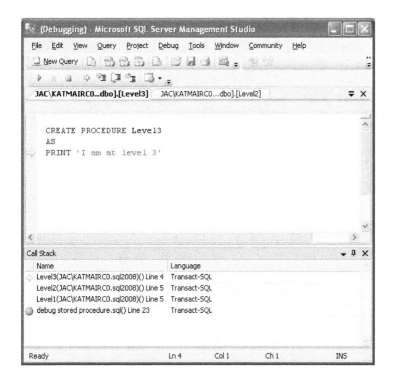

Debugging Functions

SSMS supports debugging functions too. To debug a function, select the TSQL statement that calls the function and click "start debugging" or press "ALT+F5".

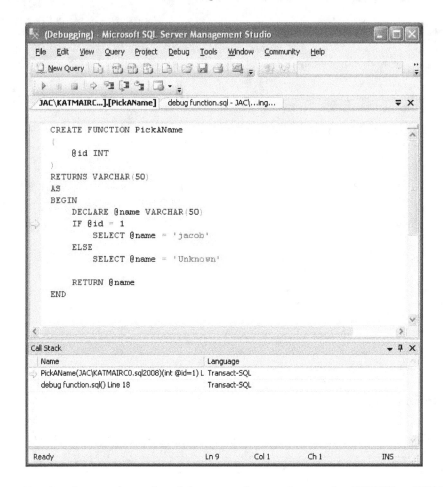

Previously, people used to debug stored procedures using PRINT or SELECT statements. So when your stored procedure behaves in unexpected manner, you could embed some PRINT or SELECT statements and find out what is going wrong with the code. However, when something goes wrong with a function, it was harder to identify.

The SSMS debugging support makes this job easier.

Debugging Triggers

Just like functions, triggers were difficult to debug too. People used to debug triggers using print statements or temp tables. SSMS makes it lot easier now. You can debug an INSERT/UPDATE/DEBUG statement and it will take you to the body of the triggers and you can step through the code.

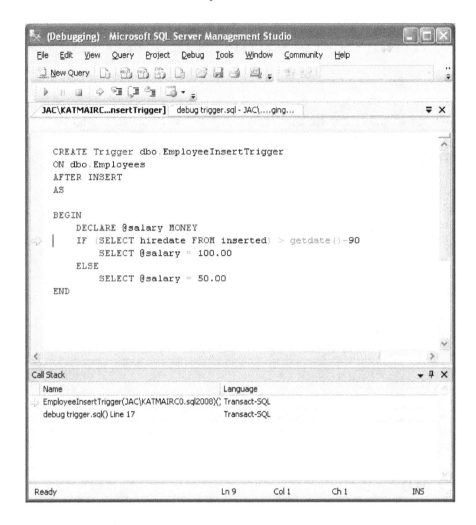

Conclusions

Debugging is something that every developer does quite a lot of times. In this session, I did not go deeper into debugging. My intention is to give a few hints and I am sure you will be able to dive deeper into it. While debugging, if I find some more interesting stuff, I will come back with another session on SSMS debugging. Till then, "Happy Debugging!".

Deploying Scripts with SQLCMD

By David Poole

I have had to deploy database applications in a variety of scenarios and very early on in my career I reached the conclusion that any means of automating the deployment process was a "Good Thing".

Manual deployment introduces a point of failure for even the most diligent DBA, particularly when that deployment has to take place in hours when most sane people are soundly asleep. Where I work at present downtime costs big money (a years salary in lost revenue for every minute) hence the early start.

This means that you would be undertaking a manual process under the following conditions: -

- Under stress due to cost considerations
- On 3 or 4 hours disturbed sleep
- Severely decaffeinated

The SQLCMD and its predecessors OSQL and ISQL offer a means of automating such deployments. However SQL Management Studio offers the facility to use SQLCMD from within SQL scripts by using SQLCMD Mode.

SQLCMD Mode

SQLCMD Mode can be activated/deactivated from a menu option within SQL Management Studio as shown below.

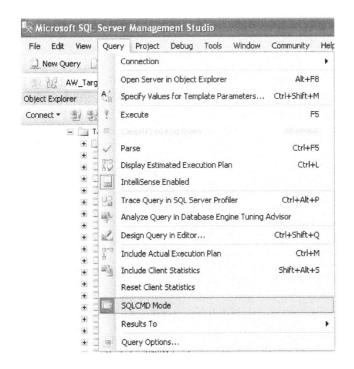

When SQLCMD Mode is engaged then the specific SQLCMD commands are shown on a grey background as shown below

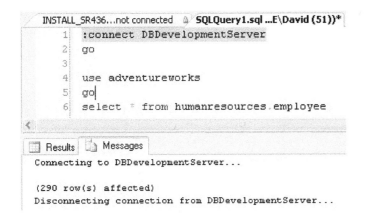

As you can see from the script above I have asked to connect to a database server called DBDevelopmentServer and run a query in the Adventureworks database.

Straight away we can see that it is possible to specify the server that a script is supposed to run on as part of the script.

This may sound like small beer but for me a typical deployment may involve tens of scripts all to be deployed to servers with remarkably similar names. Being able to state explicitly what server the scripts are to be run on gives a major advantage

An incorrect server name will show up in any peer review

The server name is "in-your-face"

User variables in SQLCMD Mode

The :setvar command is a useful addition in the SQLCMD arsenal.

We can refine our first sample script slightly to demonstrate its usage

```
INSTALL_SR436...not connected    SQLQuery1.sql ...E\David (51))*
  1    :setvar MainDBServer "DBDevelopmentServer"
  2    :setvar MainDB "adventureworks"
  3    :connect $(MainDBServer)
  4    go
  5    use $(MainDB)
  6    go
  7    select * from humanresources.employee
  8
```

```
Results   Messages
  Connecting to DBDevelopmentServer...

  (290 row(s) affected)
  Disconnecting connection from DBDevelopmentServer...
```

By itself this does not look like a big deal but it demonstrates the following

Connections can be made on user variables

Databases can be specified in user variables

Running many files from a single INSTALL.SQL script

Ultimately we want to reach the point where we only have to run a single Install.SQL script to deploy an entire solution.

Fortunately SQLCMD mode has a suitable facility to allow this to happen. To demonstrate it I created a simple script called TestSQLCMD.SQL as follows

```
DECLARE
        @UserName SYSNAME ,
        @DeploymentTime CHAR(18),
        @DeploymentDB sysname,
        @CRLF CHAR(2)
SET     @CRLF = CHAR(13)+CHAR(10)
SET @UserName = SUSER_SNAME()+@CRLF
SET @DeploymentTime =
CONVERT(CHAR(16),CURRENT_TIMESTAMP),120)+@CRLF
SET @DeploymentDB = DB_NAME()+@CRLF
PRINT '***************************************'
RAISERROR('DEPLOYMENT SERVER: %s%sDEPLOYMENT DB: %sDEPLOYMENT
TIME:%sDEPLOYER:
%s',10,1,@@SERVERNAME,@CRLF,@DeploymentDB,@DeploymentTime,@User
Name)
PRINT 'TestSQLCMD.SQL IN VSS UNDER
Solutions\SQLServerCentral\SQLCMD'
PRINT '***************************************'
GO
SET NOCOUNT,XACT_ABORT ON
INSERT INTO  Person.ContactType(
        [Name],
        ModifiedDate
) VALUES (
        /* Name - Name */ N'Dave',
        CURRENT_TIMESTAMP
)
RAISERROR('%i record(s) deployed to
Person.ContactType',10,1,@@ROWCOUNT)
```

Ignore the code before the INSERT statement, it is purely a standard header I use in all my scripts to be able to verify that a script has been run on the correct server.

However, note that there is no database mentioned or connection specified. In fact I deliberately disconnected this query and saved it in my local "My Documents" folder as follows

C:\Documents and Settings\David\My
Documents\SQLServerCentral\SQLCMD\TestSQLCMD.SQL

Our original SQLCMD mode script can then be modified as follows

This demonstrates something incredibly important.

We can control all our connections and the databases we use from a single file

Even if a release engineer downloads our project scripts to a completely
different directory they can specify that directory in a variable. Control is still
from a single file.

We can mix and match strings and variables with SQLCMD mode commands.

There is another consideration I should like to draw your attention to. In some
cases I may want to run a single script on several servers or on several
databases for a single deployment. Two specific examples come to mind.

Replication subscriptions where the @sync_type=N'none' where you have to
create objects manually.

Databases that are patterns where a fix applied to one should be applied to all.

This method of scripting allows me to run that same script many times
automatically.

Output and errors

If you are going to implement a single INSTALL.SQL script then you have to make sure that the scripts that are called from INSTALL.SQL are pretty much bomb proof. They should not produce errors and should be safe even if they are rerun by mistake. In short we have to raise our game when it comes to our scripting skills.

We have to be much more rigorous with error trapping and pre-emptive checks when handing installation scripts over to a 3rd party. Of course our output and errors will still be shown on the screen but it would be safer to ensure that the output goes to specific text files so the installation can be reviewed.

With this in mind we alter our original script one more time.

```
Install.sql - D...OLE\David (54))*  Properties   TestSQLCMD.sql - not connected
 1  :setvar InstallDirectory "C:\Documents and Settings\David\My Documents\SQLServerCentral\SQLCMD\"
 2  :error $(InstallDirectory)Install.err
 3  :out $(InstallDirectory)Install.out
 4  :setvar MainDBServer "DBDevelopmentServer"
 5  :setvar MainDB "adventureworks"
 6  :connect $(MainDBServer)
 7  go
 8  use $(MainDB)
 9  go
10  :r $(InstallDirectory)TestSQLCMD.sql
11  go
12  select * from Person.ContactType
```

Here you can see I have asked to put the errors and output into text files in the installation directory. The install.out file can be found on SQLServerCentral.com.

Conclusion

I first came across SQLCMD mode when working with Visual Studio Team Edition for database professionals. I was trawling through the various files that Visual Studio creates in order to form a deployment script and came across a file which simply listed every database object file prefixed by :r.

Digging around revealed that Visual Studio was just calling SQLCMD mode using an install.SQL file.

SQLCMD mode is useful for simple deployments where the release engineer will have access to SQL Management Studio. If Microsoft ever consider extending SQLCMD mode I would suggest that they look at error handling and some if…then…else constructs to aid automated deployments.

For this reason and given the time I prefer to use SQLCMD.EXE from a windows command file as this already has the ability to do such things.

Real-Time Tracking of Tempdb Utilization Through Reporting Services

By Marios Philippopoulos

Introduction

Although SQL Server 2005 has been around for some time, I am sure the feeling of frustration of dealing with tempdb-related issues in earlier versions of the product is a vivid memory for many DBAs. As is the case with other system objects, tempdb in SQL Server 2000 is essentially a black box. Besides access to database-file-size and free-space information, breaking down tempdb utilization to contributions from individual components, such as internal and user objects, is a challenge. This information is vital if the DBA is to make informed decisions that target, on a case-by-case basis, the main culprits of tempdb growth. This all changes with SQL Server 2005. For an excellent discussion on tempdb in SQL Server 2005 I refer the reader to this white paper: 'Working with tempdb in SQL Server 2005'[36].

Starting with SQL Server 2005, tempdb is used to store three types of objects: internal objects, user objects and version stores (new in SQL Server 2005). Internal objects store intermediate results from query processing operations, such as hash joins and sorts, as well as information related to cursors, INSTEAD OF triggers, the Service Broker and LOB variables. User objects include user-defined and system-catalog tables and indexes, table variables, table-valued-function return values and the mapping index if the SORT_IN_TEMPDB option is selected in online clustered-index builds. Lastly, version stores contain row-versioning information for features, such as snapshot isolation, online indexing, AFTER triggers and Multiple Active Result Sets (MARS). It is clear that an automated way is needed to sort through this wide array of data and target key contributions. This is where the present solution comes in.

SQL Server 2005 comes with three dynamic management views (DMVs) for probing tempdb usage at the instance, session and task level, respectively: sys.dm_db_file_space_usage, sys.dm_db_session_file_usage and

---

36

http://www.microsoft.com/technet/prodtechnol/sql/2005/workingwithtempdb.mspx#E4 CAC

sys.dm_db_task_space_usage. In addition to the three types of objects mentioned in the previous paragraph, a fourth type of utilization, mixed extent pages, is exposed by view sys.dm_db_file_space_usage at the instance level. Mixed extents consist of pages allocated to different objects (as opposed to uniform extents with pages dedicated to a single object). A high number of tempdb mixed-extent pages at any given time suggest that a large number of small tempdb objects (temp tables, table variables) is simultaneously being created and/or that there is high extent fragmentation in tempdb.

Here I combine time-sensitive information collected by the above DMVs with the power of SQL Server 2005 Reporting Services to create a tool that provides a visual representation of tempdb utilization, down to the task level, for multiple SQL instances and in an up-to-the-minute time frame. In fact, a Reporting Services installation is not even really required: the presented solution can be used from the comfort of one's Business Intelligence Development Studio (BIDS) environment, and, in fact, this is how I have created the figures for this article.

The inspiration of using SSRS to present information in real time and from multiple data sources in a "dynamic" user interface came to me from an article published in this site by Rodney Landrum some time ago: 'The Reporting Services 3-Trick Pony'[37]. Up to that point I saw SSRS simply as a tool of viewing "static" information, stored in a single repository that is refreshed at (mostly) infrequent scheduled intervals. The idea of using dynamic connection strings to selectively present data from multiple data sources, in graph format, and as events unfold, transformed Reporting Services, in my mind, to a powerful interactive tool with all the trappings of a full-blown web application, in which data is presented in ways that empower users to make timely and effective decisions.

The BIDS Solution

In the solution presented here, information is presented to the user is a highly dynamic manner that allows for the report palette to be occupied by information from multiple SQL instances, one instance at a time.

The layout of the report, as it appears in BIDS, is presented in Figures 1 and 2. The report consists of four main areas: a table listing the SQL Server instances of interest (left-most side of the screen); a group of textboxes (acting as

---

[37] http://www.sqlservercentral.com/articles/Reporting+Services/61339/

buttons), each corresponding to a specific aspect of tempdb utilization (top, under the report title); the chart area (middle); and four tables (bottom) for showing detail information (Figure 2). The role of each of these features will become clear once we get to the Results section.

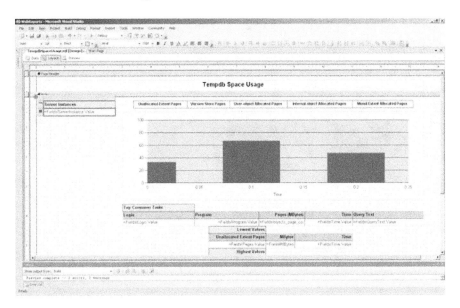

Figure 1. The layout tab (top part).

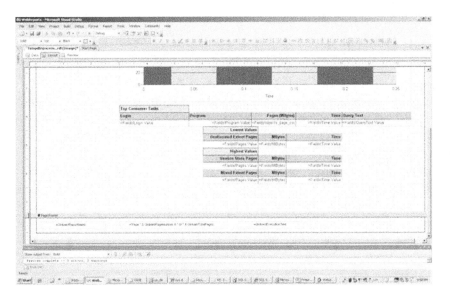

Figure 2. The layout tab (bottom part).

The Data area of the report is shown in Figure 3. The purpose of the ServerNames dataset (the one highlighted) is to populate the list of SQL instances monitored (left-most table in Figure 1). This information is stored in a central database, and is the only "static" connection in the report. The other five datasets, listed underneath ServerNames in Figure 3, populate the other areas of the report (as shown in Figures 1 and 2), and they are all "dynamic", in that they depend on a connection string that changes based on the choices of the report user.

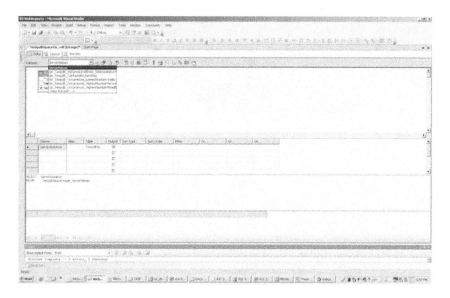

Figure 3. The *Data* tab.

The properties of a "dynamic" dataset, rpt_Tempdb_InstanceLevelStats_TimeSeriesByChartFlag, are shown in Figure 4. The query string is an expression that depends on the value of the chartFlag parameter. Report parameters are passed as input every time a report is refreshed as a result of a user action.

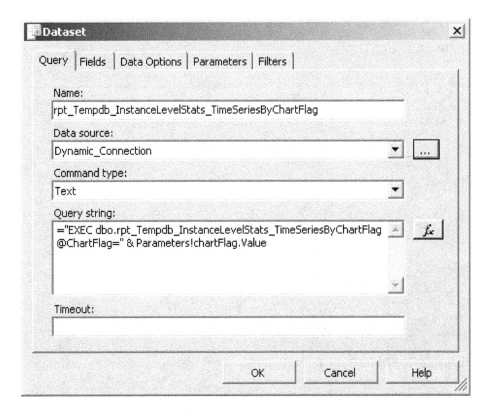

Figure 4. The *rpt_Tempdb_InstanceLevelStats_TimeSeriesByChartFlag* dataset

The Dynamic_Connection datasource is shown in Figure 5. The connection string depends on another report parameter: ServerName. This parameter represents the SQL instance selected from the list on the left-most side of the report area (Figure 1). Based on the user's selection, the connection string is dynamically constructed at run time and a connection is made to retrieve the requested data.

The 2 report parameters are shown in Figure 6.

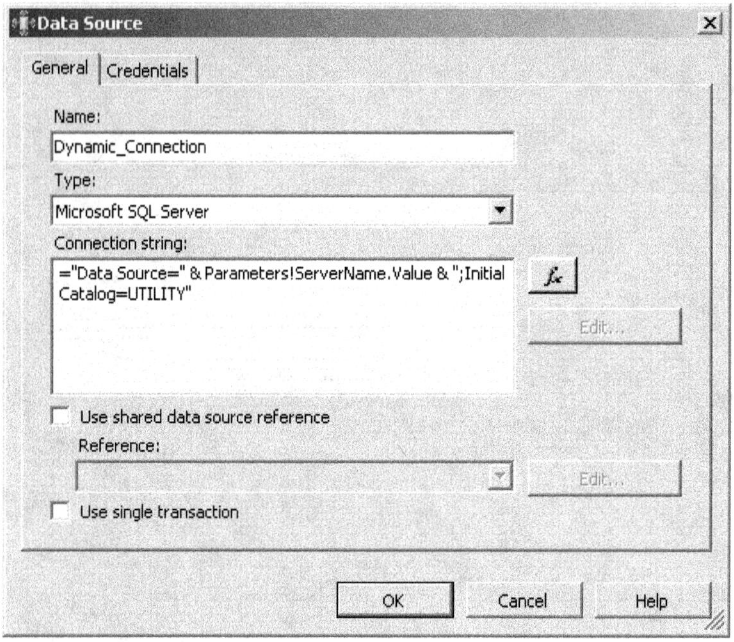

Figure 5. The *Dynamic_Connection* datasource

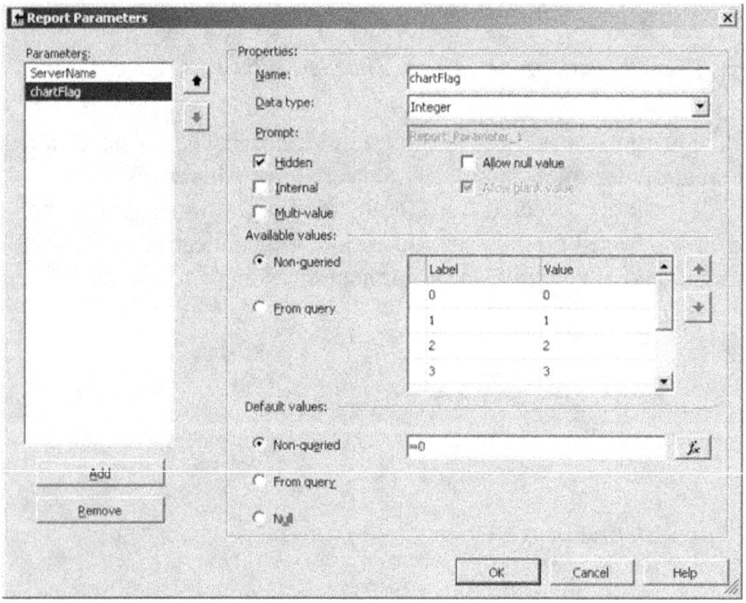

Figure 6. Report parameters

There are two regions in the report where the user is able to make requests on what data they want to see: the leftmost Server Instances table and the array of five textboxes/buttons right above the chart (Figure 1). These features essentially act as buttons/hyperlinks, in that they respond to the user's click action to refresh the report accordingly. The way this is accomplished is through the Action property. Figure 7 shows the configuration of the Action property for textbox ServerInstance. The Action property acts essentially as an event handler: it defines what should be done once the user clicks that textbox. In this case we instruct it to jump back to this report with the parameters shown in Figure 8 (obtained by clicking on the Parameters... button in Figure 7). The ServerName parameter obtains its value from the value of the ServerInstance box that the user click on; again, this will be more clear below, once an example is shown. Figure 9 shows the Parameters dialog of textbox VersionStorePagesBox (2nd button from the left at the top part of the report, Figure 7). Here, there are 2 parameters: the ServerName parameter which takes its value from that of the ServerInstance box (passed back to the report earlier as the ServerName parameter, as a result of the user clicking on a ServerInstance box, Figures 7 and 8); and the ChartFlag parameter, a value from 1-5 for each of the five "buttons" above the chart area (Figure 1).

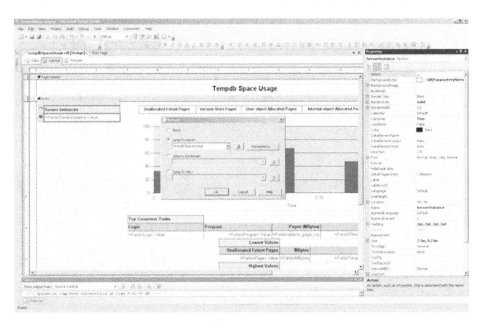

Figure 7. The Action property of textbox ServerInstance

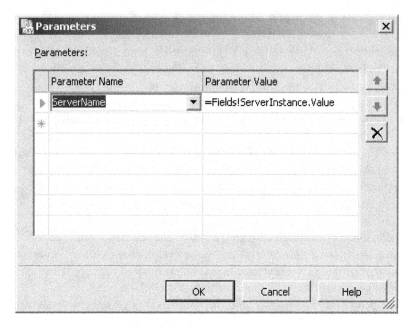

Figure 8. The *Parameters* dialog of the *Action* property of textbox *ServerInstance*

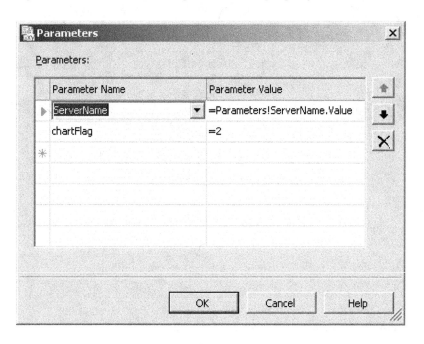

Figure 9. The *Parameters* dialog of the *Action* property of textbox
VersionStorePagesBox

Figure 10 shows the *Data* tab of the *Chart Properties* dialog box, where the name of dataset *rpt_Tempdb_InstanceLevelStats_TimeSeriesByChartFlag* is specified. This is the dataset that supplies the chart data and was briefly described in **Figure 4**.

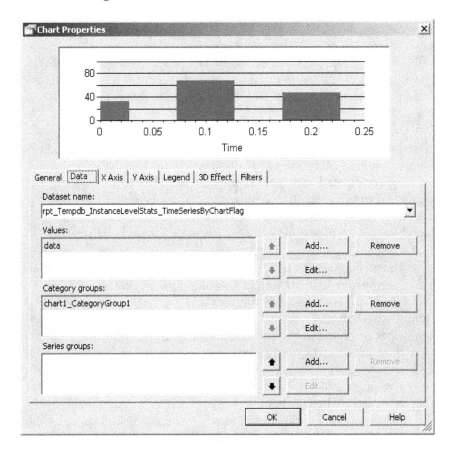

Figure 10. The *Data* tab of the *Chart Properties* dialog box

The Code

The report data is generated by two SQL jobs, running on every monitored instance: DBA - Tempdb Usage - Monitor and DBA -Tempdb Usage - Calculate Stats, Prune Tables. Job DBA - Tempdb Usage -Monitor runs every minute and collects the information presented in the report. Job DBA - Tempdb Usage - Calculate Stats, Prune Tables runs once an hour and performs two tasks: first, it calculates the mean and standard deviation values of the version-store and mixed-extent data distributions; second, it prunes data older than 24 hours.

Job DBA - Tempdb Usage -Monitor executes stored procedure Tempdb_SampleSpaceUsage, that is based on code I first saw on this link: Working with tempdb in SQL Server 2005.[38] Tempdb_SampleSpaceUsage polls system views sys.dm_db_file_space_usage, sys.dm_db_session_space_usage, sys.dm_db_task_space_usage and sys.dm_exec_sessions and stores instance-, session- and task-specific tempdb-usage data in corresponding tables. It is this information that is then fed to the report chart (see Figure 1 and Results section below).

In addition, Tempdb_SampleSpaceUsage checks whether the current number of version-store or mixed-extent pages has exceeded 5 standard deviations above the mean value (calculated once an hour by job DBA -Tempdb Usage - Calculate Stats, Prune Tables. If that is the case, stored procedure ExecRequests_Poll is executed and information about the current execution requests and sessions is stored in table ExecRequests for later analysis.

The reason for calculating the mean and standard deviation of the version-store and mixed-extent page distributions and for polling the current execution requests if a threshold is exceeded is simple: the sys.dm_db_session_space_usage and sys.dm_db_task_space_usage views provide information on user-object and internal-object page utilization, but not for version-store and mixed-extent pages at the session and task level. I therefore had to get this type of information directly by polling the sys.dm_exec_requests and sys.dm_exec_sessions views whenever "something interesting happened": when the current values exceeded a predefined threshold. At the same time I did not want to be inundated with data, so I chose to poll the current exec requests only when warranted.

Results

Figure 11 shows the opening screen of the report. Here I am monitoring five database-engine instances, which I have aliased for the purposes of this article as *alpha, beta, gamma, delta* and *epsilon*. Viewing the various aspects of tempdb utilization is made possible by the five buttons at the top. By default, the selected instance is alpha, but a different instance can be chosen (and the corresponding "button" will be highlighted in yellow accordingly).

---

[38] http://technet.microsoft.com/en-ca/library/cc966545.aspx

Figure 11. Opening screen

Figure 12 is showing the number of unallocated (empty) tempdb pages for instance *epsilon* over a period of 24 hours. In our production environment we allocate a large amount of disk space to tempdb data files to guard against unexpected surges in tempdb utilization (due to suboptimal queries, for example). In this particular case the total number of pages allocated is close to 50,000,000 (or 40 GB). The small dents visible at the top of the curve are due to tempdb usage events that occurred during the monitoring time frame. The table below the graph lists the lowest values of unallocated pages (where utilization is highest) and the times at which they have occurred.

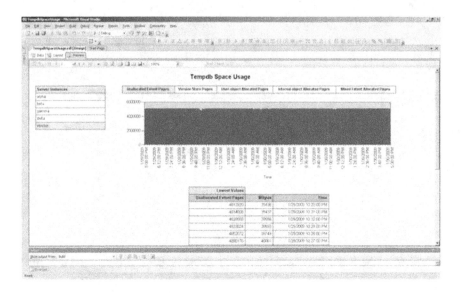

Figure 12. Unallocated tempdb extent pages for instance *epsilon*

Determination of the individual contributors to tempdb usage can be made by clicking each of the other four buttons. Figure 13 is showing the Version-Store-Pages profile of instance beta. As in the case of total unallocated pages, the table below the chart is showing the top outliers and times at which they took place.

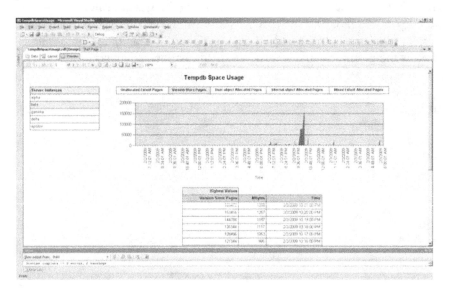

Figure 13. Version Store Pages for instance *beta*

User-object and internal-object allocated pages for instance beta are shown in Figures 14 and 15, respectively. As discussed above in the Code section, identification of the sessions and tasks consuming most of the user- and internal-tempdb-object pages is straightforward through system views sys.dm_db_session_space_usage and sys.dm_db_task_space_usage. This is why, unlike in the case of version-store (Figure 13) and mixed-extent pages, the actual top consuming tasks are explicitly shown in Figures 14 and 15. The main contributor in Figure 15 is a re-indexing job, but it could have easily been a query originating from a user application. In the past we have detected such queries, consuming tens of GB of tempdb space, and have subsequently reduced this utilization through proper indexing and code revisions.

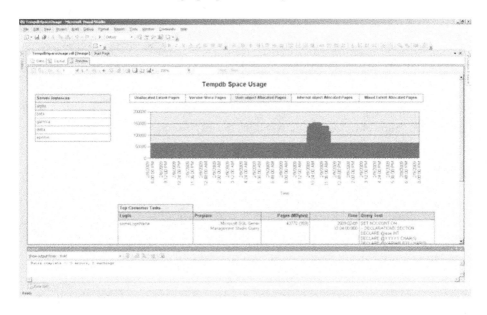

Figure 14. User-object allocated pages for instance alpha

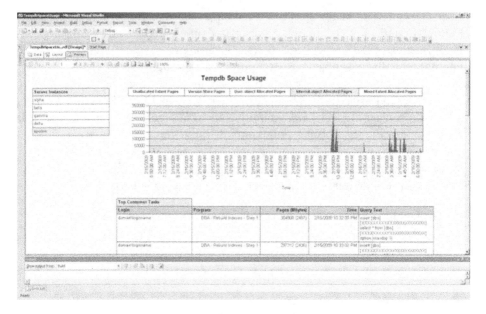

Figure 15. Internal-object allocated pages for instance *beta*

Discussion and Conclusion

Knowledge of the top tempdb-consuming processes and their times of
occurrence is an essential goal of any general database-performance monitoring
plan. Reducing tempdb utilization by targetting top consumers can result in
overall lower disk I/O, better optimized queries and a generally more
responsive and more scalable database application.

The proper in-advance sizing of tempdb files can favorably affect application
performance by: (i) preventing application timeouts that occur when a tempdb
file grows in response to an increased space requirement by a user process; (ii)
helping eliminate the physical fragmentation of the tempdb files, an
unavoidable by-product of file autogrowth, especially in situations where disk
space is shared by non-tempdb files. It is not always feasible (or advisable) to
try and prevent these adverse effects by pre-emptively allocating huge amounts
of disk space (in the tens of GB) to tempdb files, whether or not it will
ultimately be needed. Knowledge of the actual tempdb space required while an
application is subjected to production-like workloads in a testing environment
can help to more efficiently pre-allocate the appropriate disk space to tempdb
before the application is rolled out to production. In cases of applications that
have already been active in production for some time, prolonged monitoring of

tempdb utilization can help DBAs and storage engineers pinpoint those SQL instances with in-excess tempdb allocated space, in the end making possible the more effective redistribution of these excess disk resources in other areas of the IT infrastructure. Figure 12 shows this to be an issue in our environment as well.

Given the additional tempdb-utilizing components (in the form of the version store) available in post-SQL-Server-2000 versions, knowledge of application-specific contributions to tempdb usage can be especially helpful in upgrade initiatives. An obvious culprit is the heavy use of triggers. In our organization we rely extensively on triggers for auditing of data modifications, and some of our largest systems have yet to be upgraded from SQL Server 2000. Triggers do not make use of tempdb in SQL Server 2000, whereas they do in subsequent versions of the product. The tool presented in this article will help us get a reliable estimate of the additional tempdb resources needed once we upgrade our development and test environments to SQL Server 2005/2008. Armed with this knowledge, we will be able to size the tempdb files appropriately for the given application workload, hence minimizing the risk of tempdb-out-of-space "surprises" once the upgrade is finally rolled out to production. Should we also decide to switch on additional "new" features, such as one of the snapshot isolation levels, the tool will make it easy to determine the size of this extra contribution to the tempdb storage and help us plan accordingly while still in the testing phase of the application lifecycle?

It is important to note that the presented solution is beset by a couple of limitations. First, sub-minute processes cannot be detected accurately, as the monitoring job runs once a minute. These "fast" processes are far less likely, however, to end up being major tempdb consumers. Second, because of the way the underlying system DMVs are designed, session and task-level information is not readily available for version-store and mixed-extent page usage. I have been able to obtain this type of information by inference only, through polling the sys.dm_exec_requests view once utilization exceeded a statistically defined threshold. A costly trigger in one of our applications has been identified using this approach and some puzzling results shared on this forum (see 'Costly update trigger -70000000 logical reads for 30000 rows updated!'[39] and 'High count of version-store pages in tempdb'[40]).

[39] http://www.sqlservercentral.com/Forums/Topic647604-360-4.aspx
[40] http://www.sqlservercentral.com/Forums/Topic629370-360-1.aspx#bm629452

Although the importance of proper tempdb sizing is well documented and understood (see, for example, 'Capacity Planning for tempdb'[41]), it is challenging to come up with an automated monitoring plan that exposes top tempdb consumers down to the individual session and task level, in real time and in a convenient visual format. The application described in this article achieves these goals by combining the wealth of existing knowledge with much improved system-diagnostics and Reporting-Services features in versions post-SQL-Server-2000. My hope is that this will prove to be an indispensable tool for many others besides me and for some time to come.

---

[41] http://msdn.microsoft.com/en-us/library/ms345368.aspx

Transparent Data Encryption (TDE) SQL Server 2008

By Roy Ernest

Introduction

You may have heard about Transparent Data Encryption (TDE), which was introduced in SQL Server 2008. But what does TDE do? How does it help us DBA's?

One of the biggest concerns for a DBA is the "data leak". For instance, suppose your company is dealing with payment processors and stores credit card information, banking information and other personnel information of your clients. What would be your primary concerns? Likely they would be loss of data due to corruption, a hardware issue that could bring your database down, and security.

In this article we will look at the physical security of the database files. Until the release of SQL Server 2008, there was no native method of securing the physical files of the database. There were a couple of third party tools that could secure some things, but they were add-ons. SQL Server 2008 introduced a new feature called Transparent Data Encryption. We will look into some details about what this is, how to implement it, what is the impact of enabling TDE, and the known issues with TDE.

First let us look at what encryption is? Encryption is the process of transforming information in plain text using a cipher, or algorithm, to make it unreadable to everyone other than the person who has the key. There are two types of keys; symmetric and asymmetric. When the same value is used to encrypt and decrypt, then it is known as a symmetric key. An asymmetric key has two parts: one is a private key and the other is a public key. The private key is used to encrypt the data and the public key is used to decrypt the data.

> **Disclaimer**
> **Please do not execute any of the scripts provided in the article on your production environment before validating and planning them in a test environment.**

What is TDE?

TDE is a full database level encryption that protects the data files and log files. As per Microsoft documentation "Transparent data encryption (TDE) performs real-time I/O encryption and decryption of the data and log files. The encryption uses a database encryption key (DEK), which is stored in the database boot record for availability during recovery. The DEK is a symmetric key secured by using a certificate stored in the master database of the server or an asymmetric key protected by an EKM module."

One main advantage of TDE is that it does not require any changes to your existing application. This enables DBAs to encrypt data using AES and 3DES encryption algorithms without having to change the applications that will be connecting to the database.

How is the Data Encrypted?

When TDE is enabled, the Server starts a background thread that scans all the database files and encrypts them. This thread actually creates a shared lock on the database. Even when a DDL statement is executed and an Update lock is taken on the database, the encryption thread will run asynchronously using a shared lock. The only operations that are not allowed while the encryption thread runs are modifying the file structure and taking the database offline by detaching it. The scan also rolls over the virtual log file so that the future writes to the log are encrypted.

The supported encryption algorithms are AES with 128, 196 and 256 bit keys or 3 key triple DES. The encryption does not do any padding to the database file. Therefore the size of the database file will stay the same as it currently is even when TDE is enabled. But log files will be padded, thus making them bigger in size.

How do we implement TDE?

Setting up TDE is quite simple. Just four step and you are done. How much simpler can it be?

Create a master key

Create or obtain a certificate protected by master key.

Create a database key and protect it by the certificate.

Set the database you want to protect to use the encryption.

Now let us try to follow these steps. For creating a Master key, you have to execute a Create Master Key command in the Master Database. Before we create a Master Key, let us check if it already exists.

```
USE master;
GO  SELECT * FROM sys.symmetric_keys WHERE name LIKE
'%MS_DatabaseMasterKey%'
GO
```

If no other key has been created before, this should not return any rows. Now let us try to create the Master Key.

```
CREATE MASTER KEY ENCRYPTION BY PASSWORD = '';
GO
```

Once this is executed, if you run the above query, you will get one row with the column name as ##MS_DatabaseMasterKey##. The first step is now done.

The second step is to create a certificate protected by this Master Key. This is done by executing the command Create Certificate in the Master database.

```
CREATE CERTIFICATE MyTDECert WITH SUBJECT = 'My TDE
Certificate'
GO
```

This statement will create the certificate in sys.certificates. You can see the details of this certificate by executing this query.

```
SELECT * FROM sys.certificates where [name] = 'MyTDECert'
GO
```

This will return one row with the column [name] as MyTDECert and with the description as ENCRYPTED_BY_MASTER_KEY. Step number two is also done. We are now half way through.

The next step will be to create an encryption key and protect it by the certificate we just created for the database that needs to be encrypted. From here on please be very careful. You are about to encrypt the database of your choice.

By running the command below, you will create an encryption key for your database.

```
Use AdventureWorks
GO
CREATE DATABASE ENCRYPTION KEY
WITH ALGORITHM = AES_128
ENCRYPTION BY SERVER CERTIFICATE MyTDECert
GO
```

As soon as you execute this in SSMS, it will give the message below. Please read it carefully.

Warning: The certificate used for encrypting the database encryption key has not been backed up. You should immediately back up the certificate and the private key associated with the certificate. If the certificate ever becomes unavailable or if you must restore or attach the database on another server, you must have backups of both the certificate and the private key or you will not be able to open the database.

If you run this select statement, you will see that you have created an encryption key for that database. We are almost done now. The only thing that is left to do is to alter the database to set the encryption ON.

```
ALTER DATABASE AdventureWorks
    SET ENCRYPTION ON
GO
```

That's it. We are done. We have successfully encrypted the database. Let us confirm it with a couple of steps. If you execute the select statement, it should provide the name and details of the encrypted database.

```
SELECT DB_NAME(database_id) AS DatabaseName, * FROM
sys.dm_database_encryption_keys
```

When you run this query, it should return one row since we encrypted only one database. But it returns two rows TempDB and AdventureWorks. This is because when you set up one Database to encrypt, it will automatically encrypt tempdb as well. Actually in my test I am not encrypting Adventure works. I am encrypting a test database that I have with a size of 12 Gig. In my case, when I run this query more than once, I can see the last column (Percent_completed) incrementing. Once the encryption is complete, the Percent_complete column will show the value as 0.

Did it really work?

What is a better way to find out if this actually made our database physically secure other than doing a couple of small tests. The two methods we will use to test are restore and attach. First let us take a backup of the Encrypted database.

```
  BACKUP DATABASE [AdventureWorks] TO DISK =
N'D:\BackUp\AdventureWorks_Encrypted.bak' WITH NOFORMAT,
NOINIT,
NAME = N'AdventureWorks-Full Database Backup', SKIP, NOREWIND,
NOUNLOAD, STATS = 10
GO
```

Once this is completed, we will test the restore in a different Server or a different instance of SQL Server 2008. In this case, I tried a restore on a different server using this command.

```
RESTORE DATABASE [AdventureWorks]
FROM DISK = N'D:\AdventureWorks_Encrypted.bak'
WITH FILE = 1,
MOVE N'AdventureWorks' TO N'D:\BackUp\AdventureWorks.mdf',
MOVE N'AdventureWorks_log' TO
N'D:\BackUp\AdventureWorks_log.ldf',
NOUNLOAD, STATS = 10
GO
```

This will give an error like the one provided below.

Msg 33111, Level 16, State 3, Line 1
Cannot find server certificate with thumbprint
Msg 3013, Level 16, State 1, Line 1
RESTORE DATABASE is terminating abnormally.

Now we proved that the backup taken after the encryption cannot be restored on another server without the certificate. This was just the backup restore option. Let us now try the attach database option.

For this test, first we will copy both the LDF and MDF file to the other server. Then run the SQL statement to attach the DB.

```
CREATE DATABASE [AdventureWorks] ON
( FILENAME = N'D:\BackUp\AdventureWorks.mdf'),
( FILENAME = N'D:\BackUp\AdventureWorks_log.ldf')
```

```
FOR ATTACH
GO
```

When you execute this command, you will get the same error of not finding the certificate with the thumbprint as before. So now we have proven that the database files are secure. The only way to restore or attach the encrypted Database is by adding the same certificate on to the other SQL Server.

To add the certificate to the other server we have to do two things. First you have to back up the certificate onto a file and then create the certificate on the other SQL Server. To back up the certificate, execute a Backup Certificate command.

```
Use Master
GO



BACKUP CERTIFICATE MyTDECert TO FILE = 'D:\MyTDECert.cert'
 WITH PRIVATE KEY
 (
 FILE = 'D:\EncryptPrivateKey.key',
 ENCRYPTION BY PASSWORD = 'TryToUseOnlyStrongPassword'
 )
GO
```

Now you have successfully backed up the certificate. You can use this certificate that was backed up to create a certificate in the target server. First you have to create a Master Key on the Target Server. Then we will use the files generated to create the certificate.

```
USE [master]
GO
CREATE MASTER KEY ENCRYPTION BY PASSWORD = '';
GO
CREATE CERTIFICATE MyTDECert
 FROM FILE = 'D:\MyTDECert.cert'
 WITH PRIVATE KEY (
 FILE = 'D:\EncryptPrivateKey.key'
 , DECRYPTION BY PASSWORD = 'TryToUseOnlyStrongPassword'
 )
```

You have successfully created a certificate on the other server. Once this is complete, you can restore the encrypted database.

```
RESTORE DATABASE [AdventureWorks]
FROM DISK = N'D:\AdventureWorks_Encrypted.bak'
WITH FILE = 1,
MOVE N'AdventureWorks_data' TO
N'D:\BackUp\AdventureWorks_Data.mdf',
MOVE N'AdventureWorks_log' TO
N'D:\BackUp\AdventureWorks_Log.ldf',
NOUNLOAD, REPLACE, STATS = 10
GO
```

You will see that the database has been restored successfully. This proves that the database can only be restored when you have the certificate created in the target server.

Things That Need to be Kept in Mind.

Now we will look at what needs to be thought out in advance before enabling TDE. We will also look at what the after effects of enabling TDE are and the known issues of TDE.

Read Only File Groups and the FileStream Data Type

This is one known issue with TDE. If there are read-only file groups in your database and you try to enable TDE, it will not be successful. Note, I said not successful but I did not say it will fail. There is a subtle difference in this case. If you go through all the steps for setting up TDE like previously stated for a database that has read only filegroup, the encryption will not complete. If you look at
sys.dm_database_encryption_keys,
you will see that the column Encryption_state shows that the value is 2 instead of 3. Value 2 means Encryption in progress. Since the filegroup is set as read-only, the encryption state will not be reached.

When FileStream data type is used, you can encrypt the database but the actual data on the servers file system will not be encrypted.

Do you have a Maintenance/Recovery/Warm Standby plan set for this database?

Let us say that you have a simple maintenance plan where you have a daily backup and transaction log backup every 2 hrs. Let us consider a couple of scenarios.

1. **Warm Standby** - This is bound to throw errors since the database server where the backup file and transaction log is restored does not have the certificate. You have to create the certificate first before you start restoring.

2. **Disaster Recovery Plan of Weekly Back up and Transaction Log -** Let us consider the scenario where your OS on your server started throwing some fatal errors due to hardware issues. Since you have your back up and your transaction log, the decision is made to rebuild the server or migrate to a new server. When you try to restore the database backup and transaction log it will throw an error since you do not have a backup of the certificate. So make sure you backup the certificate and keep it safe for emergencies like this.

3. **Mirroring of the database will also have issues when enabling TDE.** TDE affects database mirroring. You need to install an encryption certificate on the partner servers to be able to mirror the database.

After Effects of Enabling TDE.

Every new feature will have its benefits and problems. We have seen the benefits of TDE: encryption on the physical level. Now let us look at the deficiency and problems that arises when using TDE.

TEMPDB

Even though you have encrypted only one database (AdventureWorks), when you do a

```
SELECT DB_NAME(database_id) AS DatabaseName, * FROM
sys.dm_database_encryption_keys
```

it returns two rows instead of one. One is the database that you encrypted and the other is the TempDB. This will make the non-encrypted database that resides in the same server slow down in performance when it utilizes TempDB.

Compressed Backups

Once TDE is enabled, the compression rate of compressed backups drops down drastically. Making compressed backups is virtually useless. I have shown below figures (Size of Back Up file) of a test database that I used for testing this aspect of TDE.

Full backup with no Compression, No TDE : 11.9 GB
Full Backup with Compression, No TDE : 2.18 GB
Full Backup with no Compression, TDE Enabled : 11.9 GB
Full Backup with Compression, TDE Enabled : 11.9 GB

The actual size in KB that was different between compressed and non compressed back up once TDE was enabled was 22,949 KB.

Known Issue with TDE

While I was doing my research on TDE, I stumbled upon an issue that was raised in SQLServerCentral.com. One of the posters by the name of Amit raised this issue. This issue was then posted in connect by Grant Fritchey aka the Scary DBA who is a well regarded poster. Grant then posted about this issue in Connect[42]. Therefore I am thankful to both of you. Let us look at the Issue.

If you can set a database to use encryption, we should be able to set it to NOT use encryption as well. Here is where the issue starts. To set the encryption off, we have to alter the Database.

```
ALTER DATABASE AdventureWorks SET ENCRYPTION OFF
GO
```

This will set the encryption OFF. We can double check if encryption is off by running a select statement.

```
SELECT *
FROM sys.dm_database_encryption_keys
```

---

[42]

https://connect.microsoft.com/SQLServer/feedback/ViewFeedback.aspx?FeedbackID=423249

You will see that the Encryption_state column is 1. That means that the database is now unencrypted. If you take a backup of this database and try to restore data, you will end up with an error.

```
RESTORE DATABASE [AdventureWorks]
FROM DISK = N'D:\AdventureWorks_no.bak'
WITH FILE = 1,
MOVE N'AdventureWorks_data' TO
N'D:\BackUp\AdventureWorks_Data.mdf',
MOVE N'AdventureWorks_log' TO
N'D:\BackUp\AdventureWorks_Log.ldf',
NOUNLOAD, REPLACE, STATS = 10
GO
```

This will give the Stats of how much percentage is restored and in the end, when it is supposed to finish with the restore, it throws an error.

Msg 3283, Level 16, State 1, Line 1
The file "AdventureWorks_log" failed to initialize correctly. Examine the error logs for more details.

From what I have read so far from the issue, once TDE is enabled, even after you disable it there is always a reference to the certificate. This causes the restore of backup file to fail.

Conclusion

We have seen that the Transparent Data Encryption works, but has some small issues and drawbacks. It is easy to set up, but be very careful. Make sure you have a backup of the certificate in triplicate. If one media gets corrupted where the backup of certificate is stored, you have the other two media.

Now here is a point to ponder. If you had read through the article, I had specified that compressed backups are next to useless once we have TDE enabled. That means that a small/medium sized database (Anywhere above 50 GIG) will probably have a backup file of that size itself. If someone is able to steal the backup file of that size, you have a very big issue.

Please keep in mind that you have to test everything thoroughly in a test environment before you think of setting up TDE in production.

Introduction to DML Triggers

By Jack Corbett

Being a frequent contributor to the forums, I have seen many questions about triggers and seen many trigger implementations that could be dangerous. Hopefully this article will answer some of those questions and clear up some common misconceptions.

Types of Triggers

SQL Server provides 2 types of DML triggers, AFTER and INSTEAD OF (added in SQL Server 2000). Triggers are only fired when a data modification statement is issued (UPDATE, INSERT, DELETE). There are no SELECT triggers. SQL Server 2005 also intoduced DDL Triggers which will not be dealt with in this article.

AFTER Triggers

AFTER triggers take place after the action has taken place and are the default trigger created if you do not specify the trigger type in the CREATE TRIGGER statement. When an AFTER trigger is applied to a table the action takes place, then the trigger fires. Because the trigger is part of the transaction any error withing the trigger will cause the entire transaction to fail and rollback. A typical use for an AFTER trigger is to log the action to an audit or logging table.

INSTEAD OF Triggers

INSTEAD OF triggers take place instead of the modification being made. They are Microsoft's answer to BEFORE triggers available in other RDBMS systems. If I define an INSTEAD OF trigger on a table FOR INSERT the trigger will fire BEFORE the data is inserted into the table. If I do not repeat the INSERT within the trigger then the insert will not take place. For example this trigger would be inappropriate as it never completes the insert:

Note: This code is available at www.sqlservercentral.com

If your business rules only allow for five departments in a group, you could do something like this so the insert takes place:

Note: This code is available at www.sqlservercentral.com

Coding Triggers

All of the following examples will use AFTER triggers.

Coding to Handle Sets

The first thing a DBA or Developer must understand is that triggers deal with SETS, not individual rows. The most common mistake I see made in triggers is using variables incorrectly within a trigger, which means the trigger will only handle a single row update. An example would be this:

Note: This code is available at www.sqlservercentral.com

The trigger handles this update correctly:

```
Update Person.Contact
     Set LastName = 'Corbett'
Where
     ContactId = 12
```

But it does not handle this update correctly:

```
Update Person.Contact
     Set LastName = 'Corbett'
Where
          ContactId Between 12 and 17
```

Which row update will be logged by the trigger? Your guess is as good as mine since you cannot use the ORDER BY clause in an UPDATE, thus the order of the update is not guaranteed. Here is the correct way to code this trigger to handle any UPDATE:

Note: This code is available at www.sqlservercentral.com

Now, I know someone is asking, "What if I need to process each row?". If this were posted on a forum I would ask, why? What is your desired result at the end of the process? Then I would attempt to provide a set-based option, and if I couldn't I would bet someone else could. In all honesty, if you think you need a loop (cursor) in a trigger you probably want to re-evaluate your process as that will absolutely kill performance. In my last position I worked with a third party product that handled our quality results, both from production machine processes and the lab. We used industry-standard unique keys for our products which would be re-used every 2 years, so I needed to purge data prior to the the re-use of the unique key. Since the product tied to the test results was no longer in the system I also wanted to purge the quality results, but I ended up never getting the process done. Why? Because the system had a trigger on the tests table with a cursor in it! So when I would attempt a batch delete of 1 day's data, about 10000 or so results, I would wait and wait and wait, while the server was pegged at 100%. Thankfully I had a test server, and never tried this on the production server. As I investigated why the server was being pounded by a simple delete of ~10000 rows using an index, I found the trigger with the cursor. Since it was a 24 x 7 x 365 operation I had no downtime to do this delete, so I contacted the vendor with the problem and provided a set-based trigger that did what they needed. When I tested using the set-based trigger it took minutes to do the delete with minimal server impact, but the vendor wasn't interested in fixing the problem. I wish I still had access to the database so I could give you accurate numbers regarding the improvement, but I can say it was orders of magnitude. Here is an example using the Person.Contact table in AdventureWorks:

Update Statement:

```
Update [AdventureWorks].[Person].[Contact]
     Set [LastName] = LastName
Where
     ContactID = 12
```

Set Based Trigger:

```
ALTER TRIGGER [Person].[uContact] ON [Person].[Contact]
AFTER UPDATE NOT FOR REPLICATION
AS
BEGIN
     SET NOCOUNT ON;


     UPDATE [Person].[Contact]
          SET [Person].[Contact].[ModifiedDate] =
GETDATE()
```

```
        FROM
             inserted

        WHERE
                inserted.[ContactID] =
   [Person].[Contact].[ContactID];
   END;
```

Cursor Trigger:

```
ALTER TRIGGER [Person].[uContact] ON [Person].[Contact]
AFTER UPDATE NOT FOR REPLICATION AS
BEGIN
      SET NOCOUNT ON;

      Declare @ContactId Int

      Declare c_update Cursor For
          Select
                 ContactId

          From
                 inserted

Open c_update

      Fetch Next From c_update Into
          @ContactId

      While @@FETCH_STATUS = 0

             Begin
                  UPDATE [Person].[Contact]
                       SET [Person].[Contact].[ModifiedDate]
= GETDATE()

                  WHERE
                       [Person].[Contact].[ContactID] =
@ContactId

                  Fetch Next From c_update Into
                       @ContactId

             End

      Close c_update

      Deallocate c_update
END;
```

I ran the update 6 times against each trigger and here is how they compare using STATISTICE TIME

Statistics Time Results (in ms)

	Set-Based	Cursor	Ratio
Low	5	15	33%
Avg	8.83	18.83	47%
Hi	18	24	75%

So you can see that the set-based trigger is over 50% faster on average in this case where we are only doing a single row update.

Outside Actions in Triggers

Another common issue I see in forums regarding triggers is how to send an email or do some other process that is outside the database. Any action that takes place outside the database engine -- email, file manipulation, linked servers, etc... -- does not belong inside a trigger, in my opinion. Why do these processes not belong in a trigger? I can send mail in SQL Server 2005 using database mail, why can't I use it in a trigger? You can, but you need to make sure you gracefully handle any errors that may happen when sending that email, so your ENTIRE transaction is not rolled back. Remember that the trigger is taking place WITHIN a transaction, so any errors in the trigger will, unless properly handled, rollback the outer transaction as well, so that insert/update/delete will not be successful because of the trigger. I recommend using a trigger to populate a "staging" table and then use a job or a windows service to do the emailing or other outside process. There may be a delay, but your main transaction will complete without application complexity "hidden" within the trigger.

Hidden Code

Many people do not like triggers because they consider it "hidden" code and I understand their point. I do try to minimize trigger use and when I do use triggers I try to document them well, both within the trigger, and outside in the application documentation. There are times triggers are necessary. In a current application I am working on we have a table that has a "foreign key" column that, based on the type column, can relate to either table A or table B. I can't use a normal foreign key in this case, so I use a trigger to insure referential integrity. I also use triggers for auditing changes on key tables. I could do this in stored procedures or application code, but I want to protect me from me, so I put it in a trigger.

Resources

'Trigger Trivia'[43] by Andy Warren

'Trouble with Triggers'[44] blog entry by Conor Cunningham

'Triggers...Evil'[45] blog entry by Louis Davidson

And as always, SQL BOL.

---

[43] http://www.sqlservercentral.com/articles/T-SQL/61483/
[44] http://www.sqlskills.com/blogs/conor/2008/06/18/TheTroubleWithTriggers.aspx
[45] http://sqlblog.com/blogs/louis_davidson/archive/2008/07/13/triggers-evil.aspx

Troubleshooting

By Mike Walsh

Introduction: The Problem

No matter what line of work or stage in life someone is in, we have all experienced situations that required troubleshooting. We have all seen or performed Good troubleshooting. We also have probably all seen or executed "shotgun" troubleshooting. In technology that looks a bit like this:

Happy Clicking no purpose, just clicking without order

Doing the first thing your search engine tells you to do (in production, without understanding)

An air of stressed panic adding to the confusion

Throwing the toolbox at the problem trying *everything* whether or not it makes sense

If lucky, a solution you can t explain, reproduce or understand

These same missteps or analogues of them can be seen in just about any industry and across all aspects of life. Through this article, I hope to tackle the shotgun approach and lay out a pattern that can apply to SQL and really to most any issue.

A Pattern

Design patterns are used in technology to lay out a generic solution to apply to a type of problem. We can take that pattern and apply it to our specific situation with specific code. They are supposed to help cut down some design time and help give a palette of generic solutions to use.

If we can do this with some degree of success in software problems, why not do it with our soft-skill problems? At a recent user group meeting, I struck up a conversation with someone. The conversation went to me going off on a tangent about how our problems are the same as an electrical problem or the same as an ambulance call (I am a volunteer firefighter and EMT-Intermediate though I just gave up that license for more family time). If you can boil a problem down, start at the beginning and work through it methodically, you have the majority of the problem solved. The specific skills come with learning; it s your troubleshooting ability that helps you apply those skills.

To demonstrate, I want to look at a fictitious ambulance call made up from pieces of the few hundred I have been on. We will go on that ambulance call, look at the steps taken by us, the crew, and then relate it to a pattern. Hopefully we ll find corollaries to the SQL "day job" in the process. The numbers relate to the pattern described at the end..

Patient, Instance & Tomato/Tomahto

It s 2AM; you are awakened by a high pitched tone coming out of your radio. The dispatcher's voice echoes: "Respond for the chest pain patient, 62 year old male with cardiac history. He has taken nitro with no relief of pain, difficulty breathing ". In the SQL realm, this would be our pager with an alert from a user or server. **(1)**

You start running the scenarios of this patient in your head. Asking what could cause this situation, what are possible diagnoses, what can happen to the patient? You are asking what the worst and best cases are and how do you handle each. **(2)**

As you and your partner rush to the house, you talk about who is responsible for what, what equipment you will want for this call. You talk about the severity and the scenarios you thought about earlier. You formulate your game plan so when you roll up on scene you take in what you need and you know how you will operate. You discuss that it is a possible cardiac call and you are not operating at the paramedic level and you may want backup from a paramedic unit. You let dispatch know to have one stand by or start heading that way. **(3, 4, 5)**

You arrive on scene, grab the planned equipment and head in. His wife answers the door in a panic, you calmly ask her where he is, what is happening and for his medication list plus any medical information (Doctor s name, recent hospital discharge paperwork, etc). You approach the patient and ask him bluntly, Sir what is your problem today? yeah dispatch said it but you want to hear it in his words and you want to prod him for the chief complaint; he may be nauseous, dizzy, etc. but why did he call 911? What is the main problem that woke you up from your dream of query tuning? **(6)**

As you converse with the patient, your partner is quickly assessing the patient s vital signs with the equipment you brought. The wife is panicking behind you like a nervous CIO in your cube as she reminds you, Hurry up! What are you doing?! Let s get him to the hospital!! You reassure her and quickly explain you are getting the important info. **(7)** After only a matter of 1-2 minutes you have your info and have determined this is a load and go situation. Patient is going onto the stretcher and into the ambulance. **(8)**

In the ambulance you start an IV line to have it ready should he get worse or if the medics meet up with you and want to push medicine for his pain. You do a quick electrocardiogram and the printout is pointing to what your questions and partner s vital sign checks point to: heart attack. Your differential diagnosis is based on what you perceive and what your training and equipment verifies. **(9, 10)**

Your partner begins driving to the hospital when the patient screams out and stops responding to any stimuli. You look at the monitor and it shows a rhythm that won t sustain life. You verify this with a pulse check: no pulse. You ask your partner to stop and get back there with you, unresponsive patient. He radios ahead to the medics and climbs in the back. You go through the protocol for cardiac arrest as a team. Your partner beginning CPR, you preparing the defibrillator by placing the stickers you had ready onto the patient s chest. This is a rhythm that can respond to defibrillation so you prepare to do so. You ask your partner to clear the patient, verify you are both clear, verify a second time and deliver a shock of electricity through the defibrillator. After a couple rounds of CPR, defibrillation and medicine through the readied IV, the patients pulse returns. The paramedic unit arrives, a paramedic with their added tools and training jumps on board as your partner begins to drive towards the hospital again.

The rest of the ride is uneventful. You transfer care to the ED staff, document your call and prepare the truck for the next crew. **(11, 12)**

A Pattern Emerges?

Looking at the call above we see some themes emerging in each paragraph. Correlating to the numbers in the story we see:

1. Gather initial information

2. Prepare your mind

3. Work as a team

4. Plan your attack

5. **Don t be afraid of asking for help**, better for the patient and you in the long run. Don t be afraid to ask for that help to be ready early. Give assistance time to respond even if not needed in the end.

6. **Formulate a problem statement and verify it with all parties!** Far too often I have sat through meetings with confusion, frustration and no traction on an issue only to discover we weren t all on the same problem.

7. We also looked at the entire picture and didn t develop tunnel vision. In the ambulance this looks like: focus on a flashy symptom and missing the root cause or big problem. In the database world this actually looks exactly the same: looking at a symptom and missing the root cause/serious issue.

8. Remain Calm

9. Understand priority and if the issue is stable or declining

10. **Anticipate changes and plan ahead for worsening** Readying that IV on a patient who doesn t need the meds yet is like taking a backup in the initial stages of an issue. If things go good, you don t need it and it wasn't expensive to do. if you needed it you will always wish you had it. It s more challenging to start an IV on someone with no perfusion, it s practically impossible to backup a database that is completely gone.

11. **Use all of the information** Don t formulate an opinion based on opinion or feel alone. Verify your thoughts with actual information. Look at your monitoring tools, your error logs, etc.

12. **Documentation** We hate that part of ambulance calls too. It s necessary. Helps paint a picture of what went wrong. Forms a part of the patient s medical record and covers us should the patient decide to sue. Same in the DBA world: Root cause analysis, reference for the

next time and describes what we did in the heat of the moment for change control/auditing purposes.

13. **Clean up and preparation for next call** We restocked and prepared the rig for the next call. On an ambulance this is more about preparation. In the database world this step really looks more like preventing the next call

So now we can play Johnny and Roy, what about SQL?

Hopefully it s not too huge a stretch to see the pattern emerge. The order may be different in the database realm but the principles really aren t different. When a problem emerges it may be a temptation to just start trying stuff but if you can think about the above steps you should be able to work through the problem, figure it out and work on a solution and be able to reproduce that same success with future problems.

One principle I couldn't outline from the medical call is a benefit to us in SQL Server, most of the time; Non-Production systems. We couldn t give meds or CPR to a replica dev or test version of our patient. We had to rely on training and the steps to feel good about the proposed solution (which is all the CPR, Defibrillation and cardiac drugs were). In our world, we can and should try to replicate a problem in a non-production system and verify results. Not always expedient to do so but when we can, we should.

Had the course of treatment not improved the patient we could have looked at other protocols. Perhaps other drugs, different energy settings on the defibrillator, cardiac pacing, etc. could have changed the outcome. It s the same when troubleshooting an out of control server. The first thing you do, even if reasoned and methodical, may not be the solution. Don t be discouraged. Have a backup plan, understand why it may not be working and change course.

Conclusion

Had we performed some of the sorry examples of technology troubleshooting I have seen with this patient it would have looked like this: Checking the internet for chest pain, trying the first remedy that comes up (regardless of it's danger or benefit); Throwing our drug box at the patient, injecting him with every liquid in the ambulance; shocking the patient when it wasn t prescribed; running around saying oh no! This isn t good! ; crying when the patient s wife told us to hurry up; or anger towards our partner with the patient still suffering. Yes this was a critical call but we still slowed it down, stepped back and applied a methodology. The extra 1-2 minutes in methodical approaches made the difference. Having that time back with a worse outcome seems silly.

Rushing through a critical situation will only make it worse in the end. Take the extra time to understand the problem and understand your solution path, even with the CIO pacing the cube.

SQL Server 2005 Paging the Holy Grail

By Robert Cary

Introduction

The paging and ranking functions introduced in 2005 are old news by now, but the typical ROW_NUMBER OVER() implementation only solves part of the problem.

Nearly every application that uses paging gives some indication of how many pages (or total records) are in the total result set. The challenge is to query the total number of rows, and return only the desired records with a minimum of overhead? The holy grail solution would allow you to return one page of the results and the total number of rows with *no* additional I/O overhead.

In this article, we're going to explore four approaches to this problem and discuss their relative strengths and weaknesses. For the purposes of comparison, we'll be using I/O as a relative benchmark.

The 'two-bites' approach

The most basic approach is the 'two-bites' approach. In this approach you, effectively, run your query twice; querying the total rows in one pass, and querying your result set in the second. The code is pretty straightforward:

```
DECLARE @startRow INT ; SET @startrow = 50
SELECTCOUNT(*) AS TotRows
FROM [INFORMATION_SCHEMA].columns

;WITH cols
AS
(
SELECT table_name, column_name,
ROW_NUMBER() OVER(ORDER BY table_name, column_name) AS seq
FROM [INFORMATION_SCHEMA].columns
)
SELECT table_name, column_name
FROM cols
WHERE seq BETWEEN @startRow AND @startRow + 49
ORDERBY seq
```

It gives the desired results, but this approach doubles the cost of the query because you query your underlying tables twice:

```
(1 row(s) affected)
Table 'Worktable'. Scan count 0, logical reads 0, physical
reads 0, read-ahead reads 0, lob logical reads 0, lob physical
reads 0, lob read-ahead reads 0.
Table 'syscolpars'. Scan count 1, logical reads 46, physical
reads 0, read-ahead reads 0, lob logical reads 0, lob physical
reads 0, lob read-ahead reads 0.
Table 'sysschobjs'. Scan count 1, logical reads 34, physical
reads 0, read-ahead reads 0, lob logical reads 0, lob physical
reads 0, lob read-ahead reads 0.
```

```
(50 row(s) affected)
Table 'Worktable'. Scan count 0, logical reads 0, physical
reads 0, read-ahead reads 0, lob logical reads 0, lob physical
reads 0, lob read-ahead reads 0.
Table 'syscolpars'. Scan count 1, logical reads 46, physical
reads 0, read-ahead reads 0, lob logical reads 0, lob physical
reads 0, lob read-ahead reads 0.
Table 'sysschobjs'. Scan count 1, logical reads 34, physical
reads 0, read-ahead reads 0, lob logical reads 0, lob physical
reads 0, lob read-ahead reads 0. 34, physical reads 0, read-
ahead reads 0, lob logical reads 0, lob physical reads 0, lob
read-ahead reads 0.
```

The temp table approach

The 'two-bites' approach is especially undesirable if your paged query is very expensive and complex. A common workaround is to write the superset into a temporary table, then query out the subset. This is also the most common way to implement paging pre-2005 (in this case, ROW_NUMBER is superfluous).

```
DECLARE @startRow INT ; SET @startrow = 50
CREATETABLE #pgeResults(
id INT IDENTITY(1,1) PRIMARY KEY CLUSTERED,
table_name VARCHAR(255),
column_name VARCHAR(255)
)
INSERTINTO #pgeResults(Table_name, column_name)
SELECT table_name, column_name
FROM [INFORMATION_SCHEMA].columns
ORDERBY [table_name], [column_name]
```

```
SELECT@@ROWCOUNT AS TotRows
SELECT  Table_Name, Column_Name
FROM #pgeResults
WHERE  id between @startrow and @startrow + 49
ORDERBY id

DROPTABLE #pgeResults
```

Looking at the query plan, you can see that your underlying tables are queried only once but the I/O stats show us that you take an even bigger hit populating the temporary table.

```
Table '#pgeResults
                                        000000001A9F'. Scan
count 0, logical reads 5599, physical reads 0, read-ahead reads
0, lob logical reads 0, lob physical reads 0, lob read-ahead
reads 0.
Table 'Worktable'. Scan count 0, logical reads 0, physical
reads 0, read-ahead reads 0, lob logical reads 0, lob physical
reads 0, lob read-ahead reads 0.
Table 'syscolpars'. Scan count 1, logical reads 46, physical
reads 0, read-ahead reads 14, lob logical reads 0, lob physical
reads 0, lob read-ahead reads 0.
Table 'sysschobjs'. Scan count 1, logical reads 34, physical
reads 0, read-ahead reads 39, lob logical reads 0, lob physical
reads 0, lob read-ahead reads 0.
(2762 row(s) affected)

(1 row(s) affected)

(50 row(s) affected)
Table
'#pgeResults
                                        000000001
A9F'. Scan count 1, logical reads 3, physical reads 0, read-
ahead reads 0, lob logical reads 0, lob physical reads 0, lob
read-ahead reads 0.
```

In this case, it would be better to query the tables twice. Maybe some new 2005 functionality can yield a better solution.

The COUNT(*) OVER() Approach

OVER() can also be used with Aggregate Window Functions. For our purposes this means we can do a COUNT(*) without the need for a GROUP BY clause, returning the total count in our result set. The code definitely looks much cleaner and, if your application permits it, you can simply return one dataset (eliminating the overhead of writing to a temp table).

```
DECLARE @startRow INT ; SET @startrow = 50


;WITH cols
AS
(
SELECT table_name, column_name,
ROW_NUMBER() OVER(ORDER BY table_name, column_name) AS seq,
COUNT(*) OVER() AS totrows
FROM [INFORMATION_SCHEMA].columns
)
SELECT table_name, column_name, totrows
FROM cols
WHERE seq BETWEEN @startRow AND @startRow + 49
ORDERBY seq
```

Unfortunately this approach has it's own hidden overhead:

```
Table 'Worktable'. Scan count 3, logical reads 5724, physical
reads 0, read-ahead reads 0, lob logical reads 0, lob physical
reads 0, lob read-ahead reads 0.
Table 'syscolpars'. Scan count 1, logical reads 46, physical
reads 0, read-ahead reads 0, lob logical reads 0, lob physical
reads 0, lob read-ahead reads 0.
Table 'sysschobjs'. Scan count 1, logical reads 34, physical
reads 0, read-ahead reads 0, lob logical reads 0, lob physical
reads 0, lob read-ahead reads 0.
```

Where did that come from? In this case, SQL Server implements the COUNT(*) OVER() by dumping all the data into a hidden spool table, which it then aggregates and joins back to your main output. It does this to avoid re scanning the underlying tables. Although this approach looks the cleanest, it introduces the most overhead.

I've spent most of today cleaning up and old data-paging proc that is both very inefficient and frequently called enough for me to notice it. I've explored probably a dozen other approaches to solving this problem before I came up with the solution below. For the sake of brevity and because they rest are pretty obscure and equally inefficient we'll now skip to the best solution.

The Holy Grail

In theory, ROW_NUMBER() gives you all the information you need because it assigns a sequential number to every single row in your result set. It all falls down, of course, when you only return a subset of your results that don't include the highest sequential number. The solution is to return a 2nd column of sequential numbers, in the reverse order. The total number of the records will always be the sum of the two fields on any given row minus 1 (unless one of your sequences is zero-bound).

```
DECLARE @startRow INT ; SET @startrow = 50
;WITH cols
AS
(
SELECT table_name, column_name,
ROW_NUMBER() OVER(ORDER BY table_name, column_name) AS seq,
ROW_NUMBER() OVER(ORDER BY table_name DESC, column_name desc)
AS totrows
FROM [INFORMATION_SCHEMA].columns
)
SELECT table_name, column_name, totrows + seq -1 as TotRows
FROM cols
WHERE seq BETWEEN @startRow AND @startRow + 49
ORDERBY seq
```

This approach gives us our page of data and the total number of rows with *zero additional overhead!* (well, maybe one or two ms of CPU time, but that's it) The I/O statistics are identical to querying just the subset of records.

```
Table 'Worktable'. Scan count 0, logical reads 0, physical
reads 0, read-ahead reads 0, lob logical reads 0, lob physical
reads 0, lob read-ahead reads 0.
Table 'syscolpars'. Scan count 1, logical reads 46, physical
reads 0, read-ahead reads 0, lob logical reads 0, lob physical
reads 0, lob read-ahead reads 0.
Table 'sysschobjs'. Scan count 1, logical reads 34, physical
reads 0, read-ahead reads 0, lob logical reads 0, lob physical
reads 0, lob read-ahead reads 0.
```

Compare the stats above with the stats and query below (just returning one page of data).

```
;WITH cols
AS
(
SELECT table_name, column_name,
```

```
ROW_NUMBER() OVER(ORDER BY table_name, column_name) AS seq
FROM [INFORMATION_SCHEMA].columns
)
SELECT table_name, column_name
FROM cols
WHERE seq BETWEEN @startRow AND @startRow + 49
ORDERBY seq
```

Table 'Worktable'. Scan count 0, logical reads 0, physical reads 0, read-ahead reads 0, lob logical reads 0, lob physical reads 0, lob read-ahead reads 0.
Table 'syscolpars'. Scan count 1, logical reads 46, physical reads 0, read-ahead reads 0, lob logical reads 0, lob physical reads 0, lob read-ahead reads 0.
Table 'sysschobjs'. Scan count 1, logical reads 34, physical reads 0, read-ahead reads 0, lob logical reads 0, lob physical reads 0, lob read-ahead reads 0.

Conclusion

I have found this approach to be best suited for smaller resultsets from complex queries where I/O is the primary bottleneck. Jeff Moden, Peso and others here have pointed out that with larger resultsets, the I/O cost you save is more than outweighed by the CPU cost. You definitely want to compare different approches to find the best solution for your problem.

My real goal here was to try and figure out a way to avoid unnecessary I/O overhead. I am sure that this solution is not the last word on the subject and I greatly look forward to hearing your thoughts, experiences and ideas on this topic. Thank you all for reading and for your feedback.

Hierarchies in SQL

By Gus "GSquared" Gwynne

Department management hierarchies. Bills of materials. Sales regions and offices. Data access levels. All of these and more are things that require storing hierarchical data in a database.

First, any mention of this subject needs to carry with it a mention of Joe Celko and his work on "nested sets" hierarchies. He has an excellent article on the subject at ***http://www.intelligententerprise.com/001020/celko.jhtml***.

He s completely correct that nested sets hierarchies are fast to query. The problem is, they are complex to add to or update. For relatively static hierarchies, like most bills of materials, use his method. Some organization charts or chains of command can be done that way as well.

The other general method of doing hierarchies in relational databases is the adjacency model, in which each row has the potential to have a parent in the same table. This might be built as:

```
create table dbo.Hierarchy (
  ID int identity primary key,
  ParentID int null  references dbo.Hierarchy(ID),
  Name varchar(100));
```

That s a very simple example, but it illustrates the main point, with an ID and ParentID. This can be given a natural key, and the Parent column would need to be the same data type, but the structure would still be essentially the same.

This can easily be modified to allow a single level to have more than one parent as well as more than one child. (The structure above allows multiple children, but only one parent.) I found that particularly useful when I was working for a marketing company, and many of the people we marketed for had affiliations with multiple companies. In these cases, when a customer placed an order, different sets of people would have access to that order data, and the results of the marketing campaign, depending on how each order was placed, but the individual customer needed access to all of his campaigns in one place. That kind of multi-level access is traditionally handled by hierarchies of data access, but in this case, it needed to allow multiple parents.

I accomplished this with a structure like the below:

```
create table dbo.HierarchyNodes (
NodeID int identity primary key,
 Name varchar(100));
go
 create table dbo.HierarchyRelations (
NodeID int not
nullreferences dbo.HierarchyNodes (NodeID),
ParentID int not nullreferences dbo.HierarchyNodes (NodeID),
 constraintPK_HierarchyRelations primary key (NodeID,
ParentID),
 constraint CK_NodeNotParent check (NodeID != ParentID));
```

I had to add moderately complex triggers to this to make sure no hierarchy was
created where a level was its own parent or child, regardless of how many
levels apart, but they performed quite well on such a simple structure.

Common Table Expressions in SQL 2005/8 make it much easier to resolve
such a hierarchy, whether it s a one-parent-per child or a many-parent-per-child
model.

Books Online has a great example on how to build these and how they work.
Here s one for the simple hierarchy.

```
;withHierarchyCTE (NID, PID)as
         (select NodeID, ParentID
         from dbo.Hierarchy
         where NodeID = @NodeID_in
         union all
         select NodeID, ParentID
         from dbo.Hierarchy
         innerjoin HierarchyCTE
               on NID = ParentID)
 select *
 from HierarchyCTE
```

This assumes an input parameter of @NodeID_in, and will find all children of
that level of the hierarchy. (I m using the term "node" for each level of the
hierarchy, since that s how they are often referenced in tree-views and such in
applications. I hope that doesn t confuse anyone.)

The CTE can be reversed, and run up the hierarchy, simply by changing the
relationship in the second part of it, to PID = NodeID, from NID = ParentID.

Two such CTEs, one up, one down, can be hooked together into a single view of the whole structure above and below a level.

An interesting modification can be made to the CTE to add the level of relationship, by adding a Level column to it.

```
;withHierarchyCTE (NID, PID, Lvl) as
       (select NodeID, ParentID, 0
       from dbo.Hierarchy
       where NodeID = @NodeID_in
       union all
       select NodeID, ParentID, Lvl + 1
       from dbo.Hierarchy
       innerjoin HierarchyCTE
             on PID = NodeID)
select *
from HierarchyCTE
```

This will give a number that increments by one for each level away from the root ID (the one that matches the input parameter), which can be used in Order By clauses and such. For an upwards CTE, I d change the increment to -1 from +1.

The disadvantage of these hierarchies, using the adjacency model (ID and ParentID), is that they take longer to query than nested sets hierarchies. The advantage is that they are very, very fast to add to or update. They are a little more complex to delete from in some ways, potentially simpler in others.

If you want to add a level in an adjacency hierarchy, you just insert it and give it the right parent ID, or no parent at all (for a top-level node). If you need to move a whole branch of the hierarchy, you just change the parent ID at the right point. It s quite simple.

Say, for example, your company has a Proofreading Department, and in a re-organization it is being moved from the Marketing Division to the Quality Control Division. In a nested sets hierarchy, you have to rebuild the whole department, with new ranges for every row. In an adjacency hierarchy, you change the parent ID for the department row in the table, and you re done.

To illustrate this a bit more, here s an example of a nested sets hierarchy table:

```
create table dbo.HierarchySets (
 RangeStart int not null,
 RangeEnd int not null,
```

```
constraintPK_HierarchySets primary key (RangeStart, RangeEnd),
constraintCK_RangeValid check (RangeStart < RangeEnd),
Name varchar(100));
```

For the whole company, you might have a RangeStart of 0 and a RangeEnd of 1-million. For the Marketing Division (to use the example I mentioned above), you might have a RangeStart of 1000 and a RangeEnd of 2000. Proofreading could start at 1600 and end at 1650, and there might be ten or twenty rows in the table with ranges inside that. (The whole idea is that the parent has a wider range than the child, thus, because Marketing starts its range below that of Proofreading and ends its range above, it is the parent of Proofreading.) If Quality Control is 2001 to 2100, then Proofreading has to have it s Start and End changed to some range inside the Quality Control range, and each level inside of Proofreading also has to be changed. If Quality Control doesn t have enough free space in its range to fit all the ranges for Proofreading, then it also has to be moved.

That makes moves in such a model much more difficult. They can still be done, but it involves much more IO and many more transactions, and has to be wrapped in a much larger overall transaction so any error can cause the whole thing to roll back. That means longer locks on larger parts of the table. Given enough rows being moved, it may even result in a relatively long lock on the whole table, blocking other transactions and reads.

To make up for that, selecting from an adjacency involves a number of reads at least equal to the number of levels in the hierarchy being queried, and more often closer to the number of rows being queried, which can be quite IO intensive on complex, large hierarchies, but selecting from a nested sets table requires a single-pass, single read, usually of a small range straight from the primary key.

The speed difference and IO difference can be significant on the two. For example, I have a hierarchy in one of my databases with 2,700 nodes in it, going up to six levels deep. If someone at the top of that hierarchy signs in, it takes 11 seconds for my server to resolve the whole hierarchy and determine what data that person has access to (this is a security access hierarchy that controls much of what is displayed to customers on a web site). That s using the adjacency model. Using a nested sets table, that same hierarchy takes less than 1 millisecond. (This isn t the one with multiple parents. Different company.)

If this same database didn t have a lot of updates to the hierarchies, I d definitely use a straight-up nested sets hierarchy, and have much faster web pages. But it does have a lot of updates, sometimes several per minute, sometimes several at the same time. Each nested sets rebuild takes about 20-30 seconds to finish, and locks the table pretty aggressively while it s running.

So, I came up with what I m calling a hybrid hierarchy. The table looks something like this:

```
create table dbo.HierarchyHybrid (
ID int identity primary key,
ParentID int null references dbo.HierarchyHybrid(ID),
TopParentID int null references dbo.HierarchyHybrid(ID),
RangeStart int null,
RangeEnd int null,
TempRangeStart int null,
TempRangeEnd int null,
 constraintCK_RangeValid check (RangeStart < RangeEnd),
 Name varchar(100));
```

When a row is inserted, it has an ID and (if not a top level) a ParentID, but no Range data. When a row with Range data is updated (ParentID or TopParentID changed), the RangeStart and RangeEnd columns are set to null.

Additionally, I have the insert statement figure out what the top level of the new row would be. If the row has no parent, it puts in its own ID as the TopParentID, otherwise, it resolves what level above it has a null ParentID, regardless of how many levels that is removed from it, and puts that in there. With the right indexes on TopParentID, I ve sped up the resolution of adjacency queries by up to 80%, since the recursive portion of the CTE can reference that column and greatly narrow down the number of rows it has to scan to resolve the query. (Your mileage may vary. Some queries are sped up a lot, some barely at all.)

Then, every few minutes, I have a job that looks to see if any rows exist where RangeStart is null. If it finds any, it goes through the hierarchy and set the values in TempRangeStart and TempRangeEnd. Once those are all set, it updates RangeStart and RangeEnd. That way, I don t have partial sets and all of it gets done at once, which has resulted in better average performance.

When a hierarchy needs to be resolved, the code checks if any levels exist in that hierarchy that have null RangeStart (using the TopParentID), and uses the adjacency method of resolution if it finds any. If not, it uses the nested sets method. The code for that looks something like this:

```
create function [dbo].[udf_Hierarchy]
 (@NodeID_in int)
 returns table
 as
 return
        (with
        TopSet (SS, SE) as -- Get the range for the requested
node
                (select RangeStart, RangeEnd
                from dbo.HierarchyHybrid
                where ID = @NodeID_in),
        Sets (RangeStart, RangeEnd, NodeID) as-- Nested Sets
Query
                (select RangeStart, RangeEnd, ID
                from dbo.HierarchyHybrid
                innerjoin TopSet
                        on RangeStart between ss and se
                        and RangeEnd between ss and se),
        Adjacency (NodeID, ParentID) as -- Adjacency Query
                (select 0, ID, ParentID
                from dbo.HierarchyHybrid
                where ID = @NodeID_in
                andexists
                        (select*
                        from dbo.HierarchyHybrid h2
                        where h2.TopParentID =
HierarchyHybrid.TopParentID
                        and RangeStart is null)
                union all
                select h3.ID, h3.ParentID
                from dbo.HierarchyHybrid h3
                innerjoin Adjacency
                        on h3.ParentID = Adjacency.NodeID)
        select NodeID
        from Sets
        union
        select NodeID
        from Adjacency);
```

Using this method, I get a compromise. It takes a little longer to resolve a hierarchy than a pure nested sets method, up to about 8 milliseconds on some of the bigger ones, but updates and moves are fast, and can show on the web page immediately.

After any changes, a hierarchy takes a few seconds to resolve until the range data on it gets rebuilt, of course, but customers and users have been okay with that. It s not usual for any given customer to change their hierarchy more than a couple of times per week, and changing one hierarchy doesn t negatively impact any other hierarchy.

I don t know if this will be of use to anyone else, but for the situation I have, it s been very, very valuable, so I thought I d share it. Without Joe Celko s work on nested sets, this would never have been built, so do read the article I linked to at the beginning. I'm definitely grateful to him for his work.

ROW_NUMBER(): An Efficient Alternative to Subqueries

By Francis Rodrigues

Introduction

SQL Server 2005 offers an array of ranking and windowing functions that can be used to evaluate the data and only return appropriate rows. For instance, a development cycle of a product may include hundreds of releases, and those releases may have versions associated with them: a "0" version with its many minor versions, a "1" version with its minor versions, etc. If the history of a particular product's releases is kept, then analysis can be done to see how far a version is developed before it is released. An ORDER BY clause alone cannot fulfill this need because the query would most likely still return the entire history of the product, not necessarily the last release of every version. The code is also available for download. The name of the file is *RowCountScenario1-CodeDownload.sql*.

Scenario 1 Versioning

In order to demonstrate the usage of the ROW_NUMBER() windowing function, I started with Microsoft's AdventureWorks database. In particular, I used the data in the Production.ProductCostHistory table. The products in this table are identified by the ProductID column; this is a foreign key to the Production.Product table. Using the Production.ProductCostHistory table, I mocked up some data to create versions for each Product in the table. I used a random number generation process to create attributes called Version, MinorVersion and ReleaseVersion for each product. These attributes are meant to show detailed information about the product. Together 7.0.59 represents that the 7th version of the product is currently being used, a minor version represents the iteration of the version, and the release version of this particular installation is 59. The next iteration of the product's life cycle could result with 7.2.19. I also used the existing StandardCost to create different costs for each of the Versions, to create some sense of value for the particular Version.

I created a table called Production.ProductVersion with the ProductID, Version, MinorVersion and ReleaseVersion defined as the primary key and the

StandardCost as an attribute. I inserted the mocked up data generated by the code into this table to model a simple product version/cost history.

```
CREATE TABLE Production.ProductVersion
(
        ProductID int NOT NULL,
        Version int NOT NULL,
        MinorVersion int NOT NULL,
        ReleaseVersion int NOT NULL,
        StandardCost numeric(30, 4) NOT NULL,
        CONSTRAINT PK_ProductVersion PRIMARY KEY CLUSTERED
        (
            ProductID ASC,
            Version ASC,
            MinorVersion ASC,
            ReleaseVersion ASC
        )
);
```

I used the following code to populate the table with randomized data. I created the data using a common table expression (CTE) and inserted the data into the table after it was generated.The data is based on the Production.ProductCostHistory table.

A sample of the code can be found on SQLServerCentral.com.

The ABS(CHECKSUM(NEWID())) is utilized as the random number generator; the modulus operator provides the upper bound for the random number that was generated. The NEWID() function is guaranteed to generate a globally unique identifier for each row. The GROUP BY clause is used to avoid any Primary Key constraint violations that might be encountered.

The purpose of this exercise is to avoid the complexity of certain code by using the ROW_NUMBER() windowing function. Suppose you are required to return only the latest version of a Product with its associated MinorVersion, ReleaseVersion and StandardCost. The following query will not return the correct result set.

```
SELECT
    ProductID,
    MAX(Version) AS Version,
    MAX(MinorVersion) AS MinorVersion,
    MAX(ReleaseVersion) AS ReleaseVersion,
    MAX(StandardCost) AS StandardCost
FROM Production.ProductVersion WITH (NOLOCK)
GROUP BY ProductID;
```

In fact, this query violates integrity of the rows of data in the table. It simply returns the maximum Version, the maximum MinorVersion, the maximum ReleaseVersion and the maximum StandardCost of a particular Product. This is an easy and tempting trap to fall into. Compare the results displayed in Figure 2 and Figure 3. The actual data that is in Production.ProductVersion is in Figure 1.

The following sample query captures the actual requirements, and returns the correct result, but it is long and convoluted.

This query utilizes nested subqueries in order to ensure the integrity of each row. The first subquery (lines 117-25 in the code download) provides the maximum Version for each Product. The second subquery provides the maximum MinorVersion for the maximum Version of each Product. The subsubquery in the WHERE clause ensures that the MinorVersions and the Versions match. The third subquery,

```
SELECT MAX(ReleaseVersion)
FROM Production.ProductVersion pv4 WITH (NOLOCK)
WHERE pv4.ProductID = pv.ProductID
    AND pv4.Version = (
                        SELECT MAX(Version)
                        FROM Production.ProductVersion pv2 WITH
(NOLOCK)
                        WHERE pv2.ProductID = pv.ProductID
                        )
    AND pv4.MinorVersion = (
                        SELECT MAX(MinorVersion)
                        FROM Production.ProductVersion pv3
WITH (NOLOCK)
                        WHERE pv3.ProductID = pv.ProductID
                            AND pv3.Version = (
                                                SELECT
MAX(Version)
                                                FROM
Production.ProductVersion pv2 WITH (NOLOCK)
                                                WHERE
pv2.ProductID = pv.ProductID
                                                )
                        )
```

(lines 127-46 in the code download) provides the maximum ReleaseVersion for the maximum MinorVersion of the maximum Version of each Product. Once again the subqueries ensure that only complete rows of data are retrieved. If this logic sounds too complicated, that is simply because it is. The estimated subtree cost for this query turns out to be 0.583005. This includes several

Clustered Index Scan and Seek operations. The query plan is displayed in Figure 6. The complexity of the subquery approach can increase if the requirements change.

A simplified approach uses the ROW_NUMBER() function as shown below.

```
WITH RowExample1
AS
(
    SELECT ROW_NUMBER() OVER(PARTITION BY ProductID
                        ORDER BY ProductID,
                            Version DESC,
                            MinorVersion DESC,
                            ReleaseVersion DESC
        ) AS MaxVersion,
        ProductID,
        Version,
        MinorVersion,
        ReleaseVersion,
        StandardCost
    FROM Production.ProductVersion pv WITH (NOLOCK)
)
SELECT ProductID,
    Version,
    MinorVersion,
    ReleaseVersion,
    StandardCost
FROM RowExample1
WHERE MaxVersion = 1
ORDER BY ProductID;
```

The result set for this query looks like the Figure 3.

	ProductID	Version	MinorVersion	ReleaseVersion	StandardCost
1	707	1	73	6471	12.0278
2	707	1	283	9532	13.2306
3	707	1	400	11360	13.0863
4	707	1	781	14611	13.8782
5	707	1	394	3280	15.2660
6	707	2	249	1338	14.3949
7	707	3	927	8422	29.1442
8	707	4	125	982	27.4812
9	707	4	570	10102	25.2584

Figure 1: Sample from Production.ProductVersion

	ProductID	Version	MinorVersion	ReleaseVersion	StandardCost
1	707	4	994	14611	29.1442
2	708	2	942	16616	29.1442

Figure 2: Sample from incorrect query

	ProductID	Version	MinorVersion	ReleaseVersion	StandardCost
1	707	4	570	10102	25.2584
2	708	2	802	11767	14.3949

Figure 3: Sample from properly implemented query

The PARTITION BY clause allows a set of row numbers to be assigned for all distinct Products. When a new ProductID is encountered, the row numbering will start over at 1 and continue incrementing for each row with the same ProductID. The row number will be assigned according to the sort order of the columns that you specify in the OVER clause's ORDER BY clause. The estimated subtree cost for this improved query is 0.039954. This query has only one Clustered Index Scan operation. The query plan is displayed in Figure 7.

With the OVER clause, the ROW_NUMBER() function can efficiently assign a row number to each row in a query. The fact that I've ordered the partitions by ProductID and then in descending order by Version, MinorVersion, and ReleaseVersion, guarantees the maximum version will be in the first row of each ProductID partition. This allows me to use a simple WHERE MaxVersion = 1 predicate in place of the convoluted sub-query logic in the previous sample query.

To test the effects of indexing on difference between the two methods, I used the following table.

```
CREATE TABLE Production.ProductVersion2
(
    ProductID int NOT NULL,
    Version int NOT NULL,
    MinorVersion int NOT NULL,
    ReleaseVersion int NOT NULL,
    StandardCost numeric(30, 4) NOT NULL,
);
```

I used the following query to generate a large set of randomized data to compare the estimated query costs for different record size sets.

The sample of the code can be found on SQLServerCentral.com.

The following charts show the estimated query costs for different row sizes. I chose to start at 1,000 because there are 286 distinct ProductIDs, starting at 100 would have eliminated too many rows.

The following figure shows the estimated query costs for the Production.ProductVersion. The subquery implementation actually took less than 1 second to complete where as the ROW_NUMBER() implementation took about 2 seconds to complete for 1,000,000 rows.

Row Size	Subquery Implementation Cost	ROW_NUMBER() Implementation Cost
1000	0.0652462	0.0355736
10000	0.238573	0.673282
100000	2.2258	5.97198
1000000	14.3881	83.7228

Figure 4: Indexed estimated query costs

The following figure shows the estimated query costs for the Production.ProductVersion2. The subquery implementation took 43 seconds to complete where as the ROW_NUMBER() implementation took 5 seconds to complete for 1,000,000 rows.

Row Size	Subquery Implementation Cost	ROW_NUMBER() Implementation Cost
1000	0.0355736	0.225896
10000	1.6397	0.673282
100000	44.1332	5.97202
1000000	448.47	83.7229

Figure 5: Non-indexed estimated query costs

These results may differ according to the hardware used to run the queries. A quick look at the ROW_NUMBER() implementation column shows that indexing does not significantly impact this implementation's query cost where as it is very important to the subquery implementation's query cost.

Scenario 1 Change in Requirements

Suppose the requirement changes and you need to grab the maximum MinorVersions for every (ProductID, Version) combination. Changing the subquery implementation has a large overhead, namely breaking down the logic. The subquery approach looks like this with the new set of requirements:

The sample of the code can be found on SQLServerCentral.com.

The new requirements actually eliminate some of the nested subqueries. The estimated query cost, however, does not change significantly for Production.ProductVersion.

This new change requires only a small modification to the ROW_NUMBER() implementation. This is what the ROW_NUMBER() implementation looks like for the new set of requirements:

The sample of the code can be found on SQLServerCentral.com.

In this example, the row numbers are partitioned according to both ProductID and Version. The WHERE clause is still valid here because the maximum MinorVersion for each (ProductID, Version) combination is guaranteed to be the first row. The estimated query cost did not change greatly for the modified code. The readability, manageability and the efficiency of the function make it a better choice than the subquery approach.

Estimated Query Plans

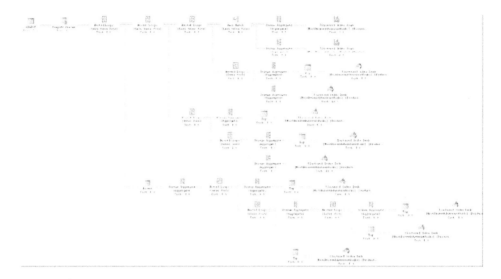

Figure 6: Subquery approach

Figure 7: ROW_NUMBER() approach

Conclusion

These examples show the critical role of indexing in the subquery approach. The ROW_NUMBER() implementation is far more readable and therefore easier to maintain. It also remains relatively independent of indexing even for large amounts of data. Since the function takes advantage of the SQL Server's ability to sort records, most queries that need to uphold a level of sequencing should at the very least explore its implementation. The sorting itself can greatly reduce or replace all together the extra logic necessary to enforce the integrity of data at the row level. The readability of the function's implementation also plays a key role in its manageability. Modifying the code with the ROW_NUMBER() implementation is easy because the logic is performed in easy to spot areas and is performed once, whereas in the subquery the logic appears in several places and could be repeated.

There Must Be 15 Ways to Lose Your Cursors... part 1, Introduction

By R.BarryYoung

A long, long time ago, it was not possible to do everything in the SQL language that a database developer or a DBA might need to do with just set-based SQL. And thus was born the Cursor. The bastard love-child of the declarative relational database language SQL and her first wild fling with a much more experienced and confident procedural programming language (whose identity is still unknown), the Cursor arrived in the early 80's amid promises and predictions to fix all manner of ills in the house of SQL. And at first, that's how it appeared. Anything that set-based SQL couldn't do on her own, her erstwhile son would step right in and handle for her. In fact he handled so many things for her, that she became convinced that she could not get by without him.

But then she began to notice some things that disturbed her. For one thing, he was just a little bit slow and a whole lot lazy. He never hurried anywhere; he always moved just one step, then another. Plus, he didn't seem capable of doing more than one thing at a time. Then there was the way that he did his work. He didn't just do it, he would lay down tarps, drop cloths, tools and toolboxes everywhere, until the whole room (and then some) was practically unusable. And this condition would persist far longer than it should because he was so slow in his work.

Which was ironic because he ultimately only ever did one thing: apply duct tape. No matter what the task, chore or repair was, he would just duct tape over it. Instead of replacing broken windows, he would duct tape them back together. When the siding needed repair, he duct taped it. Leaky pipes? Duct tape was the answer. Lost shingles? More duct tape.

"My way is cheaper" he would say when she asked him about it. "Why invest all of that time and money in new windows, pipes or shingles when with a little duct tape, we can be done now?" And because she didn't know about these things, she had to accept his word on it. But she had her doubts. First, his repairs didn't seem to work very well. The pipes still leaked some, as did the windows which she could hardly see out of. Secondly, she suspected that these cheap repairs and constructions were actually costing her more in utility bills and damage to things around them than they were saving.

And then there was the appearance. The once beautiful house of SQL, conceived, designed and built to widespread acclaim and admiration, was now a shocking eyesore. With its obscured windows, sagging fences, and omnipresent patchwork of duct tape, it looked not so much like a home as it did a duct tape shelter with bits and pieces of a real house randomly attached.

However, over the years she had been steadily learning how to do these things herself and now, not only did she realize that she did not need him anymore, she also knew for sure that there were better ways to do these tasks. In fact, the best thing for her would be to redo every single thing that he had done. But how to do it? He still insisted on doing all of the repairs himself. And after almost thirty years he was still living in her basement and showed no sign of either getting a job or moving out. "Well," she thought to herself, "there are ways of getting rid of uncooperative children..."

This series of articles intends to show you not only how to get rid of the Cursors that you may currently have, but also how to avoid ever having to use them in the first place. Up through SQL Server 2000, I would have agreed with most people that there were some things that Cursors were necessary for but, with the release of SQL Server 2005, all of those reasons have disappeared in the face of the new features and capabilities that it provides. Specifically, the new features that have enabled this elimination are:

- Large Strings(VARCHAR(MAX), etc)
- Windowed Aggregate Functions (especially ROW_NUMBER())
- FOR XML PATH

As we progress in this series, we will see how these three additions have greatly extended the reach of set-based SQL.

And although I have only mentioned Cursors so far, the same applies equally to WHILE loops as well. What I will be showing you in this series of articles is how to use the new and old features of Transact-SQL to both create and convert SQL routines that are faster, smaller, cleaner, clearer and more supportable without the use of Cursors or While loops.

What's Wrong With Cursors Anyway?

First, they are slow and resource intensive. Many of them will create a table in tempdb and copy the entire dataset into it, which can cause resource problems.

Those that do not are frequently forced to use single-record retrieval methods that can be much slower. In either event, the Cursor is forced to process the returned rows one at a time, which means a WHILE loop and that adds its own performance problems (the repeated execution overhead of multiple statements for each row). Additionally, there is locking overhead to maintaining this single record state in a database that may also have contending DML statements going on at the same time.

Secondly, they can slow other processes down as well. Using more resources (CPU, memory, tempdb, etc.) means that less is available for other uses, and using them for a longer time also means that they are unavailable to others for a longer time. Still, further, the additional locking that Cursors employ can result in blocking other processes too.

Thirdly, Cursors and While loops are blatantly procedural code in SQL, a language that was designed from the start to be a declarative language. What's the difference? Procedural languages, the more traditional approach to programming, as seen in VB, C#, Java, etc., consists of writing code in the form of procedures. That is, an ordered series of steps that individually tell the computer what to do and collectively tell it how to do it. Declarative languages, on the other hand, simply describe the results that are to be returned, leaving the optimizers the freedom to determine how best to do it.

For instance, consider the question that a cook might ask "What food should I make?" The procedural answer might be:

Get butter and sugar

Cream them together

Add vanilla and eggs

Stir

Add flour, salt and baking powder

Etc., etc. ...

On the other hand, the declarative answer would be:

Cookies, with chocolate chips

Implemented correctly, declarative code is generally much more concise than procedural code. Obviously, you don't want to use procedural answers where a declarative one will do.

Fourthly, SQL routines with Cursors and loops are, in general, harder to read, harder to understand, and harder to maintain and support. Is this just personal preference on my part? That's a valid question, but I think that the answer is no. First, look at our abstract examples above. You may notice something interesting about the procedural example; it never tells us that it is making chocolate chip cookies. That's because procedural code tells us how to do something, but not what it is that we are doing. For this reason alone, declarative code tends to be easier to read and understand. Now this single example may not be convincing, especially since it does not involve actual code of either kind, however, we will have many opportunities in this series to directly compare functionally identical procedural SQL with declarative SQL that I think will demonstrate this beyond any reasonable doubt.

Finally, you do not need them. Seriously. Let me say that again so that there is no uncertainty: As of SQL Server 2005, the only reason to use Cursors is if you actually want to slow down your code (for instance to do a big update in chunks). Otherwise there is just no reason that I can see to use them, and many reasons not to.

Why Do People Still Use Cursors?

Whenever I start to talk about the problems with cursors there are two questions that always come up. The first is "If Cursors are so bad, then why do they exist?" The answer to that question is historical, which I believe I have covered adequately above.

The second question is "If Cursors as so bad, then why do people keep using them?" That's an excellent question because no matter how often I tell SQL developers who I am training not to use Cursors they invariably do, and then end up calling me desperately to fix the problems they have caused. In fact this tendency is in my experience so powerful that it seems like an irresistible force. In short, Cursors and While loops attract developers the way that a black hole attracts matter. The cause of this is, I believe, due to a combination of reasons.

First, I believe that many SQL practitioners simply do not realize the problems with cursors or may even come from an environment like Oracle where they perform somewhat better. One of the goals of this series is to remedy that through information and education.

Secondly, I think that all developers and, indeed, almost everyone in the computer field is familiar with procedural thinking and by implication procedural programming. This is much less so for declarative programming. Even if we haven't been trained as a programmer, our job and career environment are saturated with procedural thinking and procedural perspectives. This collective procedural ambiance leads us to see procedural programming as a natural and straight-forward thing.

If you want some confirmation of this all you have to do is to look on the some of the technical support forums. It's amazing to me how many posters seeking help can only answer the question "What are you trying to do?" with a series of steps instead of an actual description of the results that they want. They have become stuck in a procedural mindset where everything can be truly described only by using an ordered series of imperative instructions. In this mindset, end-state descriptions (declarations or descriptions of desired results) are seen as inherently incomplete because they do not describe how to get to that end-state.

Thirdly, there is a phenomenon I have experienced as a (non-SQL) programmer that I like to call "Heads-Down Programming" or "Design-less Coding". When faced with a complicated task, the developer just writes a big loop to process each input row and then inserts a line or block of code for each requirement of their task. This is the essence of mediocre programming, and every developer has likely done it at one time or another. Why? Various reasons to explain this that I have heard (or have given myself) include:

"Because I am having difficulty figuring out the task or the tools and I need to get moving on it"

"Because I need to finish my tasks quickly and I do not have time to think about them"

"Because I am only being measured by my boss on how quickly I finish my tasks and problems that might arise downstream in testing, QA or production, are not counted against me"

"Because I am not very good at this, yet"

"Because I don't really care about the quality of the work"

"Because I do not know any better" (more common than you may think)

Thus, Cursors and While loops serve as a way for a developer to get their job "done" (sort of) as quickly as possible. They do not have to try to figure out what is the correct way or the best way to do something, just meet the functional requirements and move on. The problem here though is that they are reducing the cost of their initial development by adding serious or even severe costs to testing, QA, production, support, maintenance and upgrading. Developing in this way only makes the initial development easier at the expense of every other stage of the software lifecycle. And this only really works in procedural programming where you can look at things one small step at a time in isolation and do not ever have to look at the big picture or really understand what it is that you are trying to do in a purposeful context.

This is an approach that is not readily available to the declarative developer, because the individual pieces of a query cannot be considered in complete isolation from each other. The relationships between the different table sources, between the table sources and the output columns, between the output columns and the ordering columns and between the Group By clause and the rest of the query are all very significant. This means that you cannot do declarative programming without thinking about it.

The fourth reason is that because SQL is a domain-specific or special purpose language many of the developers who use it never become truly proficient in it because they do not consider it to be a central part of their expertise. I have observed this many times, even among developers who spend 50% or more of their time developing in SQL over several years. Consequently, they are frequently confronted with situations that could be easily solved with good declarative, set-based SQL, but are unfamiliar with the techniques or features that would allow them to do so. This leads them to fall back to what they knew before that started using SQL; procedural techniques and algorithms.

Homework: Exercise and Example

I know that some readers may be disappointed by the lack of code so far, so I will leave you with the following example and problem (don't worry, it's easy):

```
Declare @dummy int
Declare @X int
Set @X = 0

Declare XCursor Cursor LOCAL FORWARD_ONLY For
```

```
 Select 1
 From master.sys.columns c1
 Cross Join master.sys.columns c2

OPEN XCursor

FETCH NEXT FROM XCursor Into @Dummy
WHILE @@Fetch_Status = 0
 Begin
 Set @X = @X + 1
 FETCH NEXT FROM XCursor Into @Dummy
 End
Print @X
```

First, copy and run this procedure, measuring its run-time on your system. Next, figure out what this Cursor procedure really does (remember, that is part of the problem with procedural code). Now write a faster version that accomplishes the same task without any Cursors or loops. And don't worry if you find the homework difficult, we will cover it in detail in part two.

Coming in Part 2: "Just Put It in a Set, Brett"

We will pickup in part 2 with the simpler cases of cursor and loop based code and how to convert them to set-based or declarative SQL. I will show a straight-forward method for converting simple Cursor and While loop based procedures to declarative queries. Then, we will look at several slightly more complex instances and see how each can be easily rewritten using this technique.

My thanks to Jeff Moden[46] for his comments and criticisms in the preparation of this article.

R. Barry Young is a Principal Consultant for Proactive Performance Solutions, Inc.[47], a Microsoft Gold Certified Partner, located in northern Delaware. He has been programming for over 35 years, a computer professional for 30 years, a professional consultant for 25 years, a Systems Performance Analyst for 20 years and a Database Consultant for the last 15 years. He estimates that he has written between 800,000 and 1,000,000 lines of procedural code by now and thinks that he is finally starting to get the hang of it.

---

[46] http://www.sqlservercentral.com/Forums/UserInfo85377.aspx
[47] http://www.proactiveusa.com/

Generating Insert Statements

By Oleg Netchaev

There are occasions when on the top of scripting the database tables, insert statements for data in these tables are also needed. Consider, for example, the following scenario. During the development phase of the project the database objects are designed and created in the development database. Some of the records inserted into tables are needed for initial deployment of the project to a QA environment. These could be configuration related records or default records for catalog tables. The deployment database script should therefore include not only the code for the creation of the objects, but also a number of insert statements for the data. Unfortunately SQL Server Management Studio does not provide the option to "include data" along with object definitions when scripting the database.

There are numerous readily available scripts which will generate insert statements when executed, but typically they suffer from the cursor illness. Cursors had their place back in the last millennium, but the time has come to get rid of them and start using set-based SQL instead. With introduction of new features in SQL Server 2005, such as ranking functions and CTEs, justification of the cursors usage had become even more difficult than before. There are excellent articles by R. Barry Young[48] titled "There Must Be 15 Ways To Lose Your Cursors..."[49] published by this site, please read them if you are not convinced.

Let's first consider the design of a typical query to generate insert statements from the specified table (we will come up with a different approach later in the article):

Define a string (nvarchar) variable which will hold the statement defining the shape of insert.

Query the object containing column-related information about the table. For example, information_schema.columns view can be queried to retrieve one record per column in the table, describing such column's ordinal position, data type, name, and length.

---

[48] http://www.sqlservercentral.com/Authors/Articles/RBarry_Young/659055/
[49] http://www.sqlservercentral.com/articles/T-SQL/66097/

Open cursor and start looping through the records retrieved by this query.

For each step of the cursor loop add appropriate values from the cursor's record to the string variable. This means that there has to be a logic implemented via select case to figure whether to surround the data by the quotes depending on the column's type. Additionally, presence of the single quotes in the data needs to be handled.

Once the variable is populated, execute it against the table to generate the insert statements.

The logic described above seems to be a little bit more complex than it deserves to be. Allow me to demonstrate it by a very simple example. Suppose we have a table named t with one int and one nvarchar column in it named c1 and c2 respectively. We will insert a couple of records in it and then check how the insert-generating statement will look:

```
  create table t(c1 int not null primary key clustered, c2
varchar(50) not null);
  go

  insert into t(c1, c2) values (1, 'What''s the deal with
magnets?');
  insert into t(c1, c2) values (2, 'This is a trap, isn''t
it?');

  -- I will omit the cursor part, and will just spell out the
final statement:
  set @sql =
      'select ''insert into t(c1, c2) values ('' +
      ' + cast(c1 as nvarchar(10)) + '', '''''' + replace(c2,
      '''''''', '''''''''''') + '''''');'' from t;';
  -- at this point we can execute this rather unattractive
@sql:
  exec sp_executesql @sql;
  -- which will produce the following output:
  insert into t(c1, c2) values (1, 'What''s the deal with
magnets?');
  insert into t(c1, c2) values (2, 'This is a trap, isn''t
it?');
```

The insert-generating method described above is clearly error prone. Let's come up with the different approach based on the simple fact that the database engine, just like anything else related to data storage, does not store the values as we see them in the end. It can care less about presence or absence of single quotes, unicode characters etc because it stores everything in zeroes and ones regardless of the data types. The hex representation of any value is therefore always available. Consider the following snippet:

```
use AdventureWorks;
go
set nocount on;

declare @t table (col1 int not null, col2 varchar(30));
insert into @t (col1, col2)
values
(
    0x00000001,

0x57686174277320746865206465616c2077697468206d61676e6574733f
);

set nocount off;

select * from @t;
go
```

Here is the result:

```
col1          col2
----------    -----------------------------
1             What's the deal with magnets?
(1 row(s) affected)
```

Exploiting the fact that insert statements can specify exact binary values rather than spell them out in the "convenient for people" format, the outline for generating the insert statement routine is as follows:

1. Declare nvarchar(max) variables to hold the parts of the insert-denerating statement.

2. Populate the variables by the means of a single select statement querying the information_schema.columns view. When selecting, cast values to varbinary and use the not excessively documented, but nevertheless available function named **master.dbo.fn_varbintohexstr** to translate the binary values to their respective hex string representation.

3. Execute resulting script to select from the specified table, which will generate insert records.

The advantage of this method is two-fold:

1. There is no need to use a cursor.

2. There is no need to worry about data formatting and single quotes handling.

Here is the script implemented as a stored procedure. The script is not fast, it takes almost an entire second to generate 2679 insert statements on my box with Windows XP SP3 2 GB of RAM and Intel E6750 @ 2.66 GHz CPU, but it works well.

This code is available at www.sqlservercentral.com

I hope that someone will find this method useful. It works as written in SQL Server 2005, and it will also work in 2000 version with some restrictions related to varchar size limitations - there is no equivalent of varchar(max), meaning that there is no clean way to declare a variable of varchar type greater than 8,000 characters in length in the SQL Server 2000.

Oleg Netchaev

Dynamic SQL Merge

By Glen Schwickerath

Most seasoned database professionals have a "bag of tricks" collection of useful SQL scripts and stored procedures which are utilized to quickly solve common, but time-consuming problems. One of these tools, which was introduced in SQL Server 2008, is the T-SQL MERGE statement.

Have you ever been presented with one of the following database requests?

1. Table B is not in sync with Table A. Find the column differences and update Table B to match.

2. There are (insert number here) rows missing from Table B. Find them in Table A and insert them.

3. The rows in Table B from last Tuesday are wrong. Synchronize them with Table A.

These are common scenarios that all database professionals are confronted with in the course of our work lives. These problems are fairly easy to solve with a bit of skill using common SQL coding techniques. The issue, however, is that we are usually provided these "opportunities" at the most inconvenient times (e.g., five minutes before quitting time) or these situations place additional stress on the DBA because the problem has to be fixed "right now" or "ASAP" and there is little or no room for error.

Fortunately, SQL Server 2008 provides a new statement, "MERGE", which goes a long way towards solving the common database issues. The general syntax of the MERGE statement is as follows (Please consult MS Books Online for detailed syntax information on MERGE[50]):

MERGE "to a target server"
USING "data from a source server"
WHEN MATCHED "update something"
WHEN NOT MATCHED ON SOURCE "insert something"
WHEN NOT MATCHED ON TARGET DELETE

---

[50] http://msdn.microsoft.com/en-us/library/bb510625.aspx

After a bit of experience coding this statement, you can become fairly proficient at developing the code necessary to use this tool to solve the problems identified above.

What I wished to do was to create a process which would dynamically generate the necessary MERGE syntax to synchronize one table to another. Additionally, I wished to be able to synchronous a table on a SQL Server target server from a heterogeneous source (e.g., MS Access, DB2, Sybase, etc.)

Certainly, there are a variety of methods that could be employed to solve this problem. I commonly advise people that there are usually several solutions to any problem. A seasoned professional is able to analyze and choose the appropriate solution for any given problem. What I desired was a stored procedure that could be executed quickly and without a great deal of coding effort. SSIS packages work great for many ETL tasks, but take time to develop. Coding SQL scripts, even a MERGE statement, can be error-prone, especially when the pressure is on to complete a data correction task quickly. The Import Wizard works great in situations where the target table can be truncated and re-populated in total, but it is not always practical to do this; especially in online environments. What I envisioned for a solution was a DBA tool which could be quickly executed to synchronize a small-to-medium sized table.

The result of this effort is a stored procedure which dynamically generates the necessary MERGE syntax using schema information derived from the source table. The solution allows for a subset of the impacted data to be synchronized via a "where clause" and also output debugging and impacted row information by primary keys. Additionally, the tool would have the option to parse and generate the MERGE statement, but display it without actual execution. The result is the "usp_merge" stored procedure.

Procedure Call Syntax (Code Sample 1)

Code Sample 1

Illustrates a sample call to the usp_merge stored procedure.

I'd like to first mention a couple of general items regarding usage. This first example is a SQL Server->SQL Server direct database table merge. The @SrcServer variable is left NULL because the stored procedure is executed locally on the server. Secondly, the @TgtTable variable is left NULL and the stored procedure will default its value to @SrcTable.

Execution Result 1

Displays both the debugging output and the result of the MERGE statements OUTPUT command. The @Debug and @OutputPK flags will trigger both of these results to be output to Query Results window. If these two flags are turned off (set to 'N'), the entire process will execute silently.

One of the key features of this tool, which also illustrate the power of the MERGE statement, is the ability to specify a "where clause". This will allow you to effectively subset the scope of data upon which you will operating. In other words, if you only wish to impact a subset of the entire table, you can effectively do this by specifying a range of values. Leaving the "where clause" blank will result in the entire source table being synchronized to the target table.

Procedure Call Syntax (**Code Sample 1**)
Code Sample 2 is included to illustrate the second procedure call which utilizes a SQL Server Linked Server table source merging to a local database table destination. The additional parameter required is the Linked Servername (@SrcServer). I have modified this stored procedure to also synchronize heterogeneous data sources to target SQL Server tables via a Linked Server. However, since there are many possibilities for source Linked Tables, I did not include sample code to do this.

Finally, The Source Code

Source Code 1 is a listing of the actual stored procedure code. There is quite a bit of code involved in this stored procedure and, since the intent of this article is not to illustrate every coding technique utilized but to instead provide you with a useful tool and provide a better understanding of the MERGE statement, I will not explain every detail. However, I would like to make several comments on its construction.

A SQL buffer is built throughout the execution of the stored procedure and then executed. The optionally @ParseOnly flag can be utilized along with the @Debug flag to generate and display the MERGE SQL statement without actual execution. The DBA can then copy and paste the code and alter it prior to execution.

The steps involved in creating the MERGE SQL are as follows:

1. Determine the source columns.

2. Determine the primary keys. If the primary keys can not be derived from the source table, they will be derived from the target table. If no primary keys can be identified, the matching will take place on every column of the source and target table (not recommended).

3. Generate the SQL code for the MERGE statement.

4. Execute the statement

5. Clean up - remove temporary tables created during the above process.

There are a few caveats regarding finer points in utilizing this stored procedure that I would like to mention:

- The included code has been shortened for the purposes of this article and is not intended to be all-inclusive for every situation you may encounter. I would emphasize additional error-checking to improve robustness.

- I have not had the opportunity to test this procedure with all known data types (eg, varbinary, text, etc.)

- The buffer for the generated SQL code is 8000 characters. A table with many columns may result in code which overflows this buffer. Proceed with caution.

- Do not immediately use this stored procedure to merge the largest table in your data center. I generally advise exercising caution when using any new tool for the first time until you are comfortable with its behavior. I would not hesitate to use this on a small to medium size table but would question whether it is the appropriate tool for a 500 million row table.

- The source and target schemas must be identical. For heterogeneous linked tables, the source and target columns must have compatible data types.

- Either the source or target tables must have a primary key defined. Otherwise, the tool will utilize a match involving all columns to determine uniqueness and merge data.

- The source server may be a linked server but the target server must be a local SQL Server. This is a restriction of the MERGE statement.

- Read and understand any constraints involved in utilizing the MERGE statement. For example, IDENTITY inserts may have to be turned on for the target table. Additionally, usage of the OUTPUT clause of the MERGE statement requires that triggers be disabled on the target table.

The result of my effort is a very handy tool for synchronizing a target table with a source table. I have been pleased with the performance of SQL Server's MERGE statement. Synchronizing two SQL Server tables is an exceptionally quick operation. A SQL Server Linked Server connection synchronizing to a SQL Server table has also worked well. I have utilized this stored procedure extensively to merge heterogeneous tables via a linked server to SQL Server. As mentioned earlier in this article, additional code is required in the stored procedure to drive out column and primary key information and I have not included it in this example procedure. Performance when utilizing a heterogeneous linked server will probably not be on par with a SQL Server to SQL Server merge. However, the time saved over developing an alternative solution using SSIS may merit its usage in any event.

The code presented in this article is free to use by this publication's readers. However, if you find that this handy tool has saved you time and stress, please make a contribution of $10 to your local food bank.

The author, Glen Schwickerath, is a database professional working in the Minnesota Twin Cities area and can be reached at gschwick@aol.com.

Code Sample 1

```
usp_merge @SrcServer=NULL,
 @SrcDatabase='AdventureWorks',
 @SrcSchema='Production',
 @SrcTable='TransactionHistory',
 @SrcType='SQL',
 @TgtDatabase='AdventureWorksCopy',
 @TgtSchema=Production,
 @TgtTable=NULL,
 @WhereClause='TransactionID between 100000 and 102000',
 @Debug='Y',
 @OutputPK='Y',
 @ParseOnly='N'
```

Execution Result 1

Starting MERGE from AdventureWorks.Production.TransactionHistory to AdventureWorksCopy.Production.TransactionHistory.

Where clause: TransactionID between 100000 and 102000

Retrieving column information from SQL Server...

Source table columns:
TransactionID,ProductID,ReferenceOrderID,ReferenceOrderLineID,TransactionDate,
TransactionType,Quantity,ActualCost,ModifiedDate

Retrieving primary key information from SQL Server...

Primary key(s) utilized: TransactionID

Length of completed merge sql statement: 1463

Text of completed merge sql statement

```
-------------------------------------
MERGE [AdventureWorksCopy].[Production].[TransactionHistory] T USING
( select
TransactionID,ProductID,ReferenceOrderID,ReferenceOrderLineID,Transactio
nDate,TransactionType,Quantity,ActualCost,Modified
Date from [AdventureWorks].[Production].[TransactionHistory] where
TransactionID between 100000 and 102000) S on S.TransactionID =
T.TransactionID WHEN MATCHED AND S.ProductID <> T.ProductID or
S.Re
ferenceOrderID <> T.ReferenceOrderID or S.ReferenceOrderLineID <>
T.ReferenceOrderLineID or S.TransactionDate <> T.TransactionDate or
S.TransactionType <> T.TransactionType or S.Quantity <> T.Quantity
or S.ActualCost <> T.ActualCost or S.ModifiedDate <> T.ModifiedDate
THEN UPDATE SET T.ProductID = S.ProductID,T.ReferenceOrderID =
S.ReferenceOrderID,T.ReferenceOrderLineID = S.ReferenceOrderLineID,T
.TransactionDate = S.TransactionDate,T.TransactionType =
S.TransactionType,T.Quantity = S.Quantity,T.ActualCost =
S.ActualCost,T.ModifiedDate = S.ModifiedDate WHEN NOT MATCHED BY
TARGET THEN INSERT (T
```

ransactionID,ProductID,ReferenceOrderID,ReferenceOrderLineID,Transaction
Date,TransactionType,Quantity,ActualCost,ModifiedDate) VALUES
(TransactionID,ProductID,ReferenceOrderID,ReferenceOrderLineID,Tra
nsactionDate,TransactionType,Quantity,ActualCost,ModifiedDate) WHEN
NOT MATCHED BY SOURCE AND TransactionID between 100000 and
102000 THEN DELETE OUTPUT $action,INSERTED.TransactionID AS
[Transacti
onID Ins Upd],DELETED.TransactionID AS [TransactionID Deleted];

```
$action TransactionID Ins Upd TransactionID Deleted
---------- --------------------- ---------------------
UPDATE 100006 100006
INSERT 100007 NULL
INSERT 100008 NULL
INSERT 100009 NULL
INSERT 100010 NULL
INSERT 100011 NULL
UPDATE 100016 100016
UPDATE 100018 100018
INSERT 100026 NULL
```

9
^Number of rows affected (insert/update/delete)

Code Sample 2

```
usp_merge @SrcServer=MyServerLink,
  @SrcDatabase='AdventureWorks',
  @SrcSchema='Production',
  @SrcTable='TransactionHistory',
  @SrcType='SQL',
  @TgtDatabase='AdventureWorksCopy',
  @TgtSchema=Production,
  @TgtTable=NULL,
  @WhereClause='TransactionID between 100000 and 102000',
  @Debug='Y',
  @OutputPK='Y',
  @ParseOnly='N'
```

Note: The source code is available at www.sqlservercentral.com

Test-Driven Development of T-SQL Code

By Louis Roy

The Agile software development methodology is ever increasing in popularity among software development teams. One of the key disciplines of Agile is Test-Driven Development (TDD). The basic premise of Test-Driven Development is to develop software in many small steps driven by the requirement to make tests pass. The sequence of events goes like this: write a simple test for how a bit of code should work. Because the code to make the test pass has not been written yet the test will fail. Then, write the simplest code necessary to make the test pass. Once the test passes, refactor the code if necessary to remove code duplication and improve the overall design of the code while preserving its functionality. Once refactoring is complete, move on to the next test and repeat. If done correctly and within the guidelines of properly structured unit tests, the production code will be driven by passing tests. If done well, the resulting code is not only covered by unit tests that can be executed automatically, but is simple in design and contains only those features that are required for the application.

There are many tools available to help with the process of TDD. For the .NET developer, NUnit is a popular choice: (***http://nunit.sourceforge.net***). For the SQL Server developer, TSQLUnit is available: (***http://tsqlunit.sourceforge.net***). In this article I discuss what TSQLUnit is and how it can be used for TDD of database code.

What is TSQLUnit?

TSQLUnit is a SQL Server database testing framework based on the xUnit (***http://xunitpatterns.com***) unit testing framework. It is a free, open-source framework that is installed by simply executing a T-SQL script against a SQL Server database. The script creates a handful of tables and stored procedures that are used to enable test-driven development of database code.

Getting Started

Let's assume we are developing an application that will be used to analyze stock price trending patterns. One requirement of the application is to calculate the average price of a stock. A stored procedure will be created that takes in a stock symbol as an argument and returns the average price of the stock. In the future we may add additional arguments to account for moving averages (200 day, 40 day, etc) but because this is not currently a requirement only the most basic functionality will be implemented. For simplicity, let's assume our stock price data is stored in a table with the following table definition:

```
CREATE TABLE dbo.StockPrice
(
 StockId INT IDENTITY(1,1) PRIMARY KEY,
 Symbol VARCHAR(10) NOT NULL,
 ClosePrice MONEY NOT NULL,
 CloseDate DATETIME NOT NULL
)
```

Step 1: Create a test

In order for TSQLUnit to identify a stored procedure as a test the name must be prefixed with 'ut_'. For those familiar with NUnit, this is similar to decorating a method with the [Test] attribute. In TDD, there are essentially 4 parts to a unit test: Setup, Exercise, Assert, and Teardown (SEAT).

1. **Setup** - prepare the test conditions by manipulating the objects, tables, and/or data

2. **Exercise** - invoke the production code

3. **Assert** - check that the actual result equals the expected result

4. **Teardown** - return everything back to the way it was before the test started

In the following TSQLUnit test, test data is staged (Setup), the production code is invoked (Exercise), the actual result is validated against the expected result (Assert), and everything is returned to its previous state (Teardown), albeit implicitly via TSQLUnit's automatic invocation of ROLLBACK TRAN at the end of each unit test.

By default, TSQLUnit tests will pass unless the tsu_Failure stored procedure is invoked. Therefore, all TSQLUnit tests must explicitly call tsu_Failure when the actual result does not equal the expected result.

```
CREATE PROC dbo.ut_TestGetAveragePriceBySymbol
AS
 SET NOCOUNT ON

 -- Setup the test conditions by inserting test data
 INSERT INTO dbo.StockPrice VALUES ('XYZ', 10, GETDATE() - 2)
 INSERT INTO dbo.StockPrice VALUES ('XYZ', 15, GETDATE() - 1)
 INSERT INTO dbo.StockPrice VALUES ('XYZ', 5, GETDATE())
 INSERT INTO dbo.StockPrice VALUES ('PDQ', 100.00, GETDATE())

-- Exercise the test
 DECLARE @ActualAvgClosePrice MONEY
 EXEC dbo.GetAveragePriceBySymbol 'XYZ', @ActualAvgClosePrice
OUT

 -- Assert expectations
 DECLARE @ExpectedAvgClosePrice MONEY
 SET @ExpectedAvgClosePrice = 10 --(10 + 15 + 5) / 3 = 10
 IF (@ExpectedAvgClosePrice != @ActualAvgClosePrice)
    EXEC dbo.tsu_Failure 'GetAveragePriceBySymbol failed.'
-- Teardown
 -- Implicitly done via ROLLBACK TRAN
GO
```

Step 2: Run the test

Executing tsu_runTests will run all unit tests. Running the stored procedure above would result in a failed test because the GetAveragePriceBySymbol stored procedure does not exist. This is good since no production code should be written until you have a failing test. Therefore, the next step is to create the GetAveragePriceBySymbol stored procedure.

Step 3: Create the GetAveragePriceBySymbol stored procedure

TDD encourages us to implement our solutions by doing the simplest thing possible in order to make the test pass. After the test passes, the code can be refactored to make it better by removing duplicate code, extracting code into smaller units, etc. In my opinion, it is much more difficult to refactor SQL code than it is to refactor .NET or Java code because of the lack of tooling (i.e. ReSharper for Visual Studio, etc) and the lack of object-oriented design of code modules within T-SQL code.

```
CREATE PROCEDURE dbo.GetAveragePriceBySymbol
 @Symbol VARCHAR(10),
```

```
  @AvgClosePrice MONEY OUT
AS

  SET NOCOUNT ON

  SELECT @AvgClosePrice = AVG(ClosePrice)
  FROM dbo.StockPrice
  WHERE Symbol = @Symbol
```

```
  GO
```

Step 4: Run the test and watch it pass.

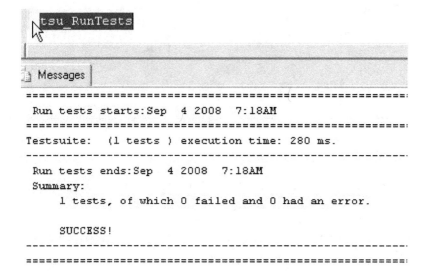

Step 5: Refactor

Now that the test passes the code can be refactored. The production code appears fine so no changes are necessary. And that's it. You now have a test that can be automatically called by invoking the tsu_RunTestsstored procedure from a NAnt[51] task or other task as part of your automated build /continuous integration (CI)[52]process.

---

[51] http://nant.sourceforge.net/

[52]

http://confluence.public.thoughtworks.org/display/CCNET/Welcome+to+CruiseContro l.NET

Now, if you want to see the unit tests that you've created so far simply execute the tsu_Describe stored procedure:

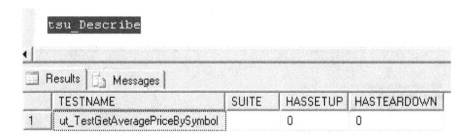

The above screen shot shows every unit test created within the current database. The SUITE, HASSETUP, and HASTEARDOWN columns are meaningful when working with test suites.

Test Suites

A test suite is similar to a TestFixture in NUnit. Individual unit tests can be grouped into test suites. Some of the advantages of using test suites are:

- Tests that exercise similar code can be grouped together.
- Individual test suites can be run independent of all other tests.
- Tests within a suite can share Setup and Teardown procedures.

Only test suites can have a Setup (a procedure that is run before each test within the suite) and a Teardown (a procedure that is run after each test within the suite) stored procedure. Setup stored procedures are commonly used to insert or update test data that the tests can use to exercise the expected behavior.

Stored procedures must adhere to the following naming convention to be included in a suite:

ut_%SUITENAME%_%TESTNAME%.

For example, if a suite called 'StockPrice' is created to group all stored procedures related to stock price then the stored procedure that was created above should be renamed to:

ut_StockPrice_TestGetAveragePriceBySymbol.

```
SP_RENAME 'dbo.ut_TestGetAveragePriceBySymbol',
'ut_StockPrice_TestGetAveragePriceBySymbol'
```

Run tsu_Describe and notice how the unit test is now part of a suite:

	TESTNAME	SUITE	HASSETUP	HASTEARDOWN
1	ut_StockPrice_TestGetAveragePriceBySymbol	StockPrice	0	0

The test can now be refactored (both production code and test code should be refactored) by creating a Setup stored procedure that creates common test data rather than duplicating insert statements across multiple tests. A Setup stored procedure must adhere to the following naming convention:

ut_%SUITENAME%_Setup

Create the Setup stored procedure and move the insert statements from **ut_StockPrice_TestGetAveragePriceBy Symbol to ut_StockPrice_Setup as** follows:

```
CREATE PROCEDURE dbo.ut_StockPrice_Setup
AS
 SET NOCOUNT ON
```

```
    -- Setup the test conditions by inserting test data
INSERT INTO dbo.StockPrice VALUES ('XYZ', 10, GETDATE() - 2)

INSERT INTO dbo.StockPrice VALUES ('XYZ', 15, GETDATE() - 1)

INSERT INTO dbo.StockPrice VALUES ('XYZ', 5, GETDATE())

INSERT INTO dbo.StockPrice VALUES ('PDQ', 100.00, GETDATE())
GO
```

Run tsu_Describe and verify our unit test has a Setup routine:

tsu_Describe

	TESTNAME	SUITE	HASSETUP	HASTEARDOWN
1	ut_StockPrice_TestGetAveragePriceBySymbol	StockPrice	1	0

Because we've refactored our test code, the test(s) should be run again to ensure they still pass. Specific test suites can be executed by passing the suite name as an input parameter (@Suite) to tsu_RunTests:

EXEC tsu_RunTests 'StockPrice'

Any additional unit tests created within the StockPrice suite will have the same test data available since the Setup procedure is run before every unit test within the suite.

Although each unit test is run within a transaction that is rolled back, a teardown procedure can be created to clean up after each test is run. Similar to the setup procedure, a teardown procedure must adhere to the following naming convention:

ut_%SUITENAME%_Teardown

Teardown procedures can be used to clean up resources outside the scope of a database transaction such as files that were created on the filesystem to support the test suite, etc.

Testing Recordsets

The example above illustrates the process for testing a stored procedure that returns data via an output parameter. Stored procedures that return recordsets are also testable by using an INSERT EXEC command. In SQL Server 2000 and above a stored procedure can insert records directly into a physical table or temp table. SQL Server 2005 and 2008 allow inserting of records directly into table variables.

For example, if the **GetAveragePriceBySymbol** stored procedure returns a recordset, the test can be written to insert the resulting recordset into a temp table or table variable that can be queried during the assertion step of the test.

```
DECLARE @Temp TABLE (AvgClosePrice MONEY)
```

```
-- Exercise the test
DECLARE @ActualAvgClosePrice MONEY
INSERT INTO @Temp
EXEC dbo.GetAveragePriceBySymbol 'XYZ' --changed to return
recordset
```

```
SET @ActualAvgClosePrice = (SELECT TOP 1 AvgClosePrice FROM
@Temp)
```

```
-- Assert expectations
DECLARE @ExpectedAvgClosePrice MONEY
SET @ExpectedAvgClosePrice = 10
IF (@ExpectedAvgClosePrice != @ActualAvgClosePrice)

    EXEC dbo.tsu_Failure 'GetAveragePriceBySymbol failed.'
```

In addition to testing stored procedures, unit tests can be written to test the existence of constraints, indexes, keys, and other table attributes to ensure database objects are scripted correctly and applied as expected. It does not make sense to test the enforcement of such constraints as this would be testing the functionality of SQL Server itself. However, on multiple occasions I have witnessed painfully slow-running queries in a production environment as a result of a missing index that was incorrectly scripted or simply never applied.

Summary

It should be evident that tools like TSQLUnit can be extremely valuable to database development. Test-Driven Development has proven to be an effective discipline for software developers across many different languages and platforms. Tools like NUnit, JUnit, Resharper, TestDriven.NET, Ant, NAnt, and CruiseControl have brought and will continue to bring tremendous benefit to development teams. TSQLUnit is a simple, yet powerful and effective tool designed to provide the same benefits as non-database TDD tools.

Resources

TSQLUnit - *http://tsqlunit.sourceforge.net*

Introduction to Test Driven Design (TDD) -
http://www.agiledata.org/essays/tdd.html

NUnit - *http://nunit.sourceforge.net*

CruiseControl.NET - *http://cruisecontrol.sourceforge.net/*

Nant - *http://nant.sourceforge.net/*

Automating tests for T-SQL code

By Ladislau Molnar

Introduction

Recently I had to write a lot of T-SQL code and I decided to approach the task of unit testing it as rigorously as possible. There are several T-SQL test tools available that seem to follow the model established by unit test tools from languages like Java and C#. Some of these are: spunit, Sqltdd, utTSQL, TSQLUnit, etc. I soon realized that in a real life environment there was a need for features that the existing tools were either missing or did not implement in a reliable way. Hence, yet another tool was born: T.S.T. (**T-S**QL **T**est Tool).

Eventually I released it as an open source project hosted at ***http://tst.codeplex.com***. At the same place you can find complete documentation and samples. A 5 minutes video demo is also available at ***http://www.youtube.com/watch?v=uGkGSkoh-CE***.

Here are some of the areas where T.S.T. improves upon:

Reliable comparison of values of different SQL types

Since T-SQL does not have method overloading, most of the existing tools use the sql_variant data type for the parameters used in the comparison procedures (think AssertEquals). Comparing two sql values of different types that were converted to sql_variant can yield outcomes that can be surprising to many people. Some of the T-SQL test tools are not prepared to handle all the possible scenarios and perform an unreliable comparison.

T.S.T. has a reliable implementation of Assert.Equals / Assert.NotEquals procedures. They automatically detect when they are used incorrectly due to incompatibility of the data types. Additional procedures like Assert.NumericEquals, Assert.NumericNotEquals, Assert.FloatEquals, Assert.FloatNotEquals are provided.

Details:To illustrate this problem consider the following procedure that tests the equality of two values:

```
CREATE PROCEDURE TestEquals
  @Expected sql_variant,
  @Actual sql_variant
AS
BEGIN
  -- We'll ignore the NULL case for this simple example
  IF @Expected = @Actual
    PRINT 'OK'
  ELSE
    PRINT 'Error'
  END
GO
```

And now invoke this validation in a code like:

```
DECLARE @MyVar float
SET @MyVar = 1.5
EXEC dbo.TestEquals 1.5, @MyVar
```

The output will show 'Error' even though you may be tempted to expect 'OK'. This is because when TestEquals is executed @Expected and @Actual will contain values not only of different data types (that in itself is not enough to fail the comparison) but values of different data type families. In this case @Expected contains a value of type numeric which belongs to the 'exact numeric' data type family. @Actual contains a value of type float which belongs to the 'approximate numeric' data type family.

Table comparison

When it comes to validating tables returned by stored procedures, functions or views many existing test tools don't provide a lot of help. T.S.T. has a convenient support for comparing results in table form by providing an API: Assert.TableEquals.

Other features needed to facilitate integration with build processes and more advanced uses

Some of the features that T.S.T. provides that are useful in this context:

- Can produce results in an XML format.
- Can run concurrent test sessions against the same or multiple databases. This is useful for cases where one or more build systems installed on the same server run concurrent build processes.

- Can be triggered from the command prompt, from SQL Management Console or programmatically.

- Test stored procedures don't have to be registered; they are picked-up automatically by the tool.

- Has a reliable automatic rollback mechanism.

Using the T.S.T. T-SQL test tool

Installing the tool

You can download the tool from ***http://tst.codeplex.com***. There go to the "Downloads" tab, and click on the link under "Downloads & files". Extract the content of the ZIP file on a local folder. The content contains no binaries - only scripts and documentation. Open a command prompt, go to that location and run "TST.BAT" This will install a SQL database called TST which is all you need to start testing your code.

Playing with the quick start sample

The tool comes with a quick start sample code. This was written to illustrate most of the features that T.S.T. offers. To install the quick start sample database open a command prompt, go to the location where you have TST.BAT and run:

```
TST.BAT /QuickStart
```

This will install a SQL database called TSTQuickStart that contains sample code and tests. Once this is done, you can treat TSTQuickStart as any regular database that contains T.S.T. test procedures. For example, to execute all the tests contained there, go in the command prompt and run:

```
TST.BAT /RunAll /TSTQuickStart
```

The output that results is shown below:

```
E:\TST>TST /RunAll TSTQuickStart
        Suite: Anonymous. Tests: 9. Passed: 9. Failed: 0
            Test: SQLTest_AssertSample. Passed
            Test: SQLTest_ExpectedError. Passed
            Test: SQLTest_GetSampleTable. Passed
            Test: SQLTest_QFn_GetEmployeeAllReports. Passed
            Test: SQLTest_QFn_GetSampleTable. Passed
            Test: SQLTest_QFn_TinyintToBinary. Passed
            Test: SQLTest_RolledBackOperation. Passed
            Test: SQLTest_SampleView. Passed
            Test: SQLTest_SimplestTest. Passed
        Suite: EmployeeOperations. Tests: 2. Passed: 2. Failed: 0
            Test: SQLTest_EmployeeOperations#DeleteEmployee. Passed
            Test: SQLTest_EmployeeOperations#UpdateEmployee. Passed
Start: 04:34:37. Finish: 04:34:38. Duration: 1026 miliseconds.
Total suites: 2. Total tests: 11. Test passed: 11. Test failed: 0.

TST Status: Passed

E:\TST>
```

Writing test procedures

Let's say we have a function called QFn_AddTwoIntegers. As its name suggests it adds two integers. Here is an example of a test for this function:

```
CREATE PROCEDURE dbo.SQLTest_AddTwoIntegers
AS
BEGIN

    DECLARE @Sum int         SELECT @Sum =
dbo.QFn_AddTwoIntegers(1,1)
    EXEC TST.Assert.Equals '1 + 1 = 2', 2, @Sum

END
GO
```

In the next sections we'll go in more detail about what we may have inside a test procedure. For now it is enough to point out that writing a test is as simple as creating a stored procedure with no parameters and a name prefixed with '**SQLTest_**'. The test runners provided by T.S.T. will recognize that stored procedure as a test based on this prefix.

There are similar naming conventions to group tests into suites and to provide set-up and teardown procedures. Let's say that we want to group all the tests regarding the authentication procedures in a test suite called 'Authentication'. The test procedures will be declared as follows:

```
CREATE PROCEDURE dbo.SQLTest_SETUP_Authentication ...
CREATE PROCEDURE dbo.SQLTest_TEARDOWN_Authentication ...
CREATE PROCEDURE
dbo.SQLTest_Authentication#LoginInvalidPassword ...
CREATE PROCEDURE
dbo.SQLTest_Authentication#LoginInvalidUserName ...
CREATE PROCEDURE dbo.SQLTest_Authentication#LoginValidUser ...
```

When T.S.T. is directed to run the suite 'Authentication', it will isolate the procedures above based on their names and will run them in the following order:

- SQLTest_SETUP_ Authentication
- SQLTest_ Authentication#LoginInvalidPassword
- SQLTest_TEARDOWN_Authentication

- SQLTest_SETUP_ Authentication
- SQLTest_ Authentication#LoginInvalidUserName
- SQLTest_TEARDOWN_Authentication

- SQLTest_SETUP_ Authentication
- SQLTest_Authentication#LoginValidUser
- SQLTest_TEARDOWN_Authentication

Important: Teardowns should be avoided unless there is a need to do more than simply rolling back changes. By default the TST framework automatically rolls back all the changes made in the Setup/Test/Teardown at the end of each test. This makes the teardown unnecessary in most scenarios. The rollback mechanism is described later in this article.

How to run the tests

You can run all the tests in a database in the command prompt by running the command:

```
TST.BAT /RunAll DatabaseName
```

You can also trigger one specific suite by running:

```
TST.BAT /RunSuite DatabaseName SuiteName
```

To use as an example the names from the previous section:

```
TST.BAT /RunSuite DatabaseName Authentication
```

Or you can trigger one specific test by running:

```
TST.BAT /RunTest DatabaseName TestName
```

An example of this would be:

```
TST.BAT /RunTest DatabaseName
SQLTest_Authentication#LoginValidUser
```

You can also run all the tests in the SQL Management Console by executing a runner stored procedure:

```
EXEC TST.Runner.RunAll 'DatabaseName'
```

Or you can run one suite by executing:

```
EXEC TST.Runner.RunSuite 'DatabaseName', 'SuiteName'
```

Or you can run one test by executing:

```
EXEC TST.Runner.RunTest 'DatabaseName', 'TestName'
```

Using the tool to validate values

Let's take a very simple case where we are going to test a function called
dbo.QFn_TinyintToBinary. This function converts an integer to a string
containing its binary representation. For example it converts 10 into '1010'.
We'll pass in a value, obtain a result and then validate it against its expected
result. We will repeat this with several values. To implement this, we create the
following test stored procedure:

```
CREATE PROCEDURE SQLTest_QFn_TinyintToBinary
AS
BEGIN

    DECLARE @BinaryString varchar(8)

    SET @BinaryString = dbo.QFn_TinyintToBinary(NULL)
    EXEC TST.Assert.IsNull 'Case: NULL', @BinaryString

    SET @BinaryString = dbo.QFn_TinyintToBinary(0)
    EXEC TST.Assert.Equals 'Case: 0', '0', @BinaryString

    SET @BinaryString = dbo.QFn_TinyintToBinary(1)
    EXEC TST.Assert.Equals 'Case: 1', '1', @BinaryString

    SET @BinaryString = dbo.QFn_TinyintToBinary(2)
    EXEC TST.Assert.Equals 'Case: 2', '10', @BinaryString

    SET @BinaryString = dbo.QFn_TinyintToBinary(129)
    EXEC TST.Assert.Equals 'Case: 129', '10000001',
@BinaryString

    SET @BinaryString = dbo.QFn_TinyintToBinary(254)
    EXEC TST.Assert.Equals 'Case: 254', '11111110',
@BinaryString

    SET @BinaryString = dbo.QFn_TinyintToBinary(255)
    EXEC TST.Assert.Equals 'Case: 255', '11111111',
@BinaryString

  END
  GO
```

Using the tool to validate views, stored procedures or functions that return a table

A more interesting case is when we have to validate a table that is returned by a
stored procedure or maybe a function or a view. T.S.T. offers a specialized API
for this task: Assert.TableEquals. Let's say that we have a stored procedure
called GetDirectReports that returns some data about all the direct reports of a
manager. Our test procedure may look something like this:

```
CREATE PROCEDURE SQLTest_GetDirectReports
AS
BEGIN

    -- Create the test tables #ActualResult and
#ExpectedResult.
    -- They must have the same schema as the table returned
    -- by the procedure GetDirectReports
    CREATE TABLE #ExpectedResult (
        EmployeeId int PRIMARY KEY NOT NULL,
        EmployeeFirstName varchar(256),
        EmployeeLastName varchar(256)
    )
    CREATE TABLE #ActualResult (
        EmployeeId int PRIMARY KEY NOT NULL,
        EmployeeFirstName varchar(256),
        EmployeeLastName varchar(256)
    )

    -- This is where we set-up our scenario. For example we
    -- could insert records in a employee table that will
    -- generate a relevant scenario for calling
GetDirectReports.
    -- ... ... ...
    -- ... ... ...

    -- Store the expected result in #ExpectedResult
    INSERT INTO #ExpectedResult VALUES(10, 'Mary' , 'Jones' )
    INSERT INTO #ExpectedResult VALUES(11, 'Michael', 'Garcia'
)
    INSERT INTO #ExpectedResult VALUES(12, 'Linda' , 'Moore' )

    -- Call GetDirectReports and store the result in
#ActualResult
    INSERT INTO #ActualResult EXEC GetDirectReports

    -- Now compare the actual vs. expected data.
    -- Assert.TableEquals compares the schema and content
    -- of tables #ExpectedResult and #ActualResult.
    EXEC TST.Assert.TableEquals 'Some contextual message here'

END
GO
```

When the table that we validate contains columns that are nondeterministic (like timestamps) we won't be able to predict their 'correct values'. We can exclude those columns from the validation by using an optional parameter of Assert.TableEquals. For example if our table contains two columns called [Create Date] and [Modified Date] we can skip them from the validation by calling:

```
EXEC TST.Assert.TableEquals
    @ContextMessage = '...',
    @IgnoredColumns = 'Create Date;Modified Date'
```

If we have to validate a table returned by a function instead of a stored procedure then the line:

```
INSERT INTO #ActualResult EXEC GetDirectReports
```

will have to be changed to something like:

```
INSERT INTO #ActualResult SELECT * FROM
dbo.QFn_GetDirectReports()
```

And if this is a test that validates a view then we will write something like:

```
INSERT INTO #ActualResult SELECT * FROM dbo.VW_DirectReports
```

Of course, in these two last cases we can explicitly specify the columns that we want to transfer in the table #ActualResult.

Using the tool to validate errors

T.S.T. can be used to validate the scenarios where we expect certain errors to occur:

```
CREATE PROCEDURE SQLTest_ExpectedError
AS
BEGIN

    EXEC TST.Assert.RegisterExpectedError
        @ContextMessage = 'Some contextual message here',
        @ExpectedErrorMessage = 'Test error'

    -- SomeSprocThatRaisesAnError is the unit under test
    -- and we expect that it will raise an error by executing:
    -- RAISERROR('Test error', 16, 1)
    EXEC dbo.SomeSprocThatRaisesAnError

END
GO
```

Note: The API RegisterExpectedError has a few more parameters that allow for a more complex usage.

Automatic Rollback

One of the important issues you will have to deal with when testing T-SQL code is how to clean-up after one test so that the changes it made won't interfere with subsequent tests. The default behavior of T.S.T is to wrap a test in a transaction and rollback all the changes at the end. That includes changes done during the set-up, the test itself and the teardown procedure. And since the roll back is automatic most of the time you should not have to write a teardown procedure at all.

If the code that you are testing does not use transactions or if it does a BEGIN TRANSACTION / COMMIT TRANSACTION, then you are fine and the automatic rollback will work as expected.

However, if the code you are testing does a BEGIN TRANSACTION / ROLLBACK TRANSACTION, that rollback will interfere with the transaction opened by the T.S.T. framework. In SQL Server, a ROLLBACK TRANSACTION executed in a nested transaction causes the rollback to propagate to the outermost level. This will in effect terminate the transaction opened by T.S.T. and have all the subsequent changes executed outside of a transaction. That will render the TST Rollback useless.

T.S.T. will detect the cases where the automatic rollback cannot function as expected. In those cases it will fail the corresponding test with an error indicating what happened. If that is the result of a bug in your test or in your unit under test then you should be able to fix it. If that is the result of a legitimate scenario you have the option of disabling the automatic rollback and do the clean-up on your own in a teardown procedure.

The T.S.T. API

Just to get another idea about the scope of the tool, here is the list of procedures that form the T.S.T. API:

- Assert.LogInfo
- Assert.Pass
- Assert.Fail
- Assert.Equals
- Assert.NotEquals

- Assert.NumericEquals

- Assert.NumericNotEquals

- Assert.FloatEquals

- Assert.FloatNotEquals

- Assert.IsLike

- Assert.IsNotLike

- Assert.IsNull

- Assert.IsNotNull

- Assert.TableEquals

- Assert.IsTableEmpty

- Assert.RegisterExpectedError

- Runner.RunAll

- Runner.RunSuite

- Runner.RunTest

- Utils.SetConfiguration

Conclusion

This tool was designed with the idea of making its adoption as inexpensive as possible. It can be triggered from the command prompt, from SQL Management Console or programmatically. It can produce XML results and it is able to run concurrent test session. All these should make the integration with existing build processes simple even for large scale projects. If you have a project that does not have an automated build process you can still run all your tests with only one command. The test runners will detect the test procedures based on naming conventions. This means there is no registration process of the tests so you don't have to incur additional costs maintaining that. Hopefully all these things will make it an attractive tool to use for anyone who wants to automate its T-SQL tests.

Database Server Upgrades the Plan, the Template, and the Task List

By Bill Richards

A wise person once said, "To fail to plan is a plan to fail". This holds true in most areas of life and is no exception when it comes to upgrading servers. The key to a successful upgrade is planning. In this article, I present practical steps to help ensure your upgrade is successful by assembling an upgrade team, making sure you have the right plan, and having a good working database server upgrade template.

Inventory your server:

The first thing you should do before upgrading your server is inventory it. Make a list of all the applications installed on your database server and make a list of all ODBC connections on your server. Note the drive letters and note what databases or files are on each drive. Note the operating system and service packs installed. After making a list of all these items, get the install documentation for each application. Print screen the ODBC connections. List the drive letters and what is on each drive. The idea is to know everything about your server. In my experience, there are often times supporting applications on database servers and sometimes a database server is not always a dedicated server. Make sure you have a completed list, install instructions, print screens, and any other necessary supporting documentation.

Map Applications To database:

Make sure you have a complete list of applications and their supporting databases. Often times, a database supports several applications. This list is important because it will help you identify application owners and application testers. After you believe you have a complete list, send out a communication to the developers, application owners, business units, and possibly other groups. The purpose of sending out a communication is to see if they have added applications that you were not aware of or if application owners may have changed since you created your initial list. They should send any corrections to the list back to you. Be sure to update your spreadsheet and send it out again to all appropriate groups, so they have a final version of the application to database list.

Identify the upgrade team:

Upgrading a database server is a team effort. Meet with each department and identify the team members who are helping you on the upgrade. As a database administrator, often times your role is to both perform the database work, and also to coordinate the effort of all the groups and individuals involved. The list below outlines the teams and individuals involved, as well as, their responsibilities.

- **DBA Role**- A DBA installs and configures SQL Server, SQL Server's service packs and feature packs. Also, a DBA is responsible for backups and restoration of databases, moving logins, setting up linked servers, moving DTS and SSIS packages, and moving jobs. In addition, a DBA is responsible for checking the integrity of each database, updating statistics and usage, and setting up any specialized sql procedures such as mirroring, replication, log reading, etc.

- **Networking Role**- You will need an individual to install the operating system, install network patches, set up drives, and set up any other operating or networking configuration.

- **Developers Role**- You will need developers who are familiar with the applications the database supports. Sometimes, developers have special setups in configuration files that need to be changed when moving to a new server. Developers can also be helpful in troubleshooting connectivity problems that arise. The developer is also utilized as the first initial tester of the application.

- **Application Testers Role** - This is a business person who uses the applications every day. Some companies have a QA department to fill this role. It is the application tester's job to use the application and collect test samples of the data before the upgrade. Test samples can be obtained through print screens or other methods. After the upgrade, the application tester once again use the application and verifies that it brings up the same information and functions comparable to the way it did before the upgrade. It is more beneficial to have a business user test the application rather than a developer. In my experience, an individual who uses the application every day uses the application differently than a developer and can catch more inconsistencies. Additionally, an application tester has a vested interest in making sure the application works correctly. Often times, it is beneficial for each application tester to create test scripts in advance, so that each part of the application is tested thoroughly. After testing, signed test scripts should be submitted to the DBA, so that the DBA has verification that the application was fully tested.

Planning and Communication:

Two of the reasons projects fail are improper planning and ineffective communication. Communication is one of the most essential components during the upgrade. People prefer to be informed about how the upgrade is progressing. Proper communication helps solve any unexpected issues that arise and allows them to be handled by team consensus rather than one individual.

Before the upgrade a number of meetings should take place. After each meeting, a summation email should be sent to all participants. The email should communicate any decisions that were made, any assumptions that were discussed, and the completion date of tasks that were assigned to individuals. At the conclusion of the email, invite feedback from the participants. Feedback ensures that what has been written is accurate and gives participants an opportunity to add any missed items, ask for clarification, or change an item that was inaccurate. Send out a final email when all the changes have been made. Below is a list of items that need to be discussed and agreed upon during the meetings.

1. Agree on when server preparation work needs to be completed. If you are moving to a new server, preparation work can be completed ahead of time. Often times, this is a coordination effort between more than one group. For instance, the networking group will install the operating system and other configurations and then give it to the DBA group to install SQL Server. The network group needs to agree upon the date by which they will have their work completed, so the next group can perform their configurations.

2. Communicate the full range of applications that are affected. End users understand application availability, whereas IT staff thinks in terms of server availability. Communicate which applications will be affected during the upgrade. If you state that a particular server will not be available, an end user may not realize that this means their application will not be available during the upgrade.

3. Agree on when a development environment can be set up that is as close as possible to mirroring the production environment, so that a practice upgrade can take place. By upgrading a development environment, you will identify steps that need to be accomplished in order to have a successful upgrade. All groups will need to be involved when upgrading a development environment. You will need to make sure applications are working and processes are running as they do in production. If you do not have the hardware to create a complete development environment, consider creating a virtual machine environment to practice the upgrade.

4. Agree on the server upgrade time and date - The DBA should propose a date and time to do the upgrade. Each stake holder will then have the opportunity to suggest alternate dates or arrange their schedule, so that the upgrade can be performed on that day.

5. Create a list of contacts - A phone list of business and cell phones should be constructed ahead of time in the event that an issue comes up which requires the input of others. It is better to get a group consensus when an issue arises than to assume you are choosing the best course of action. This ensures that the right decision was made and that it was a group that made the decision.

6. Communicate the time when each group is needed during the upgrade - Since the DBA will be performing most of the work during the upgrade, it is not necessary to have other groups involved until they are needed. Developers are not needed until the upgrade has been completed, so that they can do the initial testing. Business testers are needed to get samples ahead of time and after the upgrade has been completed. Communicate a projected time when each group is needed.

7. Upgrade Status Communication - During the upgrade, it is helpful to let team members know the status of the upgrade. It could be that the upgrade is running ahead of schedule, behind schedule, or that you have run into unexpected issues and need to alter the time for developers and testers to arrive. Also, it is good to let everyone know that the upgrade is complete and they can log onto their system. One effective way to communicate the status is to set up a voice message on a phone number. Communicate to everyone that they need to call the

phone number and listen to the message before they come to the office. The following are some examples of some helpful upgrade status voice messages.

"The upgrade is going as planned, we should be done by 8:00 pm. Please check the notification before you come in to make sure the status has not changed".

"The upgrade is running behind schedule, the new time is 10:00 pm. Please check the notification before you come in to make sure the status has not changed".

"We have run into XX issue. We need to meet and discuss what course of action to take".

8. 8. When the upgrade is complete, communicate by email to the affected groups that the upgrade was successful and that their applications are now on-line and available for use. Communicate who should be notified in the event of unexpected errors that may be related to the upgrade.

9. 9. Develop a rollback plan - Sometimes, things do not go as planned, so a rollback plan should be developed. This rollback process will need to be started if the server is not upgraded by an agreed upon deadline.

The Process of upgrading the server:

You can find an upgrade plan template of detailed steps that are used in most upgrades.on SQLServerCentral.com. When you upgrade your development environment, you will be able to customize a task list for your environment. Each task should have a projected start date and time, the task description, the person who is responsible for the task, the completion date, and comments. The upgrade plan should have three sections:

1. Pre-Upgrade preparation - This section should contain anything that can be done ahead of time. If you are moving to a new server, many things can be done. Networking can install the operating system and patches, configure drives, and do any other configurations to get the server ready. SQL Server, supporting service packs, and feature packs can be installed. Supporting applications can be installed. If you are upgrading your current server, there will only be a limited number of things you can do ahead of time. You will still be able, however, to inventory the server, generate scripts, and document any configuration options. The key to this section is to minimize the work that needs to be accomplished on the upgrade day.

2. Upgrade Day - This section should contain any task you need to perform on the day of the upgrade. In the time column, you should enter an estimated time to ensure that you are on schedule. Also, after the upgrade is completed, developers need to come in to the office to test the applications they support. They should help troubleshoot connectivity problems and application issues as they arise. After developers test their applications, business application testers arrive and test the application. Application testers should be in constant communication with the developers and DBAs to troubleshoot any issues that arise. During testing, the application tester documents each successful test by print screens or other methods. At the end of testing, the application tester sends the DBA a signed copy of the test results.

3. Rollback Plan - In the event the upgrade does not go as planned, it is important that you spend time on a rollback plan. Make sure you document where any restore backups are coming from, applications that need reinstalled and any other groups that need to be involved. A good rule of thumb is to "plan for the worst and expect the best".

Below is a birds-eye view of the upgrade process:

1. Upgrade the development environment. This will help you put a complete task list together.

2. All prep work is completed on the production server ahead of time.

3. On upgrade day, application testers follow their testing scripts and gather print screens and other documentation that will be used to compare to the results after the upgrade.

4. The upgrade begins in production. The DBA performs the upgrade.

5. Developers are notified that the upgrade is complete.

6. Developers test their applications.

7. Application testers are notified and they test the applications using their testing scripts.

8. Application testers send signed test scripts and test verification to the DBA.

9. On the first business day, after the upgrade, the DBA and developers should come in early to field any issues that arise. It is better to fix any potential problems when one or two individuals are reporting the issue than when whole departments are experiencing the problem.

In conclusion, this paper has documented ways to have a successful upgrade. The topics of discussion include successful ways to identify stakeholders, assemble an upgrade team, plan the upgrade, and communicate within the business. The best way to know when you have included all the tasks in your upgrade plan is to upgrade a development environment. Properly planning your upgrade beforehand saves time and resources on upgrade day. Every individual knows their place and what is expected of them ahead of time. I have used this method for many years and I try to continually improve the process. Since every environment is different, each upgrade plan will include different tasks. Feel free to take the template and customize it to your environment.

References for Upgrade Template:

- *http://msdn.microsoft.com/en-us/library/ms144245.aspx*
- *http://msdn.microsoft.com/en-us/library/ms144245.aspx*
- *http://msdn.microsoft.com/en-us/library/ms144267.aspx*
- *http://msdn.microsoft.com/en-us/library/ms144256.aspx*
- *http://support.microsoft.com/kb/918992*
- *http://msdn.microsoft.com/en-us/library/ms143724.aspx*
- *http://msdn.microsoft.com/en-us/library/ms143686.aspx*
- *http://msdn.microsoft.com/en-us/library/ms143699.aspx*
- *http://msdn.microsoft.com/en-us/library/ms143699.aspx*
- *http://msdn.microsoft.com/en-us/library/ms190941(SQL.90).aspx*
- *http://msdn.microsoft.com/en-us/library/ms143501.aspx*

- *http://msdn.microsoft.com/en-us/library/ms143496.aspx*

Split string using XML

By Divya Agrawal

This article would help developers looking to split strings in a single query using XML. We generally use a user defined function, which you all may have found at many places that splits the string based on the delimiter passed. But, when it comes to separate the string in a single query without any help of user defined function we often get panic. I have found a much optimized and shorter way of splitting any string based on the delimiter passed. I will be using the power of XML to do the same.

Let's say for example there is a string 'A,B,C,D,E' and I want to split it based on the delimiter ','. The first step would be to convert that string into XML, replacing the delimiter with some start and end XML tag.

```
Declare @xml as xml,@str as varchar(100),@delimiter as
varchar(10)
  SET @str='A,B,C,D,E'
  SET @delimiter =','
  SET @xml = cast(('<X>'+replace(@str,@delimiter
,'</X><X>')+'</X>') as xml)
```

Here as shown above, the delimiter ',' is replaced by </X><X> tags. When you will see the output after converting the string into XML, you will be able to see the string as shown in the image below:

```
<X>A</X>
<X>B</X>
<X>C</X>
<X>D</X>
<X>E</X>
```

Once the string is converted into XML you can easily query that using XQuery.

```
SELECT N.value('.', 'varchar(10)') as value FROM
@xml.nodes('X') as T(N)
```

This will give the output as a separated string as:

	value
1	A
2	B
3	C
4	D
5	E

Now, say if I have a table as having an ID column and comma separated string as data column.

```
DECLARE @t TABLE( ID INT IDENTITY, data VARCHAR(50))
INSERT INTO @t(data) SELECT 'AA,AB,AC,AD'
INSERT INTO @t(data) SELECT 'BA,BB,BC'
```

	ID	data
1	1	AA,AB,AC,AD
2	2	BA,BB,BC

I can use the method shown above to split the string.

```
select F1.id,
  F1.data,
  O.splitdata
from
(
select *,
cast('<X>'+replace(F.data,',','</X><X>')+'</X>' as XML) as
xmlfilter
from @t F
)F1
cross apply
(
select fdata.D.value('.','varchar(50)') as splitdata
from f1.xmlfilter.nodes('X') as fdata(D)) O
```

First of all, cast the 'data' column of table @t into XML data type by replacing the delimiter by starting and ending tags '<X></X>'.

I have used 'CROSS APPLY' for splitting the data. APPLY clause let's you join a table to a table-valued-function. The APPLY clause acts like a JOIN without the ON clause comes in two flavors:

CROSS and OUTER

The OUTER APPLY clause returns all the rows on the left side (@t) whether they return any rows in the table-valued-function or not. The columns that the table-valued-function returns are null if no rows are returned.

The CROSS APPLY only returns rows from the left side (@t) if the table-valued-function returns rows.

Executing the select statement mentioned above would display the following output:

	id	data	splitdata
1	1	AA,AB,AC,AD	AA
2	1	AA,AB,AC,AD	AB
3	1	AA,AB,AC,AD	AC
4	1	AA,AB,AC,AD	AD
5	2	BA,BB,BC	BA
6	2	BA,BB,BC	BB
7	2	BA,BB,BC	BC

This article might have made you clear of the power of XML and a very good use of 'CROSS APPLY'. There are other options to split strings in a single query using recursive CTEs.

Now whenever splitting of string is required you can easily cast the string into XML, by replacing the delimiter by XML start and end tags and then use the method shown above to split the string.

Celko's Summer SQL Stympers: Prime Numbers

By Joe Celko

A Prime SQL Puzzle

I was teaching SQL classes for YAPC-10 ("Yet Another PERL Conference" #10) at Carnegie Mellon University at the end of June 2009. For the record, I have never used PERL and had to Google up an overview before I went; it is a very different creature from SQL.

One of my students asked if you could write an SQL statement to generate the prime numbers less than 1000 (or any other limit) that scales well. He was bothered by the lack of loops in SQL and a Prime Number sieve is a common PERL programming exercise. You can Google it and see an animation at Eratosthenes' sieve[53] and some PERL code at Sieve of Eratosthenes with closures[54].

My immediate answer was "sure, but you might have to use a recursive CTE to replace the loop. Later I realized that was a really bad answer; you don't need recursion, just a little math. There are two useful facts from Number Theory:

1. The prime factors of a given number (n) cannot be greater than ceiling (vn). Think about it; by definition (vn * vn)) = n, and by definition, ceiling (vn) >= floor(vn) so integer rounding up will be safe. This says that if I look at (a * b = c) where (a < b), then I don't have to look at (b * a = c), so I can start searching for prime factors with small values.

2. All primes are of the form (6 * n ± 1), but not all number of that form are Primes. For example (n = 1) gives us {5, 7} and they are both primes. But for (n = 4) gives us {23, 25} where (25 = 5 * 5). What this does is remove the multiples of 2 and 3 from consideration.

Let's get all of that into SQL statements. Let's start with a table for the primes:

---

[53] http://www.hbmeyer.de/eratosiv.htm
[54] http://www.perlmonks.org/?node_id=276103.

```
CREATE TABLE Primes
(p INTEGER NOT NULL PRIMARY KEY
  CHECK (p > 1));
```

Now, your puzzle is to fill the table up to some limit, say 1000 just to keep it simple.

Answers

Let's assume we have a table named Sequence with integers from 1 to (n) that we can use. This is a common SQL programming idiom, so you don't have to feel bad about using it.

```
CREATE TABLE Sequence
(seq INTEGER NOT NULL PRIMARY KEY
CHECK (seq  > 0));
```

There are lots of ways of filling this table, but here is one I like:

```
WITH Digits(i)
AS (SELECT i
    FROM (VALUES (1), (2), (3), (4), (5), (6), (7), (8), (9),
(0)) AS X(i))
INSERT INTO Sequence(seq)
SELECT (D3.i * 1000 + D2.i * 100 + D1.i * 10 + D0.i + 1) AS seq
    FROM Digits AS D0, Digits AS D1, Digits AS D2, Digits AS
D3;
```

This template is easy to extend and the ".. + 1" gets rid of the zero.

Answer #1

For the first attempt, let's load the Primes table with candidate numbers using math fact #2 from above.

```
INSERT INTO Primes (p)
(SELECT (6 * seq) + 1
  FROM Sequence
WHERE (6 * seq) + 1 <= 1000
UNION ALL
SELECT (6 * seq) - 1
  FROM Sequence
WHERE (6 * seq) + 1 <= 1000);
```

An improvement which gets rid of the UNION ALL uses a table constant:

```
INSERT INTO Primes (p)
SELECT (6 * seq) + S.switch
  FROM Sequence
       CROSS JOIN
       (SELECT switch
           FROM (VALUES (-1), (+1))
        AS F(switch))S
  WHERE (6 * seq) + 1 <= 1000;
```

Now we have too many rows in Primes and need to remove the non-primes. Now math fact #1 can come into play; test the set of numbers less than the square root to see if there is a factor among them.

```
DELETE FROM Primes
WHERE EXISTS
  (SELECT *
     FROM Primes AS P1
    WHERE P1.p <= CEILING (SQRT (Primes.p))
      AND (Primes.p % P1.p) = 0);
```

Answer #2

Another way to load the candidates into Primes is to have the first few known primes hardwired into a query. This is a generalization of the math fact #2, which dealt with multiples of only 2 and 3.

```
INSERT INTO Primes (p)
SELECT seq
  FROM Sequence
   WHERE 0 NOT IN (seq % 2, seq % 3, seq % 5, seq % 7, .. );
```

The idea is that if we can limit the candidate set for Primes, performance will improve. At the extreme, if the list of "MOD (seq, <prime>)" expressions goes to a value equal or higher than the upper limit we are looking at, we get the answer immediately.

This is a good trick; many SQL programmers think that an IN() list can only be constants. You might also want to look at how many values it can hold –It is larger than you think.

Another candidate pruning trick is based on the math fact that integers with final digits {2, 4, 6, 8, 0} are even numbers; those with final digits {5, 0} are multiples of five. Let's not look at them when we build a candidate table.

```
WITH Digits(i)
AS (SELECT i
    FROM (VALUES (1), (2), (3), (4), (5), (6), (7), (8), (9),
(0)) AS X(i)
    )
INSERT INTO Sequence(seq)
SELECT (D3.i * 1000 + D2.i * 100 + D1.i * 10 + Units.i)
  FROM (SELECT i
    FROM (VALUES (1), (3), (7), (9)) AS X(i)) AS Units,
        Digits AS D1, Digits AS D2, Digits AS D3
```

Answer #3

Another approach is to generate all of the non-primes and remove them from the Sequence table.

```
INSERT INTO Primes (p)
(SELECT seq FROM Sequence WHERE seq <= 1000)
EXCEPT
(SELECT (F1.seq * F2.seq) AS composite_nbr
  FROM Sequence AS F1, Sequence AS F2
WHERE F1.seq BETWEEN 2 AND CEILING (SQRT (1000))
  AND F2.seq BETWEEN 2 AND CEILING (SQRT (1000))
  AND F1.seq <= F2.seq
  AND (F1.seq * F2.seq) <= 1000)
```

Obviously, the Sequence table in the left hand clause could be anyone of the trimmed candidate tables we previously constructed.

What answers to do you have? As a hint, there are faster but more complicated algorithms, like the Sieve of Atkin and the various Wheel Sieves.

Basically Available, Soft State, Eventually Consistent

By Phil Factor

Many special-purpose databases don't need, or use, either the relational model or a declarative language such as SQL. An interesting group of these are sometimes called BASE systems (Basically Available, Soft State, Eventually consistent) and they work well with simple data models holding vast volumes of data. Google's BigTable, Dojo's Persevere, Amazon's Dynamo, Facebook's Cassandra, and a host of others.

The 'NoSQL movement' is the latest group for developers who are working with or building non-relational BASE distributed databases, and particularly the open-source varieties. This would be no more than an interesting aside, to remind us that SQL-based relational databases are general-purpose tools and there will always be, and always has been, a thriving industry of special purpose database solutions. However, journalists commenting on the startup of the 'NoSQL Movement' cannot resist a tease. "Like the Patriots, who rebelled against Britain's heavy taxes, NoSQLers came to share how they had overthrown the tyranny of slow, expensive relational databases in favor of more efficient and cheaper ways of managing data." burbles Eric Lai over at Computerworld.

Sometimes, when the red mist of radicalism descends, it is possible to lose sight of the fact that RDBMSs such as SQL Server fit closely with the requirements of complex commercial business systems. Your system may, in fact be trivial, but hold huge quantities of data. Everyone thinks they are working with highly complex data models. It is part of our vanity as developers. It leads to absurd generalisations such as "Relational databases give you too much. They force you to twist your object data to fit a RDBMS". The problem often boils down to a developer with a filofax-sized database having to use a grown-up RDBMS. There will always be tears in such circumstances.

From a distance, an RDBMS such as SQL Server may seem like overkill, especially for a simple social-networking website. As soon as you get to the details, such as concurrency, consistency, scalability, and ease of refactoring then the idea of an open-source EAV database alternative can start to get less attractive. Even the idea of ditching the use of SQL soon hits problems. A Declarative language may seem odd to those who are only familiar with proccedural coding, but it is a fine way to allow parallel processing. I must admit that occasionally, when faced with designing an IT project that deals with data that strays from the conventional relational model, I've flirted with the use of special-purpose databases, but there always comes a time when the niggles of the details of implementation start rising exponentially, and one wakes from the dream to return to the SQL-based Relational database systems such as SQL Server.

SQL Tools
from Red Gate Software

SQL Backup

from $295

Compress, encrypt and monitor SQL Server backups

- ↗ Compress database backups by **up to 95%** for faster backups and restores
- ↗ Protect your data with up to 256-bit AES encryption (SQL Backup Pro only)
- ↗ Monitor your data with an interactive timeline, so you can check and edit the status of past, present and future backup activities
- ↗ Optimize backup performance with multiple threads in SQL Backup's engine

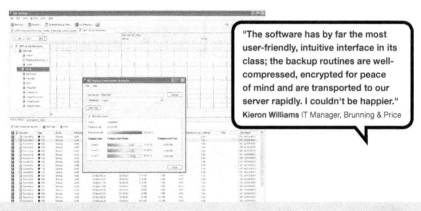

"The software has by far the most user-friendly, intuitive interface in its class; the backup routines are well-compressed, encrypted for peace of mind and are transported to our server rapidly. I couldn't be happier."

Kieron Williams IT Manager, Brunning & Price

SQL Response

from $495

Monitors SQL Servers, with alerts and diagnostic data

- ↗ Investigate long-running queries, SQL deadlocks, blocked processes and more to resolve problems sooner
- ↗ Intelligent email alerts notify you as problems arise, without overloading you with information
- ↗ Concise, relevant data provided for each alert raised
- ↗ Low-impact monitoring and no installation of components on your SQL Servers

"SQL Response enables you to monitor, get alerted and respond to SQL problems before they start, in an easy-to-navigate, user-friendly and visually precise way, with drill-down detail where you need it most."

H John B Manderson President and Principle Consultant, Wireless Ventures Ltd

SQL Compare

from $395

Compare and synchronize SQL Server database schemas

- ↗ Automate database comparisons, and synchronize your databases
- ↗ Simple, easy to use, 100% accurate
- ↗ Save hours of tedious work, and eliminate manual scripting errors
- ↗ Work with live databases, snapshots, script files or backups

"SQL Compare and SQL Data Compare are the best purchases we've made in the .NET/SQL environment. They've saved us hours of development time and the fast, easy-to-use database comparison gives us maximum confidence that our migration scripts are correct. We rely on these products for every deployment."

Paul Tebbutt Technical Lead, Universal Music Group

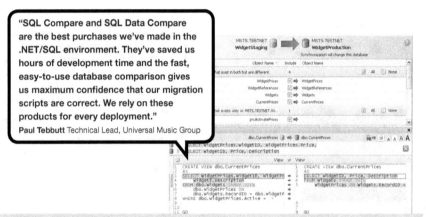

SQL Data Compare

from $395

Compare and synchronize SQL Server database schemas

- ↗ Compare your database contents
- ↗ Automatically synchronize your data
- ↗ Simplify data migrations
- ↗ Row-level restore
- ↗ Compare to backups

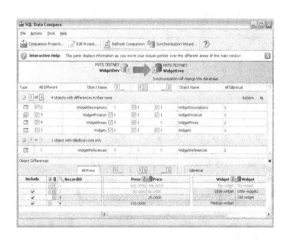

SQL Prompt

from $195

Intelligent code completion and layout for SQL Server

- ↗ Write SQL fast and accurately with code completion
- ↗ Understand code more easily with script layout
- ↗ Continue to use your current editor – SQL Prompt works within SSMS, Query Analyzer, and Visual Studio
- ↗ Keyword formatting, join completion, code snippets, and many more powerful features

"It's amazing how such a simple concept quickly becomes a way of life. With SQL Prompt there's no longer any need to hunt out the design documentation, or to memorize every field length in the entire database. It's about freeing the mind from being a database repository - and instead concentrate on problem solving and solution providing!" **Dr Michael Dye** Dyetech

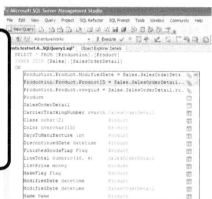

SQL Data Generator

$295

Test data generator for SQL Server databases

- ↗ Data generation in one click
- ↗ Realistic data based on column and table name
- ↗ Data can be customized if desired
- ↗ Eliminates hours of tedious work

"Red Gate's SQL Data Generator has overnight become the principal tool we use for loading test data to run our performance and load tests"
Grant Fritchey Principal DBA, FM Global

🔲 Preview of data to be generated (first 100 lines)

TitleOfCourtesy	BirthDate	HireDate	Address	City	Region	PostalCode	Country	HomeP
Title	datetime	datetime	Address Line (Stre	US City	Region	ZIP Code	Country	Phone
Dr	23/08/1963 04:0...	25/04/1992 20:0...	37 Fabien St.	Richmond	IA-CT	58907	Gibraltar	12353:
Miss	10/01/1960 23:2...	16/02/1976 11:2...	850 White Nobel...	NULL	NV-EW	39330	Tajikistan	69862:
Mr	27/07/1970 13:5...	03/12/1953 15:3...	45 Green Milton...	New York	TN-OH	60387	Liberia	529-89
Mr	27/01/2002 04:3...	24/07/1958 00:5...	43 Milton Boulev...	Sacramento	NM-JR	13294	Côte d'Ivoire	984-11
Mr	31/05/1994 04:1...	12/01/1964 04:4...	592 Rocky Cowl...	Santa Ana	MI-UU	NULL	Jersey	417-47
Mrs	17/11/1975 10:1...	27/10/1968 18:5...	69 Clarendon Pa...	San Jose	IL-TC	41768	New Caledonia	11305(
Dr.	16/05/1974 06:1...	25/11/1998 14:5...	207 Fabien Blvd.	Houston	AL-GE	04937	Belgium	89687(
Dr	27/12/1999 19:4...	03/05/1972 13:1...	53 Rocky Oak R...	Baton Rouge	MA-RT	65364	Swaziland	076-87
Dr	14/10/1971 03:1...	28/06/1978 10:0...	260 East Rocky...	Charlotte	AL-AR	97727	Benin	54684!
Mr	09/11/1981 13:2...	26/12/2001 15:0...	476 North Fabie...	Akron	MA-IU	94269	Palau	87561:
Dr	28/06/1987 01:3...	30/10/1972 00:0...	48 South Hague...	Norfolk	VT-UV	66385	American Samoa	89085(
Mr	20/10/1962 04:4...	07/09/2005 17:1...	939 Fabien Park...	Grand Rapids	HI-YT	86033	Swaziland	58415(
Mr	25/01/2001 08:0...	18/08/1983 12:0...	348 North Green...	Wichita	FL-IV	32302	Zambia	124-42
Mr	05/01/1955 10:0...	12/08/1983 22:5...	32 Cowley Boule...	Spokane	WV-DI	45980	Chile	457-22

SQL Toolbelt™ $1,795

The twelve essential SQL Server tools for database professionals

You can buy our acclaimed SQL Server tools individually or bundled.
Our most popular deal is the SQL Toolbelt: all twelve SQL Server tools in a single installer, with **a combined value of $5,240 but an actual price of $1,795**, a saving of more than 65%.

*Fully compatible with SQL Server 2000, 2005 and **2008!***

SQL Doc
Intelligent code completion and layout for SQL Server

↗ Produce simple, legible and fast HTML reports for multiple databases
↗ Documentation is stored as part of the database
↗ Output completed documentation to a range of different formats.

$295

SQL Dependency Tracker
The graphical tool for tracking database and cross-server dependencies

↗ Visually track database object dependencies
↗ Discover all cross-database and cross-server object relationships
↗ Analyze potential impact of database schema changes
↗ Rapidly document database dependencies for reports, version control, and database change planning

$195

SQL Packager
Compress and package your databases for easy installations and upgrades

↗ Script your entire database accurately and quickly
↗ Move your database from A to B
↗ Compress your database as an exe file, or launch as a Visual Studio project
↗ Simplify database deployments and installations

from **$295**

SQL Multi Script
Single-click script execution on multiple SQL Servers

↗ Cut out repetitive administration by deploying multiple scripts on multiple servers with just one click
↗ Return easy-to-read, aggregated results from your queries to export either as a csv or .txt file
↗ Edit queries fast with an intuitive interface, including colored syntax highlighting, Find and Replace, and split-screen editing

$195

SQL Comparison SDK
Automate database comparisons and synchronizations

↗ Full API access to Red Gate comparison tools
↗ Incorporate comparison and synchronization functionality into your applications
↗ Schedule any of the tasks you require from the SQL Comparison Bundle

$595

SQL Refactor
Refactor and format your SQL code

Twelve tools to help update and maintain databases quickly and reliably, including:

↗ Rename object and update all references
↗ Expand column wildcards, qualify object names, and uppercase keywords
↗ Summarize script
↗ Encapsulate code as stored procedure

$295

How to Become an Exceptional DBA

Brad McGehee

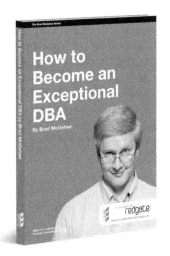

A career guide that will show you, step-by-step, exactly what you can do to differentiate yourself from the crowd so that you can be an Exceptional DBA. While Brad focuses on how to become an Exceptional SQL Server DBA, the advice in this book applies to any DBA, no matter what database software they use. If you are considering becoming a DBA, or are a DBA and want to be more than an average DBA, this is the book to get you started.

ISBN: 978-1-906434-05-2
Published: July 2008

SQL Server Execution Plans

Grant Fritchey

Execution plans show you what's going on behind the scenes in SQL Server and provide you with a wealth of information on how your queries are being executed. Grant provides a clear route through the subject, from the basics of capturing plans, through their interpretation, and then right on to how to use them to understand how you might optimize your SQL queries, improve your indexing strategy, and so on. All this rich information makes the execution plan a fairly important tool in the tool belt of pretty much anyone who writes TSQL to access data in a SQL Server database.

ISBN: 978-1-906434-02-1
Published: June 2008

Mastering SQL Server Profiler
Brad McGehee

For such a potentially powerful tool, Profiler is surprisingly underused; unless you have a lot of experience as a DBA, it is often hard to analyze the data you capture. As such, many DBAs tend to ignore it and this is distressing, because Profiler has so much potential to make a DBA's life more productive. SQL Server Profiler records data about various SQL Server events, and this data can be used to troubleshoot a wide range of SQL Server issues, such as poorly-performing queries, locking and blocking, excessive table/index scanning, and a lot more.

ISBN: 978-1-906434-15-1
Published: January 2009

Two Minute SQL Server Stumpers

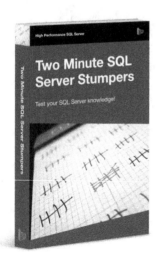

Challenge yourself in a variety of ways about the different aspects of SQL Server. Some of the questions are arcane, some very common, but you'll learn something and the wide range of questions will help you get your mind agile and ready for some quick thinking. This version is a compilation of SQL Server 2005 and SQL Server 2008 questions, to bring you up to date on the latest version of SQL Server. So read on, in order, randomly, just start going through them, but do yourself a favor and think about each before turning the page. Challenge yourself and see how well you do.

ISBN: 978-1-906434-21-2
Published: August 2009

www.ingramcontent.com/pod-product-compliance
Lightning Source LLC
LaVergne TN
LVHW012327060326
832902LV00011B/1754